# LEE EVANS IN MEXICO CITY

## The Last Protest

# The Last Protest

:

*Lee Evans in Mexico City*

FRANK MURPHY

Windsprint Press
Kansas City, MO

For information, address:

WindSprint Press
3421 Gladstone Blvd
Kansas City, MO 64123
windsprintbook@aol.com


Publisher's Cataloging-in-Publication

Murphy, Frank, 1952-
    The last protest : Lee Evans in Mexico City / Frank Murphy.
      p. cm.
    Includes bibliographical references and index.
    ISBN 978-0-9773821-0-1
    1. Evans, Lee, 1947-. 2. Olympic Games—(19th : 1968 : Mexico Ciy, Mexico). 3.
    Olympics—Participation, African American. 4. African American athletes—Political
    activity—Histoy—20th century. 5. United States—Race relations—Histoy—20th
    century. I. Title.

GV722 1968.M87 2006                                                      796.48
                                                                  QBI06-600051

Library of Congress Control Number: 2006901708



Book and Cover design by Nick Kroeker

*to Mary*

# two prefaces and a nightmare

*The first preface is childish.*
*The second preface is defining.*
*The nightmare is gratuitous, maybe.*

I

One lap around the track is child's play. It is what a child does naturally when first confronted with an oval. If another child appears, what happens next is like breathing.

There is in Alabama a middle-aged man named Lee Evans who has a rich claim on the act of running one lap, in part because he never forgot what the child knew, that the idea was to get around faster than anyone else. When Lee was young, he won race after race, leaning into finish lines and tapes with scant distance to spare, confounding and infuriating competitors who expected, always, to get past him, to win just one major race he contested. In 1968 Lee Evans set a world record in the 400 meters that would endure for two decades before being surpassed by people who competed in a sport so changed that no one knew what a record was any longer.

Despite his achievements, Lee Evans is not well known. On a critical day in his career, a day that might have made him famous, he was not on the track. He was in the stands. He watched as two other black men, Tommie Smith and John Carlos, raised their fists on an Olympic dais in Mexico City. In that moment, they left Lee Evans behind forever. This was not how it should have been! Lee should have been down there. He was the true companion to Tommie Smith, and Smith to him. They had borne hardship together, and this moment, too, should have been shared along with its consequence.

## II

The photograph showed John Carlos and Tommie Smith in black socks with bowed necks raising their black-gloved fists on the Olympic stand at the 1968 Olympic games in Mexico City. The two had exploited the games in the cause of civil rights. Rage as it might, the International Olympic Committee could not make that photograph go away. Also, in a point so important that it passes for banality, no one who was not in the photograph could wedge into it, Zelig-like. Lee Evans was not in the photograph, although contemporary reports said that he mirrored the two men on center stage by standing near his own seat, pulling on his own black gloves, and raising his own hand. Lee denies this. He stood, he says, as one among many in the stunned crowd in the Olympic stadium. He listened as the abuse began to rumble. He was angry and excited and agitated. Doubtless, he did give a black power salute. But he did not pose self-consciously to create companionship with the men in the glare of publicity.

After he won his own medals he would have his opportunity. He would command the attention of the world. His image too would flash across television screens and be frozen in still photographs, as Tommie's and John's had been. That he would protest seemed obvious. The young man was a militant, as anyone who read the newspaper knew; he was an extremist, as anyone who listened to a news report was told; he was an angry man determined to hurt his own country, a matter upon which there was agreement.

And then there was Lee. He was the man in the middle. He was the person about whom they were speaking. He had the match in one hand and the candle in the other, and he had to choose between the fire and the light. If it was the fire, he would return home a hero to the furious and the disaffected who pushed most firmly at his back and whose interest he held as his own. If it was the light, he would leave in place, undisturbed by anything he might do, the magisterial and dignified, the profound and unmoving, image created by Tommie Smith and John Carlos, and he in turn would be removed from history. He would be misunderstood, and loved no more.

In the hours and the days of Lee's decision, he would be replaced by someone older, by someone more alone, and finally by someone wiser.

### III

A man is in a car. As the result of a trivial decision the car is stopped on a railroad track. The driver in the car is looking at a map, for example, and paying little attention, until he hears the sound of a train whistle. The train is upon him. Impeded by other cars and obstructions, he cannot back up. When he looks in front of his car, with the idea of accelerating out of harm's way, he sees a small child sitting on the ground there.

# .1

*If a black man did decide to protest in Mexico City, history might explain why.*

Lee is in his lane. He is receiving a baton from those who came before him. He is the beneficiary of the progenitors! He cannot escape, but neither is he bound.

:

It is 1859 and a man is in the house, and a man is in the field. The man in the house owns the man in the field. He owns the field in which the man is working. He owns the product of the man he owns who is working in the field he owns. The man in the house is the master. As the master, he thinks not at all of his status and little of his relationship to the man in the field, the entire situation seeming correct to him. The man in the field thinks often of his relationship to the man in the house. Indeed, he thinks of little else. The injustice is burning a hole in his heart.

In July 1863, an immigrant from Ireland is living in New York. A great war is waging, and he has been conscripted to fight in it. At first, he has no objection. He has been told that the purpose of the war is to preserve the union of states, a result he endorses. Lately, he has been told that the purpose of the war is to free the slave from the master. Because he has only the slave to look down upon, he riots at the new idea. He will not die to abolish an institution that holds him aloft, however fragile the hold and immoral the grip. He and a mob of similarly motivated Irishmen burn down a black church and an orphanage serving black children.

In New Orleans, a freed black man, carried along by the tide of reconstruction after the war, holds public office. He profits little. He is derided in the streets by the citizens he is intended to represent. He will not remain long in office. His presence there has corrupted a way of life. Men will meet in council, they will hide in fraternity, and they will terrorize this man's family for a hundred years and more.

Near Clarksville, a young man was born in a shack of rough wood and set to work in the fields. He does not wish to work in the fields. He thinks that it lacks dignity and that it lacks prospect. As a young adult, he has joined the great northern migration. Unobjected, he is part of the draining from the delta of its most precious resource. He has moved to Chicago. He believes he will get a good job. He believes that he will be free of the lines that he dared not cross in the South. Soon, he will discover that the lines are up north, too, only blurred and lied about. He will find himself pushed off. He will live among others like himself. He will work hard for very little. And he will cease to dream. He will die in Chicago, a long way from home.

In Tulsa, Oklahoma, in 1921, an American citizen of African descent, a man of middle-class means and middle-class values, is entangled in a rampaging swale of white people who have nothing to do with him except that, in the way of such things, they bring his life to an end. His family is asking for reparations even yet. Repair, they know, they will never get.

A smooth brown man named Elijah says that he saw his own father lynched by a lawless crowd. After years of remembering, and thinking, and stirring, and smoldering, he has come to believe that the men who did this thing to his father, and all like them, are devils with whom it is impossible to live in dignity and peace. He has preached his message in the wilderness. By 1963, from a country of hundreds of millions of people, he can reliably count 6,000 converts. They call themselves Muslims. Because they are descendants of Africans, they make the term more precise. They are Black Muslims.

Children are holding books tightly to their sweaters and blouses. The children are walking down a corridor of people. Some of these people hold rifles. The people with rifles are accompanied by angry men and women. The angry men and women are shouting at the children. The children are going to school. It is the morning of the first day of classes. Everyone is excited by what the new year will bring.

In the year 1955, in the hamlet of Money, Mississippi, a boy named Emmitt Till thought he would pull the tail of the tiger, and did so. The tiger devoured him, most cruelly. Emmitt had seen tigers before, of course, but he had not seen this kind of tiger nor seen tigers so wholly permitted to roam free.

The youngest person ever elected to the presidency of the United States finds himself besieged by suitors. The suitors are citizens of the United States. They trace ancestry to Africa. They want to vote, to speak freely, to be educated equally, to live where they can afford to live, to travel freely, and to move about without intimidation. In short, they want the promises made to them, long denied. When the suitors leave, the young President turns to his aide. He is exasperated. He says, "Where are they getting these ideas?" The aide says, "From you, Mr. President."

A minister is speaking. He has a doctorate from a northern university, but he is a son of the South. His words echo traditional southern sermons. But he has turned those sermons to a special end. He wants to set his people free. On a chosen day, he sends wave after wave of young people and church ladies into the streets of Birmingham, Alabama, along the way from the Sixteenth Street Baptist Church to downtown. A man named Bull Connor waits there. Mr. Connor has powerful fire hoses, and he has dogs. Mr. Connor does not like these people walking in his streets. He spins the people in the street with water from the fire hoses, and he keeps his dogs on long leashes, the better for the lunging and biting. When some of the marchers break ranks, Bull Connor is delighted. "Look at those niggers run," he cries. The rest, he arrests, or near abouts.

A photograph reverberates from the streets of Birmingham. The photograph shows a young black man being bitten by a German shepherd. Doubtless, the German shepherd is a good dog. He is being used for an improper purpose. The misuse of the dog causes many disinterested people to become interested. They do not like to see dogs treated like that. Some people also notice that a Negro is being bitten.

It is Freedom Summer 1964. Idealistic college students swarm the South. They believe that they can change the world. Specifically, they believe that they can change the world by securing for black people the right to vote. Three of the students are taken at night by law enforcement officers. The three students are shotgunned. They are buried in the earthwork of a levee. After the bodies are discovered, the autopsies show that the black man, alone among the three, had been beaten nearly to death before he was shot.

The young President has been assassinated in Dallas, Texas. Democrat Lyndon Johnson now holds the office. He puts the full force of his power and his personality behind the passage of the 1964 Civil Rights Act. When the act passes in July of that year, the President turns to a companion, "I fear that we have delivered the White House to the Republican Party for years to come."

By legislation and by United States Supreme court decision, other laws are being changed. People of all races can eat together, recreate together, go to school together, and share public transportation. From one side, it is as if a floodgate has opened. From the other, it is as if a great dam still stands, cracked only slightly to allow a trickle of life-giving water. A newspaperman in Detroit says, "That 'look how much we've gained in the last fifty years' stuff—that sours on the young Negro's stomach—we're going to see violence."

"There go my people," said Gandhi, "and I must catch them, for I am their leader." The minister who led the protest in Birmingham and whose name is Martin Luther King Jr. is fond of this expression. His fondness is of a worn and wearied kind. He has claimed moral authority for his people precisely because they have not permitted themselves to engage in violence. But he cannot stop the future from arriving. He is hurrying toward it.

Some people call it a rebellion. More people call it a riot. It is August of 1965. The endless summer in south-central Los Angeles, in the neighborhood called Watts, explodes. For the remaining years of the decade, summers will be referred to as the "riot season." The expression "Burn, baby, burn" enters the mainstream.

Huey Newton and Bobby Seale form the Black Panther Party in California. They say many things. They mean some of the things they say. But it is a photograph of the two men that inflames people. In the photograph, the men pose as revolutionaries. They are wearing black clothes and black berets. They are carrying rifles. In the presentation, they are refusing old etiquette. They do not look down to the ground, they do not duck, they do not scuffle, and they do not apologize for anger.

Cassius Clay is being buried alive. Lew Alcindor is becoming a Kareem. Curt Flood is thinking about saying no. Athletes are discovering that sport is a platform on which many structures can be built.

His own time approaching, Lee Evans shifts in his lane. Everything that has happened is coming toward him. He is deciding what to do. He could move away, of course. He could stand somewhere else. He could look away and not toward. He could pretend not to see. He could not care. Or, then again, he could stand where he is. He could see what he sees, feel what he feels, and react as he does.

# .2

*A young man has to have his wild nights.*

San Jose, California, was Speed City in 1968. From all over the country fast folk drifted into town. They ran for San Jose State or the San Jose City College or the Santa Clara Valley Youth Village. One notable runner even enrolled in a local high school. Tommie Smith and Lee Evans were at the heart of the gathering. Tommie Smith was reputed to be the fastest all-around sprinter in the history of the sport, capable of winning races and setting world records at events as diverse as 500 meters indoors and 100 meters outdoors, not that he actually set world records at either of those two far-flung distances. But he could have, as no one who saw him run doubted. Lee Evans was the contrast to Tommie. While Tommie ran with silken grace, using his Tommie-Jet gear when necessary, Lee ran rough. Friends said he ran "everywhere" in his lane. Like a Tasmanian devil they thought, everywhere at once. One sportswriter was more prosaic. He said that Lee Evans ran like a man struggling out of a corset. Lee had made small changes to his motion over the years, but as long as he was moving fast, he didn't bother much with it. And he was definitely moving fast. Lee had been national champion in 1966 in the 440, only one year after graduating from high school, and he repeated the feat in 1967. With these accomplishments, Lee Evans was not a man with whom one trifled. Except that John Carlos and Billy Gaines were doing exactly that.

Gaines was from New Jersey, and Carlos was from New York. Both had been east for the early outdoor meets, and they returned to San Jose with news of Lee's imminent demise. The two Speed City sprinters had seen the first fire from the Mighty Burner, in the telling a mythical creature, something akin to a sea monster spotted occasionally in rough water, or a strange and unfamiliar piper to carry the children away, or a ship that sailed only at night, unmanned, or perhaps a light visible from the desert floor, a light that no one had seen before and no one could identify. In short, what Billy and John described was a killer of dreams. The two men were talking about Villanova University's Larry James, who was not a sea monster of course, who carried no children away, had nothing to do with ships that sailed at night, and whose light was easily identified. And what they said was not so much any of that, except in tone, but closer to this: "Oh, you should see, what will happen to you when the Burner gets you."

James was the kind of person who is the feature of every Olympic year. He was a new and sensational athlete who could shake up the existing order. A triple jumper and hurdler in high school, the second-fastest runner on a record-setting high school team, he had not even been on the national lists as a quarter-miler during his first college season. At the Penn Relays in 1968, however, the thin, gentle-appearing sophomore shocked observers by running a 43.9 anchor leg in Villanova's mile-relay victory. No one had seen anything like it. The time was said to be the fastest any human had covered the distance and superior to the world record for the open event. And it wasn't just the time, but the way he had done it. Larry James floated. This was a man who released energy with beautiful efficiency. Even the coach of the San Jose State team did not restrain his enthusiasm. Bud Winter said that Larry James was like Tommie Smith—that he had a gazellelike smoothness, "like pouring cream on a dance floor." From all appearances, Larry James could run as fast as he wanted to run, as long as he wanted to continue. When the national media got a look at Larry James they were agog. News articles and reports praised him. Implicitly, they placed him in opposition to the struggling, work-about image of San Jose State's Lee Evans.

In any case, Lee Evans was damaged goods. He and his friend Tommie—his fellow traveler, one is tempted to add—had gotten themselves embroiled in a potential boycott by black athletes of the Mexico City Olympics. In truth, the two were leading the movement, along with a professor on campus in San Jose. They called it the Olympic Project for Human Rights. And it wasn't just a boycott; it was a lot of other stuff that nobody quite remembered, but meant trouble. So it was better, wasn't it, to have a man running for the United States like Larry James, who had said nothing, so far as anyone had noted, about the subject of the boycott, his apparent purpose being limited to making the team?

:

San Jose State was running the mile relay against Villanova at Fresno, California, on Saturday night May 11, 1968 at the West Coast Relays. Lee would run anchor for San Jose State; Larry James would run anchor for Villanova. A Villanova victory would add insult to injury because Fresno happened to be Lee Evans's hometown. Naturally, the people closest to Lee thought that he would win. Others doubted. They remembered a race the year before when he and Tommie had run against each other in an event that had attracted worldwide attention. He lost that race. They also recalled a big race this indoor season, a time when Lee and two other runners came to the line together. Despite battling back from a deficit, the winner was serene, almost winged, while Lee was an anguished loser. No one cared that he had been in an early stage of his preparation, and he hadn't made much of the fact either. He just put the experience in the proper place. He put it in his memory, along with other slights and disappointments, where it could do him some good. He put it where the rage was.

Lee could be angry. He could afford that. With the high heat, he could set himself in steel. But the first task, the one that separated success from failure, was to be easy, and loose, and cool. Encouraged by San Jose State coach Bud Winter, whom he respected, Lee Evans aspired to total relaxation under pressure. In the days before a big race, he withdrew. He spent hours in each of those days rehearsing. In his mind he saw himself leaving the apartment. He saw the drive or the walk to the track; he greeted admirers and well-wishers; he practiced remarks to keep the greetings brief; he went to the warm-up area where he jogged and ran increasingly brisk strides. He felt his long spikes pierce the cinder and dirt, first at the ball of his foot and then rolling up toward his toes as he gathered his stride beneath him, and he listened always for the characteristic pock and crunch. He saw, too, the small divots kicked up in his wake, and felt them on his calves. Drawing closer, he heard the announcement of the first and second and then the final call. He took his sweats off, confirmed his lane assignment, and walked to the customary spot. The remaining seconds were occupied by his own, last, affirming thoughts. Standing behind the blocks, he stepped forward at the first command, shook himself free, and then he settled. With a relaxed, composed breath, he was off with the gun. In the hours and the days before the event, he broke the yardage down. He did this and then that and then this other thing and then he saw the tape. He felt this and then that and then this other thing, and then he felt the tape. In the end, he always won. He had seen it. The race was old to him before it was run.

:

Fresno was bubbling on the weekend. From all over California fans were arriving for the Relays. Promotional material said that the meet was where world records were broken. That was something to anticipate. This year, though, Tommie and Lee brought the meet a special fervor. All the talk about boycotts, about leveraging power, putting pressure on people who too long had been free of it, or at least secure from it, had people stirred. Some of the fans would be wild in their support. They would be raucous and joyful, and expecting a big thing to happen not only tonight but in the weeks and months ahead, a prospect they savored and shared and wished for, as if they were one of the two men in the arena, brave, forthright, unbowed. Other people, of a different sort entirely, would be apoplectic, churning and gnashing a bit, resentful. They could be angry beyond the capacity for thought. With the slightest rustle or social misstep, the whole stadium could get a little jumpy, to put the best light on it. This didn't matter. The fans came anyway. Almost 9,000 came on the Friday night to old Radcliffe Stadium and 14,000 came for the concluding Saturday session. On both nights, a show of speed brought the fans up in a sweep of unrehearsed admiration, the usual whoo's, and whee's and whistles, and the arms and the legs sweeping the air and punching into a noise that rose and fell. But always there was something held back, as if the crowd would not commit fully to the meet until the last event had been run, the one for which they had set themselves.

Fans and commentators would later say that the meet had not been quite as good as other editions. This despite the fact that the meet featured Tommie Smith on Friday night, Bob Seagren trying for a world record in the vault, and USC's stunning hurdler, Earl McCullouch, as well as Dave Patrick's Villanova two-mile relay team solidly beating Jim Ryun's Kansas Jayhawks. All this was fine, but none of it diverted the attention of the waiting and watchful crowd. Even the first appearance of Lee Evans was not enough. Anchoring his San Jose State 880-relay team to a win over Kansas, the Spartan runner was looking over his shoulder, harboring energy for the main event some fifty minutes later. Like everyone else in the crowd, Lee Evans had Larry James in mind. It was the mile relay he was thinking of.

Nineteen sixty-eight was a year of mile relays and mile-relay teams. Indeed, the Southwestern Athletic Conference (SWAC) alone—with Prairie View and Southern and Arkansas AM&N as well as Texas Southern—could put four or five teams on the track that could go faster that 3:10. Add Rice, Lamar Tech, UCLA, Villanova, and San Jose State, and the U.S. world of quarter miling was blessed indeed. All over the country great mile relays were being run. But the mile relay at Fresno was special. Special, that is, except for one uncertainty. What if the two key players weren't near each other at the last exchange? This was possible, even likely, because the teams weren't evenly matched. Villanova was much faster through the first three legs. In fact, Villanova brought a seasonal best of 3:06.1, while San Jose State had only recorded 3:10.2. Lee knew that this was a problem. He was talking to his teammates about it. Keep me close. Just keep me close. I'll do the rest.

Lee did not doubt the outcome if he was given a fair chance. He trained for this situation. While some quarter men were idling in the fall, he was doing six- and seven-mile runs. While some were running repeat 220s, he was running repeat 500s. When the imagined others were taking full recovery between repeats, he was cutting the rest interval. When they were training to race a quarter mile—or 400 meters in the Olympic year—he was training to race past the line, to assure that he dominated the last five meters. When they doubted their training or wondered at their preparation, Lee Evans was confident. "I am the best-coached athlete here. I am the best-prepared athlete here. I am going to win," he would say to himself. That was the set of his mind. This night in Fresno, Lee had something else going for him. He had known for some time that a fight was brewing, and that he was going to be in it. He did not need John Carlos or Billy Gaines to tell him anything. At the Madison Square Garden Invitational in February, Lee had watched with interest as James streaked to victory in the 500 yards. Naturally, he asked Villanova coach Jim Elliott what event the new star would run outdoors. Coach Elliott said nothing. He winked at Lee Evans and walked away.

:

At 10:12 in the evening, when the sunny afternoon had long given way to cool darkness, meet officials finally called the mile relay. Dozens and dozens of events had been run; hundreds of athletes had already run. Their work done, they stayed to watch, hypercharging an already emotional evening. As the gun sounded for the start, Lee Evans and Larry James joined them as spectators.

Lee had seen the unfolding events before. As part of his routine, he had seen them in the mind's eye. He had seen San Jose State's third man coming to the line. He had seen the darkness in the distance and the relief of the lights and the shadows on the track, moving, distorted, changing but sensible. He had seen this third man with his arm outstretched, holding out a baton, running dead even with the third man for Villanova. And there he was, arriving like a scheduled train. This third man was real, after all, as had been his two predecessors. It had not taken a heroic effort, just a willingness to do what was possible. The average split for the three San Jose State men was only 48.18, but that happened to be exactly what Villanova's three men also averaged. With a three-quarter split of 2:24.5, the two anchors were away. The peculiarity in the scene was that there were three anchors and not two. Ron Freeman of Arizona State was with Lee and Larry. Ron's presence was particularly troublesome because he got in Lee's way, a thing he had every right to do, a matter of his own interest, and the usual sorting out that relays promise and deliver, but one that produced a situation for the frontrunner to exploit. With a clear track in front of him, the young Mr. James glided away.

Bud Winter said that Lee was a tiger when he ran from behind. Lee once said he actually preferred to run from that position and that he would close any gap gradually. No one recorded what Ron Freeman said, an oversight made interesting only as the Olympic year progressed. On this night, however, Lee slipped past Ron and gave Villanova chase. Running with control and determination, he set his sights on the man every sportswriter on the East Coast thought was unbeatable. Was Larry James running as fast as he could? Or was he hoarding energy? How fast was he out? Did he have another gear? If so, when could he be expected to use it? These were all intriguing questions and would all be answered in due course, but they were not immediate concerns as Lee went into the first curve and came to the head of the backstretch. The immediate concerns were the one, two, three, four, five yards that Lee needed back.

By the middle of the backstretch, Lee Evans was running his usual raggedy run, a man in a hurry, chasing along, but he was firmly attached to the shoulder of his quarry. He had recovered the lost yards.

On closer inspection, was Lee's race all that raggedy? He had a high knee lift. His stride was long. His turnover was increasing. He was relaxed in the arms and shoulders. The jawline was loose, the neck unstrained, and the trunk was without tension. He was breathing deeply, and he was running according to a well-considered plan. Adjustments were being made as necessary. For

17

his part, Larry James was floating so softly that he barely seemed to touch the cinders. There was something elemental in this: the moving tableau, shifting fortune, an idea about the future, and so the 14,000 watchful people were lifted at last. They were standing and shouting and whistling. They were banging things, some of them easy to imagine: seats, girders, cups, each other, anything to make more noise. They were also wondering.

These were the quiet thoughts. Lee Evans was extended. He did not look comfortable; he looked strong, but he did not look easy, and now he had to deal with the ever flowing Burner, who was almost certainly going to ratchet up the cadence and the strength and the speed as the two runners exhausted the backstretch and made the circling turn toward home. Larry sprinted and Lee held. The two men went through the turn. Larry James held and Lee sprinted. Lee Evans pulled up to Larry James's shoulder. Was it a feint? A last grasp for triumph? Was it a nettle or a crown?

Lee knew the crowd was excited, to say the very least. He could hear the waves of noise. Looking up, for just a glance, he could see the ecstatic faces. Finally, a proper ending for a day now spent, they were getting their money's worth. He knew these people. Indeed, he figured he knew them all. He might not know the names, and some might be visitors, but he knew some had come out of the fields. They were picking cotton and getting paid by the pound as his family had, and as he had. He knew others had worked a long day yesterday at the factory or on the roads in the heat for little money. Others were in the armed services, some by choice and others drafted. More than a few of these boys had tickets to Vietnam, some with a wall and an inscription the only future. Lee knew some in the crowd from high school and some from college. Many in the stands were middle aged and prosperous, having made California the dream for many other Americans. Some of these people came up from Louisiana as his family had, and others, like Tommie's, from mean old sunburned Texas. He knew his high school coach, Stan Dowell, was near, and that Stan was proud of him and he of Stan.

Lee knew that Bud was crouching somewhere, of course, taking in every detail. He knew that Bud loved him and respected him.

*Three across: Larry James (left), Lee Evans (center), and Ron Freeman (right) emerge from the tangle.*

Against all this, Lee also knew that some of the people in the stands hated him. If they could, they would stop him. They did not want to see him win anything. They wanted him gone and forgotten, him and all his kind, gone and forgotten forever. Lee had said too much. He had arrogated power and taken it from them. He was uppity. He was not humble. He was not a patriot. He was not even an American. Possibly, some of these people wanted him dead. Death threats came to him now. Every day, he lived with them, as did Tommie Smith. Neither man could safely take a single stride down a single track. The decade of the bullet, the assassin, with good men in pools of blood, had proved how accessible they all were, all who wanted to make a difference, the ones who said so.

None of this mattered, not immediately, not on this night. These projections of thought, these aspects of awareness, are mere flashes, eruptions of the unconscious given expression. This is the truth: In the late evening of May 11, 1968, in the coolness of the faded sun in Fresno, California, his hometown, Lee Evans was running a race. He had a baton in his hand. He had wonderful teammates desperately interested in the outcome. He was where he was

19

supposed to be; he was doing what he was supposed to be doing. He could hear the cinders kicking under his feet. He could hear his own breathing. He could sense the relaxation of his body. Emotion rose within him. Amid the uproar, Lee Evans felt peaceful, the way a man does when walking his own property at the end of a long day.

Time was upon him. The finish line was just ahead.

# .3

*In California the people sleep out every night.*
*That's what the song says.*

Lee Evans was born in the country in 1947. The country he was born in no longer exists because the country he was born in was in California, and California is now paved, or people have built glass houses on its hillsides, or other people have burned it down in a kind of social unrest. Some of the state has fallen into the ocean. This happens every day. But, who can say? The place where Lee was born might still be the country, like it was when Lee was there. A person might be able to go see. If you would like to do this, the little place where Lee Evans was born is Madera, California. Madera is twenty-two miles north of Fresno, to be precise. When Lee was there, Madera was a good place to "go from" if you wanted to go into the fields to work, which is what Lee's mother did. In the summer, she'd take all the children out there with her. Once upon a time, she put baby Lee on a cotton sack and set him beside her when she was picking. Lee says that he was lucky not to get pneumonia, but no one listens to him when he says that. As soon as he could, Lee got his own sack for cotton or his own tray for grapes and he went to work. Lee was very young then, of course, so his mother took the money he made and she put it in a sock. She hid the sock in her bedroom. From time to time, she pulled the money out of that sock and used it to buy Lee shoes or shirts or pants, maybe some school supplies or a coat. Lee's mother, speaking plainly, was his north and south in those days. He also had a father, whom he loved. Lee's father did what fathers often do in affection for wife and children. Lee's father worked hard all his life. He was a hod carrier most of the time, but he did other kinds of work as well. Lee's father was from Louisiana. Lee had the idea that his father could never go back there, although no one would ever say why. Lee thought some about Louisiana, where his mother was also born. But mostly he thought about why his father couldn't go back there. The world was full of possibilities, of which his father admitted one. "Jim Crow back there," he would say, "Jim Crow."

In a close, happy family, Lee was a middle child among six brothers and sisters. Every one of them had the Holy Ghost to rely on, courtesy of the Church of Christ, which was bedrock to the family, giving Lee a faith he did not lose. Of course, not only in the church, but also in every way, he and his brothers and sisters were tumbled together. Who influenced whom in the family would be hard to say, only that they did. It is true, though, that one of Lee's brothers, who was five years older, was a champion runner. Maybe this older brother was where Lee had gotten his start as a runner. Or maybe Lee had been a runner all along. This might be so because Lee spent a lot of time daydreaming, and some of the daydreaming was about running. Lee's daydreamed running was mostly in the fields, filled with trees and grasses and open valleys and across streams.

The running did not have lanes, and the running did not make one person a winner and another person a loser, and it did not make that result permanent, so that a person who lost a race always lost that race and a person who won a race always won that race. Like all daydreaming, Lee's dreams looped and repeated and changed. Still, Lee was out there, in his mind. When the chances came to run in real life, he was out there too, doing that. Lee also did a lot of fishing. As a matter of fact, Lee still fishes all the time. If you want his attention, it is better to say fish than anything else. Lee was a regular boy. This is what it comes down to, but he was preparing an active, able mind and an active, able body. Maybe as important, Lee was not being damaged. Within the family and the near community, his native opportunities were being saved for him and not squandered or spirited away, as often occurs.

Lee's family moved from tiny Madera to Fresno when Lee was old enough to go to school. Of course, Lee went to a public school.

A public school is a place that records differences between children. All the children are thrown into a mix, and then they are quickly sorted out again by preference. This is a way of bringing order to what otherwise would be an unruly rabble of children. At the school Lee went to the white kids sat in the front near the teacher, while Lee and the other two black kids sat in the back. From there, Lee had a good view of the whole room. He saw that the white kids didn't get in trouble for the little bits of mischief that got him and his two seatmates in trouble. One time Lee said to the teacher, "I do not want to sing today," but the teacher made him do it anyway. But when the white kids said that they did not want to sing, the teacher said nothing and they did not sing.

This is a small matter to be pulled out and examined, you might say, but the small events are the components of memory, and memory is what makes a person. It comes to this: The young Lee Evans was noticing the way he was being treated. More to the point, he was noticing that he was being treated differently than the white kids. Knowing this, he did not rustle or fight because his nature was quiet. The things he noticed, he noticed for himself. But they were important. Later, when Lee was well known, the stories of his childhood would say: Lee had bad shoes, and other kids had good shoes, and Lee had one shirt and one pair of pants, and other kids had many sets of clothes. This is likely true, but Lee does not talk much about that anymore. He says that his family was not rich and was not poor. That is where he leaves the question. But that back-row seat assigned to him and his two classmates? He talks about that.

Lee was growing outside school as well. The days in the school belonged to someone else. Outside, much of his time was his own. Some days he and his brother Dayton Jr. would collect Coke bottles and turn them in for cash. With the little bit of cash generated, the two boys would move through the town all day, sitting or talking and walking, exploring, mostly waiting for something to happen. Sometimes, they fished. Sometimes, they played games alone or with other kids they knew or met. But, together, they were making something of themselves. In Lee's case, he was developing a habit of exercise and movement. He was learning specific lessons, too, from Dayton. One day, the road outside the Evans's house was being paved. Out there in the road at day's end, the contractors left a nail. The nail was stuck in the road. Lee went out there and worked a bit at that nail, trying to get it for himself. He did not budge the nail, and he left it where it was. Then, Dayton Jr. went out to the nail. He worked and worked and worked until the nail came out and Dayton Jr. had himself a prize. Lee looked at what his little brother had done and he understood something. He understood that the nail had come out because his brother had tried harder than he had tried. He made a note of this. He reminded himself, next time, to try harder.

:

Lee was a good athlete when he was a child. But he was too small to be much good to anybody, despite what he might say now. What Lee says now is that even into high school he was small, but he was fast. That is fine, but it is not good to be fast and small, when the alternative is to be big and fast. To make this point, Lee's high school had a special place they put the little kids. They called the place a C league. It is hard to believe that any kid wants to run in a C league. What do you get when you beat all the other little kids in a C league? Anyway, Lee did this for two years. He was one of the best little kids in the state! But the summer after his sophomore year, Lee's family went to Oregon. Up in Oregon, where you can be very, very certain some fishing took place, Lee got big. Lee did not get big like Too Tall Jones, but thirty pounds of muscle big. And then you know the rest. Lee went back to high school, and he was not little Lee any more, not that he was big Lee either, but it was pretty easy to see he wasn't big and he wasn't little, and that he was still very, very fast. He was fast enough and big enough to play tailback on the football team, or whatever they called tailback, and when they gave Lee the ball, he would run for a long time before they pulled him to the grass, but it was not an easy thing they did.

This football Lee played wasn't in Fresno. He was in San Jose, California, enrolled in a new school by then. The entire family had moved after the summer because his mother had caught "valley fever" from the chemicals in the fields outside Fresno. She could not work in the fields any longer and as a result neither could Lee. It didn't matter much, except that Lee had to find other ways to make money, like caddying, which he did not like. What he didn't like were the golfers, who often tipped him like the money was a charity for which they should be congratulated. They reached down and gave him a little or a little bit more than a little, but rarely a lot. But always they decided what to give, and he took what they gave. This routine wasn't suited to Lee's temperament, which was a bit prickly from pride and self-respect.

The business about the golfing, the carrying, and the men is another of the little stories that a person ought to get past, but most don't. And maybe most shouldn't after all, because it is important to learn that somebody has to carry the bag, and somebody's bag has to be carried, and young people have to decide at what end of that business they want to be on, if they can. And if they can't—if they have to live always as a bag carrier or always as a person whose bag is being carried, that is important, too—but this particular experience should not grow too large in the telling. Much more important was that Lee soon met some pretty smart people in San Jose, and some of them were prepared to help him along the way. One of those pretty smart people was named Stanley Dowell. Stanley Dowell had been in the Army, but he must have gotten knocked on the head because when he, a white guy, came out of the service, he thought, "Well, I will teach school. I will teach school to kids who really do need a guy like me, an ex-army man who has filtered, if you get me, all the nonsense out of me." Given the chance, this is exactly what he did.

Stanley Dowell took a job as a teacher and a coach at a high school on the east side of San Jose, where most of the students were black or Hispanic. And one day passed, and time passed, and then some more time passed, and students were coming and going, and Stanley Dowell was sitting in the stands at Overfelt High School after a practice of some kind on a fall afternoon. The sun was shining right in his eyes, but in such a way that if Stan Dowell shaded his eyes with his clipboard, he could make something out headed his way. And when the coach shaded his eyes with the clipboard, it wasn't just the sun he was blocking out. He was blocking out the entire head, neck, shoulders, and torso of this not big but not little fellow walking in his direction, and he was looking just at the legs of this fellow, whereupon he said out loud, "I can tell from the legs alone that you are a runner."

If this were the Bible, and the whole of the Bible were about Lee and his being a champion, which of course would make it something of a new Bible with a different kind of message, this might be the place where the words would be: In the beginning. You understand, of course, that that would not be strictly true, because there is never a beginning except that someone comes along with a different idea and backs the whole story deeper into history. But a story has to start somewhere. So start with the clipboard, the sun, the shaded eyes, and the appraisal. Beginning there, the fact soon became obvious that Coach Dowell was a hard one, for all his good intentions. He thought that speed in a runner was a good thing. In fact, he loved the idea of people running fast. But he was very, very interested in making fast people strong. If you are the runner, you know what this means: You might want to call your parents because you will be home later than usual.

At first Coach Dowell had to work through another coach who had responsibility for the track and field program. But eventually, Coach Dowell was able to give advice to this boy he had seen behind the clipboard. If Coach Dowell said, "You do this, and you will win," the boy would think it over, because this was a smart kid after all, and then he would say, "Well, you have said it." He would then do what was required. And soon this boy, whom you no doubt have figured was Lee Evans, came into his own kind of power. He joined a community of men, many gone, others only older, but all with much to teach him.

# .4

*A fond farewell to Dr. Wint and a tip of the cap
to Hustling Herb.*

Arthur Wint was a giant Jamaican who was said to run in seven-
league boots with nine-foot strides. Actually, as you, being no one's
fool, might have guessed, Wint wasn't really a giant. He was only 6
feet, 4 inches, although he might have appeared taller than that
because he was slender, even to the point of being spindly. And he
never ran in seven-league boots. In all likelihood, Arthur Wint did
not even know what a seven-league boot was or where one, or a
pair, might be acquired or to what purpose they should be put.
Rather, Wint ran in the standard-issue leather, black, spiked track
shoe common for his day. Perhaps as a boy he ran barefoot over
grass tracks on the warm island he came from. Finally, doubt may
exist about the length of Arthur Wint's stride. Maybe he ran with
nine-foot strides and maybe he didn't. Maybe he ran with nine-
foot strides some of the time and other times he didn't. Without
doubt, Wint did win two Olympic silver medals in the 800 meters,
and he did lose both those races to America's smooth-striding Mal
Whitfield. Win or lose, the gentleman from Jamaica was a favorite
in England, to which he had come in 1944 to fly for the Royal Air
Force and in which he had remained to complete his medical
studies at the famous St. Bart's. There, in his studies, making time
for training at the local tracks, surrounded by his mates from the
club for which he ran, the future Dr. Wint was but a glance across
the ocean from a great adversary and teammate, a man who had
taken a different course but with whom he was destined to collide.
  Herb McKenley was also a tall Jamaican, although no one called

him a giant. More often they suggested, without exactly saying, that Herb was deranged. He was a sensation at the University of Illinois, where he received his education and his competitive blooding, and it was at Illinois that his wondrous nature was confirmed. Herb was a sprinter who just could not keep his hands off the quarter mile, but neither could he stay away from the 100 or the 200. Like many people of many gifts, McKenley appeared anxious to do everything at once, as if concentration on the one event would bore him. In Olympic finals, McKenley was fourth at 200 meters in 1948 and a narrow second at 100 meters in 1952. In the Olympic 100-meter final, observers figured that if the race had been one meter farther, the victory would have gone to Herb. Even when he settled on the quarter, Herb ran like a man who had money burning a hole in his pocket. He had one fixed imperative: He wanted to spend whatever energy he had as fast as he could. Meaning, McKenley went out very fast indeed in his one-lap races and then crawled in. A four-second differential between first and second halves was not unusual.

Arthur Wint, the giant, ran a race at 400 meters against Herb McKenley, the brilliant dabbler, at the 1948 Olympic Games in London, England. This being the first Olympics after World War II, London was still bombed out, hungry, and deprived. It was also, however, England, and England was capable of putting on a good show and was enthusiastic about the challenge. The track events were held at Wembley Stadium on a cinder track made soft by periodic rain. These Games gave the sporting world Zatopek in his first edition, a jazzlike improvisation in form who made his competitors seem old and joyless; the teenager Bob Mathias, tired under his blankets waiting for the final events in the decathlon; the veteran hurdler Don Finley, a true Brit if ever there was, now back from the war with his best years behind him; and the Swedes in the 1,500, representative of a state that stayed out of the war, save the few individuals, like Raoul Wallenberg, who did the right thing in the entire country's behalf, and perished. If it seems like a cloud to mention the war, to mention a death with the Olympic Games of Wint and McKenley going on, you must remember that in London in 1948 nearly every mature person in the stands, surely, had a death in mind, and many competitors, too. Loss and pain fell from the sky.

:

Track fans have always argued about the quarter. Was it for strong runners or fast runners? Was it for sprinters moving up or for middle-distance runners stepping down? Buried in the debate was the assumption that every quarter-miler was either fast or slow, strong or weak, in disproportion. Famously, Ben Eastman was the strong runner, and Bill Carr was the fast runner when the two met in 1932, in the Intercollegiate Association of Amateur Athletes of America meet (IC4A), at the Olympic trials, and in the Olympic final in Los Angeles. Eastman was assigned the role of the strong runner because he was the world-record holder for the half mile. Carr was assigned the speed role because he had been, prior to moving to the quarter, a respectable sprinter. Carr won all three confrontations. In Los Angeles Carr came away not only with the gold medal but the world record of 46.2. The advantage here was to the sprinter. Rudolf Harbig balanced the result and maintained the debate between speed and strength. That Harbig had exceptional speed is agreed, but that he was oriented to the longer distances is evident in his training and his results. In the winter, Harbig was accustomed to taking forest runs of between ninety minutes and two and a half to three hours, sometimes through snow, changing pace throughout from hard running to easy jogging. And Harbig ran 800 meters in 1:46.6 in 1939, a world record until 1955. The record for the 800 meters joined his other record, the one for 400 meters. That one was 46.0, and it remained the world record until 1948 when Herb McKenley beat it by running 45.9.

:

In 1948, Hustling Herb McKenley, the faster runner, was reckoned to be unbeatable in the 400 meters at London. Herb McKenley knew better. If he slipped, his fellow Jamaican would take advantage. Tall Arthur would cast his shadow on even the coldest

29

and wettest of London days. On August 5, 1948, the rain came down in Wembley Stadium, the cinders grew wet and then soft, and a capacity crowd of 67,000 people showed up anyway to see Herb McKenley race Arthur Wint. McKenley had his world record for the event, and he had the favored lane two. Wint had his silver medal in the 800 meters in 1:49.5, and he had lane three. What was a man with speed to do in such a situation? What was a man like the second Jamaican, the one not from the RAF, not running with a local club, not living in London, not cheered with every breath, not a doctor being trained at the local hospital, not lionized for past victories, and not joined by mates and friends crowded on the rail, to do but burn it up? At the gun, Herb did what he was compelled by nature and character to do, although another man might have attended Arthur Wint and waited. True to himself, uninhibited by circumstance, McKenley went out very, very quickly. Some officials put the 200-meter split at 21-flat, a time faster than the 21.1 Mel Patton ran to win the 200 meters in these Games. Others had the split at 21.4 to Wint's 22.2. McKenley entered the homestretch with a four-yard lead over Wint and an eight-yard lead over Mal Whitfield, who was also doubling down from the 800. Then, McKenley did what runners do on soft tracks. He got tired. When he got tired, he got nervous. When he got nervous, he started looking over his shoulder, or maybe he wasn't so much looking over his shoulder with intention as he was wrenching and struggling. In short, McKenley, the surest bet at these Olympics, tied up, and Arthur Wint cut him down in the homestretch. The respective times were 46.2 and 46.4. The half-miler had won. A second half-miler, Whitfield, had closed brilliantly to take the bronze. McKenley was unhappily in the middle.

:

Herb McKenley was the loser in London, but he had a measure of revenge. From that day in London in 1948, the developing story of the quarter mile was all about speed and its proper application over the distance. McKenley had speed, he had great speed. He had just mismanaged it. If McKenley had run even 21.4 for the first 200 meters on the wet track in London, how fast would that split have

*All the doctors are good, but this one is golden. Wint wins.*
*McKenley is second.*

been on a modern, tuned surface? Arthur Wint, of course, had speed, too, but it was speed of a different and lesser magnitude. Prominently, Arthur Wint had strength, and it was that strength that took him past Herb McKenley in Wembley Stadium. Nonetheless, Arthur Wint was outmoded by the time he reached the finish line. Herb McKenley made him so, even as he trailed. It was Herb who captured the imagination. How much better would Herb have been, fans asked, if he had been more temperate, if he had been more selective, if he had become strong enough, somewhere along the line, to match his performance to his impetuosity and ambition? All that speed is gone to waste, the implication went, for want of the secondary qualities. And so Herb McKenley, in his disappointment, sinking into the dead track in London, created a kind of grail, a goal to be quested after. Even now, some track fans refer to Herb McKenley as the man who should have been the first to run a 44.0 quarter mile. When people say this, the pure speed of the man impels the belief. Likewise, the speed of the man creates the regret.

McKenley ran the 400 meters again at the Helsinki Olympics in

1952. After his narrow disappointment in the 100, he lost to George Rhoden, yet another Jamaican and a man with legitimate sprint speed of his own. Arthur Wint was fifth. Thereafter, every four years, sprinters lined up and took the medals: Charlie Jenkins, a tough veteran of Villanova relay teams and indoor events, won the gold in 1956 over favored teammates; Otis Davis, erstwhile basketball player, high-jumper, hurdler, and sprinter, outleaned Germany's Carl Kaufmann in the 1960 Rome Olympics in a world record 44.9 (45.09 electric phototimer). In 1964 at Tokyo, Mike Larrabee beat Wendell Mottley of Trinidad-Tobago in 45.1. A 220 man of national note, Larrabee had run 44.9 for 400 meters earlier in the year to equal Davis's world record. If these winners were not quite as fast as some who came later, neither were they slow. Nor were they people with established reputations in the half mile or 800 meters. That day was over. And should readers line up to object, an historical note is added: When he won both events in 1976 at Montreal, Alberto Juantorena moved up to the 800 meters from the 400 meters, where he had previously been ranked best in the world. The direction of the journey makes the difference.

:

As a freshman in high school, Lee Evans weighed eighty pounds, and he ran the 660-yard dash in 1:29.2. As a sophomore in high school, Lee weighed between ninety and one hundred pounds, and he ran 330 yards in 36.0, a San Joaquin Valley record for the C class. With the additional weight and power acquired in the summer after his sophomore year, in the football season that fall and early in the track season, Lee was ready to do much more. Although he flirted with the idea of becoming a half-miler, Lee finally set his eye firmly on the quarter mile. Here he would be required to summon reserves of speed, strength, endurance, work ethic, coaching, and competitive fire. But of these, the first was speed. Strength was critical, and on the important day it could distinguish a winner from a loser, but the purpose of strength was to sustain speed; it was not a separate value. In this critical regard, Lee Evans received the entire benefit of Herb McKenley's experience.

Coincidentally, there was another man in San Jose who was closer yet to Herb, a man who would take not only the benefit of Herb McKenley's experience but also its burden. This was a man of many events, like Herb had been, with many records, as Herb had been, a man of possibility and promise. This was a man who teased people into believing that he had range and speed beyond any previous experience. Even when he did less, people assumed he could do more. More tellingly, people expected him to do more, and demanded it. If people like Herb McKenley lightly dappled Lee's athletic ambition, providing a texture that might not otherwise have been there, this other man cast a direct shadow. He was the continuation of the quest, the grail itself, the end of the quest for the perfect quarter-miler. And he was not Lee Evans.

# .5

*Nobody Knows the Trouble I've Seen*

When Lee Evans was running as a young boy in the C class in Fresno, his team went to Lemoore, California, for a track meet. At that track meet, Lee Evans looked up into the height of Tommie Smith for the first time. Handsome, 6 feet, 3 inches, with more leg than trunk, graceful, moving from event to event, Tommie Smith was in casual motion, not so much competing against the other boys as rising above them. Here he was lifting from the blocks and exploding to win a dash. There he was standing at the head of the long-jump runway, deigning to land in the unseemly sand and to permit others to measure his effort. And there he was again, in the homestretch, snapping over the hurdles, and several times in the long afternoon taking the baton for the anchor leg of a relay. Tommie Smith was set apart, the phenomenon. No one in attendance could miss it, and certainly not the boy from Fresno who saw everything. It is tempting to discern on that first occasion an affinity between the two boys, as if they were moving unavoidably to each other, sharing parallel formative experiences, developing a similar drive, nursing the same injuries, and making the same promises to themselves and to their families and friends. But that is to impute the future to the past, to pose as inevitable a circumstance that could have been tipped a different way hundreds of times.

The certainty is that Lee saw on that day in Lemoore one of the few geniuses of physical motion, a man distinguished even in a nation complete with sprinters and with an unbroken history of producing them. Moving through that history, Jesse Owens comes to mind, to raise the question of capacity and precocity consistent with genius, but then along comes Eulace Peacock who might have derailed the myth of Owens if only he had remained healthy. If Peacock had done so, if he had run with Owens in Berlin, would anyone speak of Owens in terms of genius or exceptionalism? Perhaps they would, but the possibility shrinks, precisely because there would have been two of them. In any case, after Owens, who next? Surely there are other geniuses to account for, Bob Hayes or Henry Carr or Steve Williams, but they do not come to mind as swiftly, except to offer qualifications or doubts. Anyway, the hesitation itself says, no, they were not of the absolute highest order, no matter how remarkable the accomplishments or how impressive in performance, not truly set apart by birth and by the special gift of spirit. They fail the instant tilt test, in which genius is immediately recognized and inarguably so. Tommie Smith passed the test. As his career developed, coaches, athletes, fans, and sportswriters grasped for comparisons, going in desperation even to the field of science fiction and to cartoons. The natural comparisons may be the more useful ones. Nature gives us the ordinary examples: A bird so light and soft perches at the end of a thin branch, barely moving that branch, but the bird has the power to rise up and fly at will. If all birds are alike, save the few that cannot fly, then none are geniuses. But all are miracles.

:

Tommie Smith was born in a small town in Red River County, Texas, on June 6, 1944. The family moved to California and settled in Lemoore, near Fresno. In Lemoore, Smith worked in the fields, as Lee was doing. From a distance, an observer can sprint past this fact in the case of both boys to trivialize the days in the field by leaving them with the experiences of youth. That would be a mistake. Working in the fields was not only hard, hot, repetitious work, but it was activity for which the only satisfaction was being done with it. At the end of a day in the field, Tommie would collect his earnings and slip a nickel aside for an ice-cream cone. Walking into town, he heard the voices. They tried to tell him who he was. He was a nigger out on a lark and therefore fair game for every catcall. "Where you going, nigger? What're you doing, nigger? You got some place to be, boy?" Once upon a time a classmate even told Tommie the straight fact that a nigger could not possibly enjoy ice cream, so what was he getting it for?

Every day along the roads and in his work, hearing the calls and ignoring them or taking them to himself, letting them turn him to purposes of his own, Tommie was in fact conducting himself in an unpardonable way. He was acting human. He was acting like a regular young person, with wishes and dreams, and slight satisfactions and pleasures, the kind of guy who might like an ice-cream cone bought with a hard-earned nickel at the end of a long day. How very radical of him. Not much to be done, not immediately anyway, so stack it away, as Lee was doing too. On the question of affinity between the two, Tommie says he met Lee Evans out in the fields, so close were they to each other, physically, in those days, and so close were they to become, personally, later. Lee doesn't recall it. But he could have met Tommie, like one black boy meeting another black boy, looking deeply or slightly into another face and seeing kin.

People wonder at the black monolith, the way Americans of African descent tend to stay together, to walk a line a little closer to each other than might be expected, especially on social issues. Well, there the monolith is, out there under the hot sun with Lee and Tommie. Stressed like this, people fold, becoming bitter and half cocked, maybe not so prone to conversation on the fine points of life. Or, people survive and make something of the hardship. When Lee worked in the fields until he was 16 and moved away, he valued the little bits of money he made. He says that if he could earn a dollar for gas and a dollar for bait, he could eat for a week. Fishing, you got to know! This is the lesson in self-reliance. Tommie, too, saw value later in life. As a sprinter of unusual strength, he was often asked whether he lifted weights. He said no, but he meant yes. The weights he lifted, time after time, in a repeated motion, for money to make ends meet, were light tufts of cotton settled in big bags of cotton, or little grapes, heavy in trays. Maybe not so much weight that if you lifted it once, you'd bother. But lift it often, and the strength will come.

:

In the idleness of time and the isolation of experience, what color you are doesn't make much difference if you can run fast. So long as you are on the track, you have friends. These, you understand, aren't true friends; they aren't the kind of friends you can rely on. Fact is, they'll melt faster than ice cream on a summer day when the pressure comes. Still, the fast running has its own satisfaction. At the highest speeds, sprinters separate from time, the pull of which is stronger, even, than gravity. On those rare occasions, sprinters are alone. The world moves around their quiet selves, but they are not truly part of it.

:

Tommie Smith was fast, and he did run. By the time he graduated from high school in 1963, he had already run 9.5 for the 100-yard dash, 21.1 for 220 yards run on a straightaway, and 47.3 for a quarter. He had also long-jumped 24 feet, 6 inches. His quarter time was the fastest run by any high school boy in the country. His 100 time was tied with nine others, including a youngster named Charles Greene, running for O'Dea High School in Seattle, Washington. In the long jump, Tommie was third in the country. He also anchored his school's 880- and mile-relay teams to national prominence. At the West Coast Relays, he brought the 880-relay team back from a ten-yard deficit to win, and in the mile relay he ran a split estimated between 46.8 and 47.1, starting in fifth place and running on the outside the entire lap. His team lost the race by a tenth, but his anchor was all anyone talked about. It was all anyone saw. These are estimable performances, indeed. They are especially so for a young man who spent entirely too much time playing basketball, where he was also a promising performer. Graduating, he had choices. He could have played basketball at any number of colleges or universities; he could have sprinted for even more of them, and long-jumped. But, really, how could Tommie Smith have gone anywhere except San Jose State University? Why would he, when San Jose State offered this potential sprinter extraordinaire the services of a likable, ebullient, knowledgeable legend, a man who literally wrote the book on the sprints?

# .6

*etc. life and times.*

Lloyd "Bud" Winter coached track and field first at Watsonville (California) High School, moved on to Salinas Junior College, and finally made his way to San Jose State University in 1944, where he coached for thirty years. At Salinas, Winter coached Hal Davis, a local boy who was nicknamed the California Comet. The Comet was known for his atrocious starts and his lightning finishes. He was also known as a person who rarely lost. Between 1940 and 1943, Davis never lost a race at 200 meters or 220 yards and only had one important loss at the 100. Barney Ewell beat him in the 100 meters in 1942 at the AAU meet. All told, Davis won seven national championships between 1940 and 1943, three at 100 meters and four at 200 meters. He equaled the world records for both 100 meters and 100 yards, running 10.2 for the former and 9.4 for the latter. In 1942, he ran 200 meters in 20.4. Some of what Hal Davis did was due to natural talent, the rest, surely, was Bud Winter. The coach was interested in sprinting. He liked to study the intricacy of the sport. For him, sprinting was not a mad dash down the track, but a carefully constructed series of movements and decisions that, when taken consciously and enforced by practice, created a favorable result. In books, articles, lectures, and in individual training sessions, Winter deconstructed the art and science of running fast. In other words, he broke the sprints down, the better to see what was actually happening. With that, it was possible to improve. In his influential book, *So You Want To Be a Sprinter*, Coach Winter used simple language and rudimentary

*Bud Winter of San Jose State University.*

illustrations to teach people, particularly young people, how to run as fast as they were capable. He started with the easy part.

To get better, he said, you must either move your legs faster or cover more distance with each stride. Or, obviously, you may do both. With regard to stride length, he cautioned the ambitious athlete against leaping. Rather, the stride should carry the runner close to the ground. Maintaining a long stride over the ground, and not hopping along above it, was the secret to sprinting, the way Coach Winter saw it. To make the secret effective, the coach packaged it with reinforcing principles:

1  *Use high knee action.*
2  *Use good foreleg reach.*
3  *Run high on toes.*
4  *Have good arm action.*
5  *Maintain good forward lean.*
6  *Bound forward, not up.*
7  *Run tall, with back straight.*
8  *Be relaxed, with loose jaw and loose hands.*

With the rules in place, the coach then preached relaxation, he prescribed exercises, he analyzed starting techniques, and he told the athlete how to finish a race. The proper way to finish, he taught, is to drive past the line. To get this done, Winter asked his athletes to take a deep breath twenty yards from the finish, to say to himself the words "faster, looser," to get up on the toes, to reach out with the arms, and to try to lengthen the stride by rolling the hips. Thoughts like these would incidentally crowd out panic or anxiety, and even the purposeless yearning that causes a person to try harder and tie up. Despite his attention to detail and to the way things should be done, Bud Winter was not a theoretical man. He wanted results. He wanted people to run faster. He wanted the athletes to learn the lessons so well that they became intuitive, or something like it, almost as if the learned behavior had cut a deep groove from which departure was unlikely. In his thirty years, the coach's work produced 102 All-Americans, twenty-seven Olympians, forty-nine NCAA records, and an NCAA team championship.

:

Bud Winter was an assistant coach for the United States Olympic team competing in Rome in 1960. Ray Norton of San Jose State University was America's favored sprinter. After an exceptional performance at the Olympic Trials, he was touted to win gold medals in the 100, the 200, and as a member of the United States 4 x 1. A great deal of this was boosterism, and some of it was an exaggerated view of Norton's ability relative to his competitors, but some of the hopes were legitimate. The hopes were certainly more legitimate than what Norton produced in Rome: last in the 100-meter final, last in the 200-meter final, and one of two men implicated in a bad handoff that caused the disqualification of the relay team. His explanations made matters worse. He tied up, he said about the two individual events, and as for the relay, he was overanxious. This explanation was bitter not only for the athlete, for whom it suggested an inability to handle pressure, but for the athlete's coach, who was responsible for anticipating problems and avoiding them. The explanation was especially bitter for Bud Winter who emphasized relaxation as a key to success. Indeed, he later wrote the book *Relax and Win*. And here was Norton, his own athlete, a San Jose State sprinter with whom he had spent years in preparation, too tense to run; here was his very own athlete moving early. "That didn't make me look too good," Winter admitted, although he had a second opinion about the bad handoff on the relay. He thought that the incoming runner had slowed. This was nuance, however, to which little attention was paid. Norton was the goat of the Games. Everyone seemed to agree on that point.

:

A man—someone like Ray Norton, for example—slowed on a day when he had hoped to speed up, he reacted less well to a gun, and he forgot, for an instant, the mechanics of his sport. These are ephemera. The man lives on. He has his kindness and his generosity, his time to exercise good judgment, and his time to make mistakes. He takes good jobs, and fails, and bad jobs, and succeeds. He makes his way. But the athlete who has failed carries the memory of the day with him and is often reminded, and the coach who has coached him carries the day, as well. He too is reminded. But the coach unlike the athlete has more days, as he has more athletes. After Rome, Ray Norton said that he was finished, and he was. Bud Winter went on. Going on, he came upon a new sprinter capable of easing old memories, of softening their sharpness, indeed of blurring them to indistinctness, as if all had been but a dream before the dream. What does a sprint coach want most from life? The usual, and one thing more: speed to take his breath away.

## .7

*Flight and fight*

The story passed out along the way was that Tommie Smith didn't even know Bud Winter when he decided to enroll in San Jose State in the fall of 1963. The story is that the basketball coach brought him in, the basketball coach arranged his scholarship, and the basketball coach arranged to loan him in the spring to the track team. For that, the basketball coach got one good season. He got the freshman season, when Tommie was the leading rebounder on a team limited to freshmen. This was in a day when the NCAA, wisely, required freshmen to refrain from varsity participation, until they had the important first year accomplished. The rule gave students the chance to adjust to new work habits, to learn their way around campus, to locate a social world in addition to the gym or the field. More generally, the rule gave students the chance to mature before athletics thrust them into the limelight, where temptation and distraction beckoned.

The quiet year of restricted performances, however, was less critical in the nonrevenue, or minor, sports because no one was paying attention anyway, or rarely so, taking into account the experiences of Jim Ryun or Gerry Lindgren or to a slightly lesser extent Tommie Smith. Lesser, that is, in the case of Tommie Smith because he was an object of attention less for what he had done, but for what he could do, as his performances in that freshman year were modest. He ran 46.5 for the quarter, and 21.0 for the 200 meters. That being so, Tommie Smith appeared in 1964 much as he would when he started to run fast enough to bring the media in.

He had the long thighs and short foreleg, the high calves. He had the exaggerated knee lift "that seemed to climb to his throat," as it was later described. He started poorly and spent his time catching up, a pattern that gave the impression that he exploded past his fading opponents in the final yards. When Tommie Smith subsequently described his running by saying, "I run on top," that was true of his freshman version as well. In his tenure at San Jose State, Smith would get stronger and faster.

He would better learn the mechanics of the start. He would gather experience from indoor running. He would move up and down in distance outdoors until he settled on a specialty. Always, he would astonish people the way ballet does. How was it possible, people wondered, to generate so much power so beautifully? In the middle of all this was a sprinter who was but a sliver of the man. In the middle of all this was a man. Duly, that would become a problem as the man asserted himself and attempted to relegate the sprinter to lesser consideration, however impressive. And here of course is the fact, once more, the critical fact that is in one way or the other applicable to all athletes. Although it is the man who is important, no one heeded the man without the man's speed. To that degree, Tommie Smith may have had many talents, but he was captive to the one.

In an athlete, potential is like the ownership of a stock that has no value, really, until it is converted to cash by dividend or sale. Performance counts. Tommie Smith began to move from potential to performance in the outdoor season of his sophomore year at San Jose State in the spring of 1965. After running 20.6 for 220 yards in February, Tommie ran 200 meters on the straightaway in 20.0 to tie the world record held jointly by Dave Sime and Frank Budd. Thereafter, Tommie ran his specialty eight times, with results between 20.6 and 20.0. His only loss was to Dick Stebbins of Grambling College, a respected runner in his own right. When the season ended, Tommie Smith was ranked second in the world at 200 meters/220 yards. For good measure, Smith lowered his 100 yard time to 9.4 and anchored his San Jose State team to a 4 x 1 NCAA victory over Charlie Greene's Nebraska Cornhuskers. This much should be added, however. The victory in the 4 x 1 was only crust and not the bread itself. Smith was hurt going into the relay. He actually slowed in the final strides of that short dash to save his leg, or to protect it from further damage, and was unable to run well in the 220 even though he used a standing start to avoid strain. He didn't survive the heats. "How can I run," he asked, "when I am wrapped up like a mummy?" It was a grumpy but understandable question.

If Smith was upset at the NCAA meet, he had a right to be. Why hobble through a vain effort? If other people were upset, it was because they did not get to see the man as advertised. Here is what the proud coach had said before the meet:

*I feel that Tommie is possibly the world's fastest human right now. It's quite probable that he has the fastest maximum speed of any sprinter in history, and he seems to be able to sustain the speed for a longer length of time. Bob Hayes, for example, is reported to have reached about 26 mph top speed, which he would hit at about 70 to 75 yards. But he would begin decelerating after that. I believe Tommie is faster than that, and that he can maintain this peak speed for a longer period. The wall doesn't hit this guy. The tension that hits most sprinters at high speeds doesn't seem to affect Tommie.*

The few doubters did not see Tommie accurately, the coach said, because Smith had been stumbling out of the blocks and losing precious time, a situation that could be fixed. The solution was to have Tommie lift his knees higher right after he left the blocks rather than driving low for the first several strides. What worked for shorter men was simply not the best way for a man of Tommie's stature. Once safely on his way, the coach added, Tommie could take advantage of his two major talents: stride length and competitive ability. As to stride length, the coach offered Hal Davis's as the longest ever at 9 feet, 6 inches, but was anxious to measure Tommie's stride because he believed that it would be longer. Given remarks like these—the kind that herald a unique talent—even a number two ranking in the world for a college sophomore hits like a thud. This is especially so if the new man finishes the season by taking standing starts while wrapped like a mummy. Seasoned observers of the sport had seen athletes like Tommie Smith before, no matter how enthusiastic Bud Winter was, and how fervently he sought to distinguish his charge from the runners who had preceded him and whose talents Smith was intended to exceed. They had all seen flashes across the night sky before. They would not argue with the coach about his student's skills and would not deny having seen the light, but they would not rely on that light for steady illumination or count on it to shine at the moment it was needed. The young man was fragile! So thin boned and high striding and sensitive, it would be better to wait and see.

:

With a flick of the wrist, a reader of a leading sports magazine found a place for the latest story about Tommie Smith, the young man who had been injured at the NCAA. He threw the magazine across the room and into the trash. The reader meant no offense, and perhaps the vigor of his action is exaggerated, but there would be new stories next week and new heroes, and one had to make room.

:

With all the difficulty of nurturing a talent like Tommie Smith, at least the topic is running and the ambitions are consistent with the purpose of sport. There was another kind of ambition that was powerful in 1963 and 1964, culminating in 1965. This other kind of ambition had nothing to do with sport, although sport was its excuse and its means of expression. The controversy is almost forgotten now. The combatants should wish it so. This old ambition, with its fractiousness, has a place here only because it has roots, or it has vine, or it produces seed. One way or the other, it connects to what came later.

:

When Tommie was running as a sophomore at San Jose State University, the Amateur Athletic Association was the sanctioning body for open track and field competition in the United States. The NCAA administered track and field events for its participating institutions. The NCAA, and at least some of its member institutions, became disenchanted with the AAU. For that reason, the NCAA created, or fostered the creation of, the United States Track and Field Federation. The benign purpose of the USTFF was to improve conditions for track and field athletes, coaches, and fans, but the unavoidable and therefore actionable intention was to undermine the authority of the AAU. This, the USTFF did by setting itself up as a separate and autonomous sanctioning body. A series of decisions followed:

1 The NCAA claimed that it had the right to tell an NCAA athlete when he (and they were all "he" in the day) could or could not compete. The claim extended beyond the school year and specifically included participation in the AAU national championships.

2 The NCAA said that no college athletes within its authority could compete in the AAU championship in 1965 unless the meeting was separately sanctioned by the USTFF.

3 When the AAU refused—predictably—to share its national meet with the USTFF, the NCAA let it be known that sanctions would be levied against any affiliated athlete who crossed the line and ran at the "unsanctioned" AAU meet. To an athlete, as the NCAA would have known, the ultimate sanction was loss of scholarship; to a university, it was loss of affiliation.

In every real sense, the NCAA was enforcing a boycott of the AAU meet by all university athletes. As it happened, a good number of college athletes defied the NCAA and suffered no sanction, but other collegians stayed home, including three who had won national collegiate titles the week before the AAU. In every case, the hard choices to compete or not were forced upon people who had little or nothing do with the controversy.

Of course, these events happened in the '60s, when boycotts

were in the news. There were boycotts of diners in North Carolina, for example, and boycotts of bus services in Montgomery. But here, we have a different kind of boycott. The NCAA boycott of the AAU meet was not in service to social justice. It was not intended to make the world a better place. It was about power. This being the case, the questions and the conclusions necessarily follow: Was boycott a legitimate instrument by which to adjust reality, to move people and events? The black people in Montgomery who boycotted the bus services thought so. The black people in Wilmington who boycotted the diners thought so. And, in the specific context of track and field and a petty, internecine scramble for power, the NCAA evidently thought so. Years earlier, Dick Gregory, the comedian and activist, had called for a boycott of the 1960 Olympic Games by black athletes; in 1964, other black leaders agreed, arguing that black athletes should refrain from participation in the Olympics until they had justice and fairness at home. In 1960 and 1964, the voices of protest and boycott were dismissed as coming from the margin. But now, were things not different? How could these calls for organized resistance by black athletes not be heard with greater sharpness after the NCAA legitimized the concept of the boycott, and did so in the specific context of sport?

# .8

*Before you can be somebody,*
*you've got to be somebody.*

Lee Evans was a junior in high school when Tommie Smith was a freshman in college. Lee Evans was a senior in high school when Tommie Smith was a sophomore in college. The two young men were traveling toward each other, but Lee had farther to go. Unlike Tommie, he was no one's idea of a phenomenon. When he ran, no one spoke of gazelles or uncommon grace. They spoke, when they spoke at all, of toil. Lee would be required to earn what Tommie was granted as if by right. But there was unfairness in the juxtaposed images of natural talent and visible labor. Lee Evans was not a house painter seeking to shake hands with Michelangelo. He was an equal artist with different gifts. It just so happened that one of those gifts was the capacity to undertake and to survive hard work. Lee's high school coach saw the young man's potential almost immediately. He saw a runner, surely, but he also saw the man in the boy.

By contrast, Lee's first impression of the coach was downright startling. Lee was playing on the football team at the time and fully occupied, but on a fading afternoon he happened to hear the cross country coach at work. "You can run one more," the coach was shouting, "you can always run one more." The coach was directing this wisdom to a group of kids who were nearly spent. Some of them were leaned sharply over, retching. "You can always run one more," Lee was thinking to himself, "Man, this guy is mean." Still, because he thought the man might be the track coach, as well as the cross country coach, and he planned to run on the track team, he went over to introduce himself. He also wanted to take a closer look at what was happening, perhaps even to cast a commiserating eye on his forlorn, exhausted schoolmates. As he approached, the man raised a clipboard above his eyes. Lee soon learned that he had made a mistake; the man would not be his first high school track coach after all. No one could blame him for breathing a sigh of relief.

:

The first track practices that spring were easy. In this regard, they were like track practices all over the country at the time. The sprinters would warm up in a leisurely way, do a little stretching, run a dash, maybe half a lap, and then sit on a bench until it was time to do another dash. They would do that other dash. And then they would sit on the bench or in the grass a bit more. Maybe the group would do 5 x 220 in total, often much less. Later, they might do some starts, jog down, and drift away. The ritual was called "working out," but the name suggested more than the reality. Lee neither failed nor succeeded on this training. He just ran and won. In the sprints and in the quarter, he won his early races against kids who lacked his talent. The times were not fast. His best quarter hovered near 51, for example. Stan Dowell only watched these performances as a result of school regulations that prevented him from coaching the track team because he had already coached cross country. The regulations were strict enough that he was not even supposed to go to practice, but he could go to the meets. Each day passing, watching Lee race, Stan stewed. He feared that a boy was being lost, that the talent in the youngster would be left to founder and be unknown; he feared that work and dedication and hardship would not carve out the talent and make it visible. He feared that a special boy would never know the qualities he had, that he would take his diploma across the stage and walk out into an ordinary life full of never and never knew. In the situation, Stanley Dowell was bound to go over the side. He could not help himself. Lee says that the occasion was the Hill Invitational, a regular meet but this year marked by the fact that a boy from another team had run a 9.6

100, a low 21 in the 220, and achieved good results in the quarter. Stan Dowell decided that the time was right to rock Lee Evans.

:

At the meet Stan found Lee and talked to him a few minutes before Lee was to line up. Stan was saying to Lee that it was just too bad that he was in such terrible shape. He was saying that Lee was not to blame that he had not worked hard enough, and that now it was too late. He was saying that next year, when he was in charge, Lee would work. Next year, Lee would be prepared to win a race against such an athlete as he faced this evening. Next year, next year, next year, Stan was saying. In every single respect, Stanley Dowell was speaking to Lee as if this race had already been run and Lee had lost it. He was speaking to Lee as if the season were over, in fact, and Lee had wasted it. Lee did not feel that this was an acceptable series of suggestions to make to him. Rather quickly, Lee became furious. Lee was thinking, "Who is this guy? I have never even seen him, he has not been at practice, and he shows up here just before this race, with this 9.6 runner, and he's blowing smoke all over the place and saying all these things to me, and he doesn't know what he is talking about, and I am going to show him exactly what I think of him." Forty-nine point five seconds later, Lee Evans went looking for Stanley Dowell. He wanted to talk to the coach about who had won what race and about the season, the way a young man would to an older fellow who was all wet.

:

The man for whom he was looking had been a quarter-miler for Bud Winter at San Jose State University before entering the service. As a runner, the young Dowell was good but not great. When he was fit, he could shade 50. Dowell had done the workouts at San Jose State as prescribed, but he had never been exhausted, nor even stretched, by them. He became convinced that the quarter guys could handle more volume, that they could work harder without sacrificing speed, and that in doing so they would develop strength that would make the difference in close races. Not content with his experiences, Stan studied training methods as a coach and looked for ways to make his athletes better. If a student had talent, Stan Dowell could help.

After Lee ran the 49.5 quarter, everyone agreed that Stan should begin writing his workouts. Lee was already fast. As he continued with his career, he would get faster, finally arriving at a day when he could run 200 meters in 20.4. To that speed, Coach Dowell began to add strength work. In Lee's case, this orientation prompted the coach to add workouts of 300s, 400s, and 600s. For Lee the change in his workouts meant two things. The first was that he went home tired almost every night. The second was that he started to improve. In the coming weeks, Lee qualified for the state meet by running 49.0. For that meet, he and his primary coach, Frank Olsen, drove the five hours to Los Angeles together. This was the first time Lee had eaten in a restaurant and the first time he had slept in a hotel room. He was a stranger to the experiences, just as he was a stranger standing in the middle of the Los Angeles Coliseum where California schools of all sizes would compete together. Getting a look at the track inside the huge stadium, Lee turned to Mr. Olsen and said, "Hey! This track's bigger around than a quarter!" Olsen assured him that it was not, and that it only looked that way. Lee was doubtful, naturally, but there wasn't anything he could do about it, so he let it go. Or, it might be more accurate to say, he persuaded himself that the coach was right and his eyes were wrong. On the big track, Lee had a better experience than his eyes had suggested he would. He qualified for the finals easily, and he even got a little jolt for free. The little extra was that when Lee came around the turn for the homestretch in his semi, he heard his name on the loudspeaker: "Lee Evans of Overfelt is leading. Lee Evans is leading." He would hear this call often over the years, but this was the first time, and special, but only for the moment because Lee didn't win the semi. He only came out of the turn first. Spencer Williams from Chaffey High School in Ontario won. And Lee didn't win the final either. He tied for third with Grundy Harris of Jefferson, Los Angeles, with both of them finishing behind winner Fred Banks, also of Jefferson, and behind Williams.

A loss is a loss, and Lee Evans never liked or accepted losing. That fact aside, Lee enjoyed the experience at his first state meet. For one thing, he had never heard cheerleaders at a track meet before! "Go, Go, Go Jeff! Fight, Jeff! Go, Go! Go!" This gives a high school boy an entirely new attitude. No wonder he had such problems with Grundy Harris and Fred Banks. And then there was the time. He had run 48.2 for 440 yards at the state meet. When the season ended, Lee's time would be among the top ten run anywhere in the nation by high school boys. The prospects were good for an even better senior season.

:

With Stan keeping a watchful, disapproving eye, Lee again played slotback for the football team his senior year. When that season ended, Stan set Lee back to work. Early on, Lee and the other track guys were assigned overdistance runs of three or four miles. While some on the team were jogging, hiding, and cutting through, Lee and his closest friend, Calvin Robinson, took the work seriously. Robinson had been the star on the football team and ran the 100 in sub-10. He was also the person who introduced Lee to push-ups and other exercises designed to put strength in his upper body, which was lightly muscled. Generally, Lee was subject to the three-part program Coach Dowell had developed for him: volume, transition, and speed. Influenced by the German Woldemar Gerschler, Dowell used interval work as the foundation for all three stages of the program. The first part of the program was high volume, measured by the number of reps as well as the distance covered in each rep, and a short rest period between each. The transition period maintained some of the volume of the first period and some of the short intervals, but feathered in shorter distances with slightly longer rest periods. Finally, as the championship season got underway, the volume was cut, the distance covered in each interval was shortened, and the rest between each interval was lengthened.

When his senior season opened, Lee ran the 440, a leg on the 4 x 2, and the 880, although the 880 was something he did for the points and the conditioning. He was content to win in the low two minutes. Only one time did Stan ask Lee for something extra in the half. The story has a traditional quality: At an Overfelt home meet, a competing coach showed up with a kid who had run 1:55. Stan decided that he did not like this coach and that he did not want his kid to win. Particularly, he did not want this kid to beat Lee Evans. In fact, the result was never in doubt. Lee knew how Stan felt and intended to take care of the coach. He was going to borrow a pair of spikes from a teammate, and then he was going to go out and win. Lee borrowed shoes because the school did not provide equipment and because the money he made from caddying met other needs. In any case, his teammates were happy to have their shoes win races even if they did not. Tonight was different though, and Lee would not be running in borrowed shoes, nor hand-me-downs of any kind. Five minutes before the big race, Stanley Dowell called Lee over. Stan held in his hands a box. He put the box in Lee's hands. And from the box Lee took 9.9s: adidas, reverse kangaroo, velour, like a second skin, so light as to be unfelt.

The race was over. The poor fellow from the other school had his 1:55, but he had no chance now. Lee followed him through a slow first lap, and then dashed the second for a final time of something like 1:58, the time being unimportant, and the win being everything. Later, Lee heard the boy's coach giving him hell for letting the pace drag, and he felt a bit bad about that, like maybe he should intervene and tell the coach that it wouldn't have mattered. The kid could have gone out in 51 and Lee would still have been right there on his heels, being careful with the clean white shoes on his own feet. When the time came he would have kicked, if for nothing else, for the pleasure of seeing those shoes move beneath him and feeling the newness of the spikes punching into the cinders. No need yelling at the boy, coach, not tonight. Maybe later, maybe when the shoes have a scuff or two, but not tonight.

This was a major event, this gift. Lee knew that Stan Dowell had not only given him a pair of shoes. The coach had put a charm on him. He had recognized worth and value, and the shoes were an indication of the trust and friendship that now existed between them. For his part, Lee did what was necessary in return. He put the shoes to good use. Three decades later, he still recalls the experience with emotion. Lee Evans has owned many track shoes since. Most of them have been given to him; many others he has been paid to wear. Later, he would find himself in the center of a controversy about shoes and payments and challenges to his amateur status. Shoes would become a commodity. But no shoes replace the first shoes, the magical 9.9s that Stanley Dowell bought with a teacher's salary and gave to his student.

:

As the senior season progressed, Lee Evans emerged in his mature configuration. He was the winner whenever he set foot to track. This was no boy, but a young man. Was it speed that was wanted? Lee ran 20.8 for 220 yards on the straight, albeit wind aided. Strength? The young man put a 46.9 on the board before the California state meet where he expected to run faster than the national record of 46.1. Watching from meet to meet and looking at the times Lee recorded, an observer would be forgiven for concluding that he was looking at a finished product, one whose adult accomplishments were as certain as his high school triumphs. But that conclusion would be wrong. Lee lacked a critical experience. He had not suffered disappointment on his own account. He had never overreached and fallen short. He had never earned a victory then been denied it. He had never suffered accident or injury or misfortune to take from him something he had considered uniquely his own. He had sailed and not wrecked. He had flown and not walked, walked and not stumbled, stumbled and not crawled. He had not been furious at misfortune. It was time for all that to change. The state meet, the first treasure for even a would-be Olympic champion, was the perfect time, place, and circumstance for Lee to get what he needed.

The lesson started innocently enough. A coach and an athlete sat down and concluded between them that three wins were possible and that three wins might be enough to win the entire competition, with the points being cut up so fiercely among the competing schools. The coach and the athlete decided that the favored sprinter, Harold Busby, who led the nation at both the 100 and the 220, was nonetheless vulnerable at the 220. Whenever the 220 appeared on the schedule, the athlete would win it. The coach and the athlete next concluded that the athlete could run his signature event, the 440-yard dash, faster than any schoolboy ever had. Further, the two decided that the occasion to run that record 440 was in the semis. With the record for the 440 safely in hand, the athlete could win the final conservatively the next night. With his energy thereby harbored, he could anchor the mile relay to a high finish. This is an ambitious plan, to be certain, but innocent. Unfortunately, the innocent plan lasted all of 150 meters into the semifinal of the quarter, where Lee had hoped to set a national record. His sartorius muscle, which had been sore before the race, pulled violently. Lee's state meet was over before it properly began. He never got the chance to contest any final. Despite his promise and his ability, he would never be a California state champion. The most that could be said is that the time he brought into the state meet, the 46.9 that he had hoped to make outworn and tired, was sufficient to hold his place among the best high school quarter-milers in the country. His time was second fastest. The fastest time belonged to one Ron Freeman of New Jersey.

# .9

*Separate but equal isn't equal;*
*it's faster.*

Lee was prepared to graduate from high school in the spring of 1965. Every night Dick Hill was on the phone. Once the coach of sprint sensation and Olympic champion Bob Hayes at Florida A&M, he had returned to his alma mater, Southern University in Baton Rouge, Louisiana. Dick was telling Lee what he believed Lee needed to hear in order to pick up and move south. He told Lee of the Southwestern Athletic Conference, a collection of schools providing postsecondary education for black people from all over the United States. He told Lee about the successful track programs, particularly the one at Southern, and about his future teammates and their meets and performances; he told Lee about the classroom expectations and how other people from California had adapted. Dick told Lee that he, too, could be successful and that he would be used wisely, trained well, and cherished. In sum, he told Lee what college coaches tell athletes. Hovering above the conversation were two words familiar to Lee from his father's use of them. "Jim Crow," he had said, "Jim Crow down there." By 1965 Jim was dying, but he was not dead yet. In his death throes he might still be dangerous, perhaps even more dangerous than in the past when the issues that had given him life were settled, days when everybody knew where to sit and where to stand, and more important, where not to sit and where not to stand. Ironically, these last few years, the years of Jim's paroxysm, were days of glory for the teams of the SWAC, especially in track and field. Soon enough, the SWAC schools would find their athletes carried away to the Southeast Conference, to the Southwest and Big 8 conferences, even to the Big Ten and the Pac. But the years before full integration were special. The dream was articulate but not fulfilled, the opportunity was promised but not yet fully delivered, and the SWAC was alone with its black athletes for the last time. Most of the athletes were southerners, but a surprising number arrived from other parts of the country. Or maybe it would be more accurate to say that they were coming home again, to reverse the migration of their parents or grandparents.

:

Dick Stebbins and his Grambling Tigers made a national impression for the SWAC. Stebbins made the Olympic team in 1964 at 200 meters and finished seventh in the final. His Grambling 440-relay team equaled the world record at the Mt. San Antonio College Relays and ran a nation-leading 1:23.4 for the 880 relay. Other SWAC athletes and teams were also nationally ranked at year's end, but they were not numerous, and the times were not outstanding. Nothing from 1964 predicted 1965, when the SWAC teams really hit their stride. A suggestive note did come from Oakland, California, however, when barrel-chested James Hines of McClymonds High, who was the fastest schoolboy in the country, decided to enroll at Texas Southern in Houston. Hines had run 9.4 for 100 yards and 20.9 for the 220 yard on the turn. When Clyde Duncan, a 9.5 100-yard man from Iowa, decided to join Hines at Texas Southern, Coach Stan Wright had the foundation for solid sprint-relay teams that might challenge even Southern University, which had exploded since Dick Hill started making his nighttime telephone calls.

Lee knew two of the athletes who went to Dick Hill's Southern and were running as university freshmen while he finished high school. Southern had lured Fred Banks and Grundy Harris from Jefferson High. Banks brought 9.6, 21.2, and 47.3 credentials. Harris had run 48.0 in high school, but quickly established his talent in college by running 21.0 for 220 and lowering the quarter to 46.9. These two joined so many other sprinters and quarter-milers that Banks boasted that Southern could field three separate teams capable of running faster than 3:10 for the mile relay. Manning those teams would be sprinters like Theron Lewis, 46.1; Robert Johnson, 46.3; Webster Johnson; 46.5 (relay); Everett Mason, 46.2; and George Anderson, 9.3 (yards), along with hurdler–jumper–sprinter Harvey Nairn. All the attributed times were effective June 1965, and all were noted in the aftermath of a college season in which Southern recorded the following performances: 440 relay in 40.0 (a tenth off the world record), 880 relay in 1:23.2 (seventh fastest ever run with splits broken down as 21.9, 20.5, 20.4, and 20.4), and a mile relay in 3:04.5 (tied the world record). In the world-record mile relay, anchor Theron Lewis slowed before the line, there being no apparent reason to hurry, and still recorded 45.1 for his leg. In all, Southern had three men run faster than 9.6, five faster than 21.3, and seven faster than 47.3, with a total of fourteen faster than 48-flat. At that, Southern participated in a conference so deep in the quarter that 46.3 failed even to qualify for the finals at the conference meet in May 1965. In the coming several years Southern would hold its tempo; Grambling would falter slightly; Texas Southern would step up, led by Hines; and other black schools from the SWAC and elsewhere would make their presence known. Prairie View, in particular, would become powerful. By the time 1967 arrived, it would surprise no one that SWAC member Arkansas AM&N could produce three quarter-milers at 46.0 and faster for yards, another one who could beat 47.0, and that at the national NAIA meet all these fine runners would lose to two other athletes attending black schools, Vince Matthews of J.C. Smith, 45.4, and Thurman Boggess of the SWAC's Prairie View A&M, 45.6. In the years 1964 through 1968, the heat kept on coming from the SWAC, with echoes to and from other blacks schools.

Here, ultimately, is the point. When San Jose, California, later became known as Speed City, it was the second gathering of talent sufficient to justify the name. The first was in Baton Rouge, Louisiana, the city of Southern University, lead star of the SWAC, the school that wanted Lee Evans in the spring of 1965. He didn't go, of course. Lee didn't leave San Jose. Stan Dowell had no intention of letting his prize student trot down to Baton Rouge, Louisiana, no matter how attentive a recruiter Dick Hill might be, no matter how fast his prospective Southern teammates might be, and no matter how tempting it might be to go back down to Louisiana, from where his mother and father had both come. To meet the challenge, Stan offered the continued presence of the Evans matriarch at his meets, the general support of family and friends, familiar routines, and not least, his very own watchful eye. Lee said, essentially, fine. But he was not prepared to foreclose later reconsideration. He agreed to run a year at San Jose City College, a junior college, to live at home, to work on his studies, and to get additional time and distance from which to view his future prospects. The decision to enroll at San Jose City was clinched when the coach at the college helped Lee find summer employment at the Lockheed plant, and when he talked strongly to Lee about the value of an education. For all these reasons, the SWAC would have to get along without him for a year, after which he would reconsider. By then, of course, when he looked again, he would be a new man, not a man of possibility, but of accomplishment.

# .10

*Lee takes a place in line.*
*He will jump it.*

The purpose of spending a year at San Jose City College was academic, in part. For a variety of reasons, now almost traditional among urban high school students, Lee was not prepared for a university curriculum. He needed to learn how to study, and then he needed to study. If he failed, his future would be jeopardized no matter how fast he ran. The commitment to become a better student, to become a student at all, became part of who Lee Evans was. While Lee was intent on running well, he started building the man who could speak truth to power. He was reading *Cry, the Beloved Country* and taking its messages about the people and the land to heart. He was reading *The Autobiography of Malcolm X* and being scalded by the recognition of his own turmoil. And he was also reading tracts and newsletters and articles and books being pressed into his hands. He was taking the information and gathering context for his own experiences. He was growing up, that's what he was doing. Lee was daydreaming still, unavoidably, but his dreams were growing wider and richer, and more varied. The dreams were reaching beyond himself to other people's lives and other people's troubles, especially as they concerned social justice. In his own family, resistance to injustice had two faces: his mother's, which counseled patience and dignity, those being the values and apprehensions of her Louisiana childhood, and his father's, which was angry and near fed up with waiting. And if Lee felt a special anxiety to get settled and choose his own course, to decide for example between his mother's view and his father's, there was a reason for that. He had acquired a family of his own. In the summer after high school, Lee married an intelligent, attractive woman with whom he soon had his first child. Necessarily, Linda was part of the sculpting of the man she married. Sometimes she was in front of him, pulling, and sometimes behind, pushing, but she was a force in either case in the young man's life, as he was in hers: strength meeting strength.

Running track remained important to Lee, however. He had immediate goals and immediate needs. Absolutely as soon as possible, he was determined to become the fastest 400-meter man in the world. He needed to become the fastest performer in the world because he could not envision a day when losing to anyone, under any circumstance, would be acceptable to him. To keep that possibility away, he had to prepare to beat everyone all the time. Stan Dowell had encouraged Lee to attend the City College, but he did not coach him there. That job fell to the capable Charlie Baker. When speaking of Coach Baker, it is tempting to describe his career backward, starting with the many years he spent as an assistant to the estimable Sam Bell at Indiana after leaving San Jose. But to do that would be to diminish the man in his own right. A native of Sublette, Kansas, in the area of Goodland and Liberal, and a graduate of Emporia State, Baker was a protege of track coach Fran Welch, a man from whom Bill Bowerman once said he learned more track and field from than any man alive, Arthur Lydiard included. Baker learned from Welch that good running starts with the fundamentals and works outward. These lessons included the ones often quoted but little enforced: Run with good posture, run relaxed, run over the center of gravity, extend the stride without compromising turnover, increase power off the driving leg, swing the arm fluidly and without tension, and run ten yards past the line. To these, Coach Baker added sophisticated lessons picked up from coaches like Payton Jordan of Stanford, from neighboring Bud Winter of San Jose State, from Bowerman himself, and from any source that helped him teach people to run faster. With Lee, however, the coach would have to restrain himself, at least initially, because Lee continued to be bothered by the serious injury suffered at the state high school meet. The affected muscle ran from inside the knee past the groin and to the outside of the hip. The health of the sartorius is a critical factor in determining if an athlete can reach and then hold a full stride. In other words, Lee could not hope to excel if that muscle were not reclaimed.

Coach Baker was in his first year at City College. The previous year he had coached at a rival school to Overfelt. Having seen Lee run many times, he knew that the young man was unusually talented, one of the few who could be world class if properly trained. But he also knew that Lee's injury had frightened away a lot of the big California schools whose coaches had seen it happen. He knew, as well, that the first doctor who saw Lee concluded that Lee would not run again. The first job, then, was to rebuild Lee. Baker originally had Lee run cross country, but the leg did not respond, so the two sought additional medical advice. Unlike the first doctor, the one who thought Lee would not run again and scared some coaches away, the second doc thought Lee would be fine if he were conscientious about rehab, which he prescribed. Lee did pull-ups, sit-ups, push-ups, and V-ups, of which the V-ups were the most important. More than 100 times a day, in three or four sets, Lee rested on his back, then lifted his straight arms and straight legs into a V and held this position for the purpose of making his abdominals stronger and the troublesome muscle less so. Lee also did controlled running and striding. He did nothing fast in the first months of school and nothing to appeal to his competitive instinct, one that had been satisfied by playing football in every autumn of his high school career. Not surprisingly, Lee got bored and restless and discouraged. He wanted to stop; he wanted to leave school. He wanted to do something or anything other than what he was doing. But he didn't. Every day he showed up for practice and every day he did what the coach asked until one day, finally, in December, he got a chance to race. It was not, after all, a quarter, but the anchor leg of a sprint-medley relay. Lee handled the half mile with an easy 1:52, split 60, 52. Within the next several weeks, Lee anchored the College to a couple of indoor wins, and he was back on track. The leg was better. In fact, the leg was fine.

With the improvement, Lee was able to take full advantage of Coach Baker's program. The coach was convinced that Lee needed to be fast, above all things, in order to reach his potential. This philosophy complemented, and to some extent, exploited the work that Lee had done in high school with Stan Dowell; an athlete coming to Coach Baker with a foundation based on strength could expect to progress faster than one who lacked that background. Further to the point, Coach Baker expected that Lee would get stronger by running more reps and cutting the rest interval. Baker also integrated drills into each workout. For stride length, for example, the athletes started with distances of 20-20-20 yards, with the middle 20 yards used for high knee lift and quickness and the other yards used as entry and exit from the exercise. Eventually, this drill became 40-40-40 as the athlete grew accustomed to the burden, and the reps increased to four. If an athlete failed to do the drill correctly, he and his teammates would go again. For Lee's program, Coach Baker used a primary distance of 165 yards around the turn, to which Lee adjusted well. Eventually, he was doing fifteen or twenty of these runs and using a brisk trot across the infield as the only rest.

Always, Coach Baker was watching. If Lee's form got sloppy, he stepped in. If the form continued to be a problem, the coach changed the workout. On a day, he might send the athlete off for overdistance or use a longer interval or permit longer rest, but he would not let a bad habit become engrained. Just as uniformly, the coach insisted that Lee finish each effort fast. He wanted Lee to run his hardest when he was most fatigued, because that was the way to win big races. In the entire regimen, the coach was assisted by the fact that Lee Evans was a good student who picked up instruction quickly, was consistent in his workouts, did not beg off for minor illness or injury, and concentrated on his work. The coach was also assisted by Lee's physical nature. Even now, after these many years, the coach says that he could distinguish Lee's beating heart from that of any other person. That large heart, he says, was a gusher. More lyrically, he says that the heart was a "devout pump" that permitted Lee to work harder, to recover faster, and to do more, more quickly than any athlete he had ever coached, or ever would coach.

This, then, was Lee Evans as a freshman at a junior college in California. He was a 5-foot, 11-inch, 175-pound man with world-class speed, a relaxed if eccentric motion, and sturdy strength that had been reinforced by good training. He was promising, ready for his first outdoor season, recovered from injury, lately bored and now excited, and somewhat more mature than the 46.9 performer of the previous season, and he was confident. Still, to anyone but himself, his confidants, and his coaches, he was just another high school champion trying to claw his way to the top.

But Lee was different, a fact that would soon become apparent. On race days, he took the lessons learned and joined them with the advantages of his nature. He avoided tension, seeking control and ease and choosing the instant to apply power. In the race itself, he ran the first 100 fast, he lengthened his stride in the second 100, and he used the third 100 to get into position for the homestretch. He made adjustments as necessary. In the last 100, he ran with emotion and intensity, battling deceleration and driving through the finish line. Race after race, Lee Evans ran to this pattern, and race after race, observers came away with the belief that they had seen a veritable dervish in action, a man violently throwing himself around the track. His head rotated on his neck, they said, like it might come off. His arms grabbed and clutched and swung from lane to lane, they said. His face was anguished and painful to behold.

He lurched and twisted and drove. Lee didn't care about any of this. While other freshmen might struggle to establish themselves at the next level, Lee handled the experience easily. He beat collegians and accomplished open runners just as surely as he had beaten high school sophomores, juniors, and seniors the year before. Seven times before the national AAU meet in 1966, Lee Evans ran his 440-yard race, and seven times he won, including championships at the Coliseum Relays, the West Coast Relays, the California Junior College Championships, and Compton. All of his winning times were between 46.1 and 46.9. These were among the fastest times in the nation. As the national AAU meet approached, the young man, late of Overfelt High, now from the smallest junior college in its junior college league, was a favored athlete with a developing reputation.

:

Lee was a favored athlete, but he was not *the* favored athlete.

69

Although he was undefeated in the quarter and had run fast times, Lee Evans would disappear if Tommie Smith, for one, lined up next to him at the AAU meet scheduled for late June on Randall's Island, New York. Tommie was on a tear in 1966, putting his mark on every distance from the 100 to the 440. "Tommie is more than just fast," wrote one columnist. "It's as though he possesses three gears while other sprinters are stuck with only two. Once on his way, he has demonstrated the same great acceleration and pure blazing speed that has characterized many great sprinters in the past. It's that special third gear that sets him apart." If he could get his start under control, Smith was an athlete capable of holding or sharing world records for every running event from the 100 through the 440, the writer suggested. This, the writer concluded, would confer immortality of a rare blend. In fact, Tommie would be the fulfillment of the old ambition. He would be the short sprinter with sufficient range and strength to move up to the quarter, something along the lines of Herb McKenley, but with finer design and therefore more control.

Accolades like this were prompted by a startling series of performances, the most outstanding a 19.5 in the straightaway 220 at an all-comers meet. The time was a full 0.5 second faster than the record previously shared by Frank Budd and Dave Sime, and was considered the greatest performance ever achieved by a track athlete, measured by the Portuguese Scoring Tables then used to compare results from disparate events. Along with the world record for the 220, Tommie recorded 9.3 for 100 yards, 10.1 for 100 meters, an early-season 20.3 for the 220 on the turn, and a long jump of 25 feet, 11 inches. Somewhat gratuitously, Smith ran the third-fastest 440 yard ever run when he posted a 45.7, with an intermediate time of 21.7. At that, most observers thought he had coasted the last twenty to thirty yards. If Tommie did rest at the end of his quarter, the decision was understandable because he was in the middle of a long and ambitious season, culminating in the NCAA outdoor meet. At that meet, Bud Winter hoped to win a national championship by entering his star in four or five events including the 100, the 220, the long jump, and one or both relays.

Peeking past the NCAA, Tommie might look forward to the

AAU meet as something of a relief, a chance to take a risk or stretch a little. This might be the time to run a championship quarter, or at least the fans thought so. Once upon a time, Tommie had said that the 440 might be his best event. This, of course, was alluring talk from an athlete who had run the 220 in 19.5 on a straightaway and 20.0 on the turn, and it called to mind a true exhibition, something different, more difficult, more remarkable, than a mere sprint. To run the quarter as well as he thought he could, Tommie would have to establish his speed and then hold it, not for a mere fifty meters after fatigue set in, but for a longish time measured by how soon he got into trouble, which he surely would somewhere in the course of the lap. The inevitability of fatigue raised the question of discretion, for how tempting would the backstretch look to an athlete like Tommie Smith, and what would happen if he gave way to temptation and blew it out? Could he hold then? Coach Winter had said that the sprinter was distinguished by an ability to hold his tempo while others, less talented, faltered. The AAU was a chance to test the conclusion. Collectively, in 1966, track fans were saying, "Do it."

And what of the specialists in the quarter? Might they view Tommie as a poacher of sorts, a person whose presence diminished their own efforts? Was he making sport of them, by moving up and taking whatever he wanted, whenever he wanted it? Wouldn't there be a special incentive to bring the sprinter down to earth? In this regard, for example, what of Lee Evans, the young man of estimable but quite human talent, despite his outsized ambition and his string of surprising victories? Tommie Smith knew who Lee Evans was, certainly, and what his ability was. They were in the same town, after all, running the same meets, seeing each other often, and reading the same newspapers that included race results. But Tommie had no reason to be concerned about Lee. His own quarter time was faster than anything the specialist had run. And in the shorter distances, he had already given the junior college runner a lesson. In Sacramento, California, on June 11, 1966, a week before the NCAA, he had run against Lee in a 220 on the turn, on an evening that was mild and calm and the track hard clay.

With the eagerness and optimism of youth, Lee burst from the blocks and took a yard or two from Smith. For the sake of posterity, it would be good to lock the image in, to see it as one does a still photograph, to give Lee his moment, but the moment would not be stilled, and nothing could stop Tommie Smith and his famous Tommie-Jet gear which, when it kicked in, sent its bearer and its passenger flying to the front. In the critical stride, for that is all it seemed to encompass, Tommie took four yards from Lee. Everything else was anticlimax. Tommie's winning time was 20.0, another world record, achieved so casually that no one even seemed to notice it, except for the effect it had on Lee, who, reports said, hardly looked like a sprinter at all compared to the incomparable Tommie Smith, as if to say, here is reality, referring to Lee, and here, referring to Tommie, is something unreal. Lee was credited with only 21.0 in that 220, but observers thought his time must have been faster, as he had finished only six to eight yards behind the winner. Perhaps Tommie had so stunned the timers that they neglected the second-place runner until he was well past the line, and then said, "Oh!" and turned their attention back to him and his pedestrian performance.

No matter, some good came of it. Lee had seen the high-stepping Smith up close. One instant he had the man on his shoulder, the next instant, in that one great explosive stride, the fellow was yards and yards ahead. It was not possible, but it had happened. Talking about it now, Lee has the thrilled aspect of a man who has survived a tornado, happy to describe how his car was blown through the top of a tree and landed on a house half a mile away. Nevertheless, if Smith moved up to the 440 at the national AAU meet in New York in 1966, Lee would take him on, and Lee would expect to win. At worst, he would hang around to see what happened on the homestretch. Maybe Tommie Smith would be like Herb McKenley, when finally pressed. Maybe he would run too fast too early and tighten like a bow in the last few meters, leaving the opportunity for Lee, or someone else, to come through. These were faint hopes, resting on faith that Tommie Smith would make a mistake. The plain fact is that Tommie would almost certainly not do that. He wasn't going to get out there at the head of the stretch with an empty tank, the victim of a friendly relationship with the backstretch. He was too old for that, a person who had jumped chronological age by force of experience, a premature caution having settled on him by having been watched closely for so long and evaluated so minutely. When Tommie Smith put caution to the side, it was because he had to, by force of circumstance, not because he created the circumstance. Running with true unwanted and unnecessary abandon was for intrepid souls or those less heedful of consequence, which Tommie would one day prove to be in social terms, but which he decidedly was not when he was on the track, suited up and ready to run.

:

Theron Lewis was a strongly built young man with long legs and long arms and a partiality to dark-rimmed glasses. From a watchful distance, he had a quality approaching grandeur, an upright, regal bearing that suggested dignity, although equally it might have been aloofness, or detachment, or indifference, differing slants that nonetheless left the man impressive. Lewis, who was sometimes called T-Bird by his teammates, not a very dignified nickname after all, had been fourth in the United States Olympic Trials at 400 meters in 1964, but was left off the 1,600-meter relay in favor of Henry Carr, a matter of no controversy for anyone, it seemed, except the people who esteemed Theron and had hoped to protect his interests. At the next year's AAU, Lewis's misfortune continued. He had been misinformed about the schedule, showed up late for the finals of the 440, missed his warm-up, and decided to let it rip anyway, a decision that eventually left him struggling down the homestretch, his one-time commanding lead whittled down and then destroyed, as he was left fourth behind, among others, Ollan Cassell. So, he lost, but he had been the show, and then the showstopper. If Tommie Smith decided not to run the quarter at the AAU, and in any event it was only the sheerest fantasy that he was even considering it, Theron Lewis might provide the excitement. This possibility was enhanced by the running Theron Lewis had done in the early spring of 1966 and by the performances of his Southern University teammates.

*The young Theron Lewis.*

There was something remarkable about these runners. Just as Icarus had gotten too close to the sun from ambition, causing his wax wings to melt, the runners from Southern also got carried away by enthusiasm and ambition, and fell mighty hard. But, Icarus had actually flown, and that was Southern as well. Whether rising or falling, these Southern University runners were part of Lee's world, they down south and he in the West, but they were gathering reports about each other and thinking of the possibilities in New York, of who would do what and whom to watch and whom to let go. And in New York, a sprinter would be wise to watch closely for any person wearing powder blue and gold with an S and little wings along the side of the emblem.

:

At the Texas Relays, Southern University was everywhere. The team ran 39.9 to win the 440 relay, equal to the second fastest ever run. They ran a qualifying round of the 880 relay in 1:22.9, only 0.3 off the world record, and then narrowly lost the final to SWAC adversary Texas Southern. With Jimmy Hines anchoring for Texas Southern, both teams ran 1:23.4. Undeterred, Southern won three more relays: the mile, the two mile, and the sprint medley. The mile relay was 3:04.7, the third-fastest ever run, behind Arizona State's world record and a previous time by Southern. The sprint medley was 3:16.5, a collegiate record and second only to the 3:15.5 by the Santa Clara Youth Village. Theron Lewis contributed quarter-mile legs of 45.3 and 45.6, a half mile in 1:50.1, as well as anchor legs in the heat and finals of the 880 relay. At this, Lewis had to share the limelight with teammate Robert Johnson from tiny Princeton, Louisiana, who ran legs of 45.8 and 1:48.7 on day one, and 46.0 and 1:47.0 on day two. These performances were fine in their own right, but they were also preparation for the Drake Relays.

Drake was the highlight of the spring relay schedule, in part because it was last on the schedule and in part because the fans in Iowa jammed the stadium, giving the meeting a festival feeling. In 1966, some of the fans came, as they always did, to see the high school teams, others to cheer for Drake or the large universities of the Big 8 or the Southwest Conference or the many small, liberal arts colleges that swarmed Des Moines from all over Iowa and the Midwest, but knowledgeable fans came with a special eagerness to see the Southern Jaguars run in the college division. Such was the strength of track and field in the mid-1960s that even a collection of fliers like Southern would be challenged. Texas Southern actually beat the Jaguars in the 440 relay, 40.2 to 40.6, but Southern reversed the result in the 880 relay, 1:22.7 to 1:23.0 with Theron Lewis on anchor. Southern also won the college sprint medley in 3:19.2, the college two-mile relay in 7:31.2, and college mile relay in 3:07.4. As ever, the devil, as well as the fun, was in the details.

In the sprint medley, for example, Southern's Robert Johnson stunned the crowd when he took his anchoring half mile out in less than 50 and then finished in 1:51.5, a spectacular way to run a half, to say nothing of the discomfort the runner would have experienced. In the two-mile relay Theron Lewis did his teammate one better by running the first lap of his anchor half in 49.0 and the second lap in 63.2! As the quipsters say, "That had to hurt." In Drake's feverish atmosphere, two other half-milers also ran the first lap faster than 50 and the second slower than 60: George Hunt did it for Texas Southern, and Martin McGrady for Central Ohio. Any fan who saw this kind of unbridled enthusiasm got fair return for money spent. That's the ticket: spring, youth, hope, excess!

The summary of Southern University's speed and comportment emphasizes the stature of Theron Lewis, who was its leader. Later in the spring of 1966, Lewis took his team to the NAIA National Championships in Sioux Falls, South Dakota, and won the individual 440. Lewis's victory was no mean feat; he beat Kentucky State's Jim Kemp, who the previous year had won the NCAA championship and been ranked second in the world to Lewis's fifth. Kemp was a little banged up at the time and might have wished to run another time, but he still got beat, 45.2 to 46.2. If the times are converted to meters, the result was 44.9 to 45.9, making Lewis's time the second fastest ever run. He was in the company now of Adolph Plummer, who had the record, and Otis Davis, Carl Kaufmann, and Mike Larrabee, who shared his time. This was good news for a man aiming toward an AAU national championship later in the season.

What was Lee Evans to such a competitor? He was a threat, as many were, but only that. Theron Lewis should have loomed larger in the imagination of Lee Evans than ever he did to Lewis. And what of Tommie Smith? Theron Lewis would lose to Tommie Smith if Tommie stepped up. He must, or Tommie Smith would cease to be Tommie Smith. But there is more to consider. The mystique of Tommie Smith was that he appeared unnatural, so distilled and plain were his gifts; the wonder of Theron Lewis was that he was entirely natural—a talented man who made remarkable tactical choices, some good, some bad, but all invested with the vigor of youth. If there was only one Tommie Smith to appreciate and marvel upon, the world could wish for a thousand like Theron Lewis and be richly rewarded.

:

In the glimpse of what the quarter mile looked like as Lee made his ascent, another race catches the eye as if it demands that a marker be put down, so that the significance not be overlooked. Dave Crook of the University of Nebraska, one of the fine quarter-milers in the country, was scheduled to run the NCAA and the AAU meets later in the season, but first he too had Drake, where he would anchor the mile relay in the university division. Crook didn't have to worry about Southern, which was in the college division. Therefore, he could be comfortable, even serene. He had nothing to do but run as well as he was able and to win. As the third runners finished and the anchors prepared to take off, Crook looked up to see: what? He saw just another runner at Drake in a singlet of no distinction, not an Iowa State or a Kansas or a Kansas State, schools with tradition whose appearance would be enough to alert Crook to the necessity of concentration, but really a nothing, a blur with no meaning except that a loss would be hard to explain to anybody back home. Not that it made a difference, but the school was Central State in Ohio, a college that didn't even have its own track and had to make do with occasional practices at Ohio State. A man named Martin McGrady was its anchor. From the look of things, McGrady actually thought he was going to win, or at least he was making an effort commensurate with the intention. What exactly, in this regard, the weighing of possibilities, is a doppelganger? Is it a mirror of one's self, an alternate version, or only a memory of another self? Whatever it is, Martin McGrady had one. The second shadowy version of himself was only hours old, and it showed him running the first quarter of a half in less than 50 and the second, oh, a woeful carry indeed. And this in addition to the baton, and the weight of Crook's presence, was a burden on McGrady as he ran down the homestretch. In the circumstance—and indeed in any other, for that matter—no one expected Central Ohio to win. Maybe Crook would have to claw a bit, lean more fearlessly, dip close enough to suggest a tumble to the cruel cinders, but he would win in the end. And that is exactly what happened. Although both men ran splits of 45 and change, and both teams finished in 3:09.9, Crook came on strong in the last yards, and Nebraska got the call. After the race the anchor for Central Ohio went one way, quiet for a while now, and Crook the other, two talented young men, one of whom was enrolled in a school that gave him a full opportunity to achieve, and the other enrolled in a school that could not do that. Crook would go on to win the Big 8. He would go out to Compton, California, as an invited runner and there get beat only by UCLA's Bob Frey and by a junior college kid named Lee Evans, who beat them both. But the marker at Drake is not for Dave Crook. It is for Martin McGrady.

:

The last meet before the AAU answered the question whether Tommie Smith would run the 440 in New York. He wouldn't. At the NCAA meet, Bud tried to win a national championship with the one great talent available to him. Tommie finished third in the long jump, second in the 100-yard dash, ran an impressive heat of the 220, and then hurt his leg in the 440 relay. He never even got to the finals of the 220, his favorite event and the performance everyone looked forward to. The injury was relatively slight, a strain with swelling and bleeding. But it was the end of Tommie's NCAA in 1966, and the end of his AAU before it even started. The other leading contenders for the AAU quarter did better, or at least they emerged unhurt and ready to move on. Dave Crook finished second to Dwight Middleton of USC in the quarter, 46.3 to 46.4. Jim Kemp rebounded from the loss to Theron Lewis at the NAIA to take third place in 46.9, and Bob Frey arguably did better than any of them.

Frey stayed out of the individual events. Instead, he ran legs on UCLA's winning 4 x 1 and 4 x 4 relay teams. He was especially impressive on the mile relay, where he got the baton a couple of yards behind Cal's Forest Beatty, shadowed him until the homestretch, and then went past to win by three yards. The splits were 45.6 to 46.3, satisfying, even though Beatty had been injured and was not in his best condition. More satisfying yet was the UCLA victory over Brigham Young for the team title, 81 to 33. San Jose State was third with 31, a losing margin wide enough to cast doubt on Coach Winter's decision to enter Smith in four events. The national press noticed and critically evaluated not only the extensive use of Tommie Smith but also one of the coach's malapropisms. Winter said that Tommie looked so good running relays that he occasionally got standing innovations. The observation begged the question whether one such innovation might have been the exercise of caution with so talented an athlete.

# .11

*Mr. Smith Goes to Washington*
*The Philadelphia Story*
*New York, New York!*

The glow of the postwar years was faded, and the poets and painters were settling in. Cherished buildings were tumbling down. The neighbors let Kitty Genovese die, closing their windows to muffle her cries. The famous central park was dangerous, and no one went in, least of all at night. The people went from place to place underground, hanging on straps while the women stood, like men. The buildings formed caverns, and it was hard to get a glimpse of the sun or a breath of fresh air, or so it would seem to one who had never been there, but knew the place from newspapers, magazines, and black-and-white television. For these and many other reasons, New York City was an unlikely site for an AAU outdoor national track meet. No one would be comfortable, not like they would have at home. What was needed was an island, near the city but not too near, something that was in New York but not. What was needed was Downing Stadium, set adrift in the middle of the East River on Randall's Island. The organizers could freshen the cinders, add paint to the stands and seats, pick up the blowing trash, and then bring out Jim Ryun for the world record attempt he was rumored to make every weekend. Add a few odds and ends—the sprinters, the jumpers, the throwers, some of the skinny guys to run the five-mile or whatever—and you got yourself a track meet. Success would come from presentation and from packaging, the ordinary conceits that New York had long since mastered.

In 1966, the track meet was pretty decent after all, with old lights blinking and new ones lit. Two-time Olympian Dyrol

Burleson blinked in the mile. After a promising heat, the final proved that Burleson could not run with Jim Ryun. Ryun himself was blinking a little, like a star seen at night but extinguished already, the light a mere trick of time and space. He would annihilate himself eventually, the burden of expectation too heavy. Here, for example, his national championship was prominently described as doleful. He let the pace dawdle. He had not set a world record. So there was Ryun in the middle of images: a man pushing a stone up a hilltop knowing as he approaches the peak that the stone will slide down, a man whose debt was renewed each time he came near to paying it off. Beneath the surface of the AAU champion on the island was a man not yet revealed, but there nonetheless, the Ryun who could not win for losing, a man whose lion heart would cease to beat the moment he shuddered to the back of the field in Mexico City and ran for second. Perhaps the light blinked earlier than Randall's Island, but there, definitely, it did, despite the fact that the glory days were yet ahead. How can a man continue to run when he knows only disappointment, even in triumph?

Other fine runners too were on display at Randall's Island. Charlie Greene had not lost a final since the 1964 Olympic Trials, when he had been hurt. He did not lose this AAU either, although it looked like he might. He gave Jim Hines a head start—which is to say, he got a mediocre start to Hines's better one—then ran him down for the win, using, in the last twenty yards or so, his Super-Satellite gear. That particular gear was a reference to Tommie Smith's Tommie-Jet gear and a reminder that the injured sprinter's absence hung over the meet. The absence hung most forlornly over the 220, in which Jim Hines beat 440 record–holder Adolph Plummer, with both runners in 20.5. About that victory, one reporter openly called the specter to mind. "Hines ran the turn," the writer noticed, "as if he expected Tommie Smith to come barreling after him down the straight. One can only speculate what might have happened if he had, since Smith had a 0.9-second margin over Hines in his 20-flat record race the same night two weeks earlier. Would you believe 19.6w?"

Joining Hines with one first and one second in the weekend was young distance runner Tracy Smith. Smith lost the three mile narrowly to George Young and then beat Billy Mills, Dave Ellis, and John Lawson for the six-mile championship. Meanwhile, distance star Gerry Lindgren was home in Spokane, Washington, recovering from a lingering viral infection. Lindgren did have the grace, however, to send a successor. Rick Riley ran 29:11.4 and thereby became the second-fastest Spokane high school six-miler in history. Otherwise the winners at Randall's Island read like a who's who of American track and field in the '60s, including luminaries like Ralph Boston, Al Oerter, Tom Farrell, Ed Burke, Otis Burrell, Art Walker, Randy Matson, and Willie Davenport. Into this mix came Lee Evans, somebody new.

:

In the 440, Robert Johnson misjudged the finish line and was eliminated in a heat. Ron Freeman just didn't run fast enough, and he too went out. The other contenders passed uneventfully through the heats and semifinals. The final included, from the inside, Ollan Cassell, Vince Matthews of the New York Pioneer Club, Crook, Evans, Rupert Hoilett from the 49ers Track Club, Lewis, Kemp, and Frey. The temperature was eighty-five degrees, and the wind was negligible. The news was Lee Evans, who had run 45.8 in his semifinal. The time tied the AAU record, beat the junior college and freshman records, and left people wondering whether the young fellow had shot his bolt, which he probably had. Ollan- -Cassell–

– sprang out quickly with the gun, (and there you go with him, from a crouch!)
as the man in the first lane always seems to do, as if to deny the reality of the disadvantage; Crook began the race by running up Lee's back, an enthusiastic gesture that he must have realized would cost him; Theron Lewis ripped along, as did Kemp, and the others, moving too. They were like eight men scurrying from the line to take the smoke and the echo away with them. The runners were in their own worlds, but pressed into each other nonetheless, keenly aware of what was going on around them, making

adjustments on the fly. With the calculating and moving, coming around the bend and into the backstretch and beyond, Lee finally realized in the third 110 that he was out too slow and that he had to do something quickly. Nearing the second turn, he accelerated with enough suddenness and power to bring the 12,000 fans up out of their seats. Evans was either going to hold this new speed or he was going to double up, and either way it was going to be a lot of fun. It made sense to bet on the collapse. This was a young man from California, after all, only a year out of high school, and his run in the semifinal and his record were but temporary triumphs. Lewis was leading now, moving up to take control right on schedule. Kemp was running well. Lee was extended. The others were unlikely to mount further challenge, and the race continued on its way. Theron Lewis looked supreme, in fact, long and graceful and powerful. Only a person familiar with Lee Evans would know that Lewis was in trouble because Lee's real racing began only the moment the two men hit the top of the homestretch, where Lewis had a three-yard lead, which, depending on the condition of the person who holds a lead of that length could be described either as scant or commanding. In this case, it was scant. Lee was charging, and Theron Lewis had passed the time where that could be said about him. Oxygen debt is cruel no matter how it reveals itself, but it is most cruel when it comes fast and when it takes a long-sprinter and jerks him backward as if by a rope. That is the most cruel form of oxygen debt because, when that happens, an accusation has been leveled that the runner has made a mistake, that he has been a fool, that all of his training is washed away because he forgot the essential fact that races are won in the last fifty yards. Ten yards from the finish Lee ran right past Theron Lewis, who was almost walking by then. No one else challenged, and Lee Evans was national champion. The time was slower than he had expected, at 45.9, but Lee had run two races the day before when the weather had been even hotter. Theron Lewis did hold second, although he barely avoided the late charge made by Bob Frey and was only another step or two in front of Vince Matthews who finished fourth. Dave Crook was fifth. Kemp, Cassell, and Hoilett occupied the final spots.

:

The remaining summer of 1966 was a season for Lee to spend in shadow. Lee Evans was national champion, he had won every race he had entered in the season, and he would win all those remaining to him. But Tommie Smith lived and breathed, his leg having healed sufficiently for him to join the United States national team, and he was the main attraction, no matter what Lee did. The only person who could stand with him was Jim Ryun, but Ryun was a miler and of no concern to Lee except that, sometimes, it did seem that Ryun could get a cover story for having a cold when other athletes, black ones specifically, went unnoticed. Be that as it may, at the All-American Invitational, 19-year-old Jim Ryun earned his publicity. He took an astonishing 2.3-second chunk out of Michel Jazy's world mile record. With his injured leg firmly wrapped, Tommie Smith won a 200 meter on the turn from Jim Hines, Edwin Roberts, Harold Busby, Adolph Plummer, and Bill Toomey. Lee beat Lewis, Frey, and Matthews, among others, in the 400. That done, the two men from San Jose joined Frey and Lewis to win the mile relay in 3:04.7, with Lee contributing 46.9, Tommie 46.3. Frey 46.3, and Lewis 45.2. The next weekend, the relay team decided to break the world record in the 1,600-meter relay. It was as simple as that. The world record they had in mind had been set in the Olympic final at Tokyo under intense international pressure with the best 400-meter men in the world tuned and primed and given every encouragement. The record-setting American team included two Olympic gold medalists, a national champion, and a world-record holder. At the Los Angeles Times International Games, by comparison, Lee was the only national champion on the relay. Furthermore, the U.S. team would be opposed only by Australia. Effectively, the attempt would be made as part of a well-attended time trial.

Bob Frey led off. He ran 46.3 to the Australian runner's 49.0, and any notion of competitive spur fell away. The clock controlled. At that, Frey and Lee Evans, who ran the second leg, almost gave the game away. Frey faded a bit coming in, Lee got a little anxious, and the two barely connected. When that crisis passed, however,

Lee was winging. Running once again in a way that made later commentators fear his head was going to wobble off, Lee split 44.5, and gave the baton to the fastest third leg in history. The United States team might have lacked national champions, but it had Tommie Smith. With his recovered leg now unwrapped but still feeling the effects of a three-week layoff, Smith altered his usual tactics. He ran harder on the backstretch, pushed the final turn, and settled for steady progress on the homestretch rather than the usual high-stepping jet gear. The result was a lap in 43.8. With that, all anchorman Theron Lewis had to do, in order to secure the world record, was a sedate 46-flat. He ran 45.0 instead, and the world record for the 1,600 meter was complete. The final time was 2:59.6. "A tremendous race," said Coach Stan Wright, "I've got the baton with me and I wouldn't take a $1,000 for it." As for the team, they jogged the traditional lap, waving and smiling, then separated and finished the season in meetings of their own.

:

By year's end, Tommie Smith had run fifty-three finals notwithstanding the injury at the NCAA and the enforced layoff. He lost four competitions in total, one at 100 yards, one at 100 meters, one at 220 yards, and one long jump. He was the tenth-rated man in the world for the 100 meters/yards, the number one man in the world for the 200 meters/220 yards, and the number three man in the world for the 400 meters/440 yards. Lee Evans in contrast was one thing and one thing only. He was the number one ranked performer in the world for the 400 meters/440 yards. Lee ran fifteen major races. He won every one of them. He had been disqualified once, at the Coliseum for running out of his lane, but this had been minor, and he, after all, had been first across the line. Everyone who had seen the race counted the win. All this, the clean sweep against the world's best, came from a man who had been in high school the previous year.

# .12

*I went fishing, but all I pulled up was
an old boot.*

Talk of shadows, of primary forms and secondary ones, of people in
the sun and people thereby darkened, is perception only. Lee Evans
acknowledged no shadow, which is not the same as saying that he
failed to notice Tommie Smith's talent. He had seen that talent
from the time he had been a boy. More recently, he had seen
Tommie go past him in a 220 as if Tommie were, in Lee's
description, riding a motorcycle, such was his speed and power.
And of course, proceeding apace, he had handed Tommie a baton
this past summer and seen Tommie run a quarter in 43.8, so
smoothly that it was like a stream trailing into a river and a river
into a sea. But Tommie Smith, when all was said and done, plucked
at the quarter, teasing with it, running the distance only so often as
to raise the question of what he could do if he concentrated on it,
but not so often as to answer the question. By comparison, Lee did
run the quarter as his true event. By fair accounts, he ran it so well
that he was the best in the world. This was not a status given to
him, not handed to him because he looked good running around a
track, a paean to his grace and beauty. It was work that got him this
far, and his ability to endure and benefit from it. If ever Tommie
Smith stepped into his event, Lee meant to beat him, and it would
be work that produced that result as well. Work being something
he controlled, able to escalate the volume and intensity at will, Lee
saw little limit to its effect. For that reason, as well as trust in his
own talent, Lee did not fear Tommie, nor did he feel a covering
darkness. Lee saw light and meant to bask in it. Furthermore, he

meant to do his basking as a teammate of Tommie Smith at San Jose State University, from which he had accepted a scholarship. The decision made sense. Linda and he had friends and family in the San Jose area. Stan Dowell, with whom Lee continued to be close, was in San Jose, as was Coach Baker. Sprint expert Bud Winter was at SJS. Also, Lee relished the opportunity to run as Tommie's teammate. With him, Tommie, Ken Shackelford, and Bob Talmadge on the same team, San Jose State could think reasonably of world records.

:

San Jose State University had an enrollment of 21,000 students. In 1966, the school was a caldron in a caldron in a caldron, a great mix of students settled in a city that was undergoing rapid change in a state that was culturally shifting from one extreme to the other. In this case, of course, the state was Reagan's California. The actor had won the primary in August, would win the general election in November, and take the governor's office a minute or two after midnight on January 2, 1967. Being a man who took direction, the newly sworn governor turned to his aides and supporters and asked, "What do we do next?" In that instant, the summers of love that had lured so many young people west were forever complete. An energy that had promised to sweep everyone along with it was replaced with an energy designed to resist, to control, to retrench, and certainly to limit the exercise of influence. The tide goes in, the tide goes out, in social events as in nature. Many people, who had found themselves lifted by the first strong stirring of hope, who had a particular dream for example, now found themselves on the wrong side of the tide. In the cafeteria at San Jose State when Lee or Tommie talked with a white coed, as they might occasionally, about a class or a teacher or themselves, in an ordinary way, many of the young white men in the room grew somber and watchful. When Tommie and Lee each looked for apartments, the good ones disappeared the moment either of the men knocked on the door. Time after time, they approached. Time after time, they were rejected and trod back down steps and sidewalks. If California was known in the rest of the United States as a state where a black family could relocate to avoid the open hostility of the South or the de facto discrimination practiced in the East and Midwest, the individual experiences would be different, and Tommie and Lee, no less than any two other young men, had stories to tell.

:

For an athlete whose season is in the spring, even languorous training in the autumn has moral implications. After all, someone, somewhere is doing absolutely nothing. When the season comes, the victory will drop into the arms of the waiting worthy. Lee was training in the fall of 1966. He was building a belief system that would later permit him to say "I am ready." If the system was in part delusion, based on the belief that someone else was less ready, it mattered little. The strength of the conviction was important, not the facts behind the strength of the conviction. Lee ran regularly with the San Jose State cross country team, which was coached by Tracy Walters. Walters was well known for having produced Gerry Lindgren in high school. Lee ran overdistance on the roads, he ran the hills at the football stadium, and he ran longer interval workouts at a controlled tempo. He did his V-ups and push-ups and sit-ups. As the indoor season approached, Lee turned more to the track and to shorter distances. Almost immediately, he had a problem.

From Lee's perspective the workload was inadequate for the approaching indoor season. As bad, he was too shy then and reserved to challenge the coach, or even to talk to him openly, so he did not. However, Lee had trusting relationships with Stan Dowell and with Charles Baker. In the troubled first semester, he turned to both men. In due time, Lee even went to Coach Baker and considered the possibility of transferring back to San Jose City to complete the second year there. Feeling uncomfortable, and knowing it to be the correct course, Baker called Tracy Walters, with whom he had a good relationship, and talked about Lee's unhappiness. The upshot was that Coach Winter, Coach Walters, and Lee had a meeting designed to clear the air and set direction.

From Lee's perspective, the meeting had the salutary effect of putting his coach at San Jose State on notice that he might leave if something didn't happen. More important, Lee soon realized that he could continue to use the workouts from his past. He especially began to rely on Stan's strength workouts to supplement the speed work he was otherwise doing.

Despite his world ranking, Lee was not necessarily the best quarter-miler in the country in 1966. All that could be said was that he had been the best quarter-miler in the country the prior season. That means something, but not everything. Lee understood the reality, and this was why he maintained his concentration. Tommie Smith was one thing, but other challengers were also gathering strength in the fall of 1966. Theron Lewis and Martin McGrady were preparing for a pre-Christmas 600-yard dash at the Senior Bowl in Mobile, a race that McGrady would win in 1:09.3, just 0.3 slower than the national record he now owned in the event he had come to dominate. Larry James was enrolled at Villanova as a freshman, having completed an outstanding high school season the previous spring at White Plains, New York. Led by Otis Hill and by James, White Plains had run prep national records in both the 880 relay and mile relay, with times of 1:25.4 and 3:12.7. Vince Matthews entered his second year at Johnson C. Smith in North Carolina. Largely unknown in 1966 despite his high finish at the AAU meet, he was getting ready for a breakthrough season in 1967. Ron Freeman was at Arizona State as a sophomore. Presuming further improvement, he would pull up to Lee's shoulder unless Lee, too, improved. Don Domansky was enrolled at UCLA. The SWAC was loaded with quarter-milers on every school's shelf. Perhaps it would be fair to say that Southern was fading from its crest, that Texas Southern was in ascent, and that Prairie View A&M was a gathering force. Prairie View had two freshmen of unusual promise, Thurman Boggess and Felix Johnson. Arkansas AM&N was strong. Elbert Stinson led that team. In the state of Texas, Lamar Tech, Abilene Christian, the University of Texas, and Rice had strong quarter-milers getting ready for the next season. Conley Brown from Rice was particularly tough, but all could put four fast men on the track. From the Big Ten, Mike

Mondane and the University of Iowa had high, and reasonable, expectations.

Soon enough, the training done, the expectation established, and the goals fixed, the fall was memory. The indoor season opened. The indoor season in 1967 bears no relationship to the tattered version now in place. Then, the schedule was deep, the crowds were enthusiastic, the tracks were boards, the boards were banked, the turns were sharp, and the performers were interested. Achilles in Vancouver, Cleveland KC, Maple Leaf, All-Eastern, Mason-Dixon, Golden Gate, NYAC, LA Times, Dallas Invitational, Oregon Invitational, Will Rogers, San Diego Indoor, USTFF, Seattle Invitational, Philadelphia Inquirer, Albuquerque JC, and the names of meets just roll and roll. Lee ran a few meets open and perhaps a few more as a member of San Jose State's emerging relay unit of Smith, Evans, Shackelford, and Talmadge. Appraising his new runner, Coach Winter occasionally referred to Lee as a strength runner, despite his obvious speed. The one thing that became obvious in this, Lee's first extended indoor season, was that he wasn't much good at it yet. More tellingly, he wasn't much good at it even compared to his gangling teammate Tommie Smith, who might have been expected to be flummoxed by the tight turns and banked elevations of the country's various indoor arenas, with tracks likely to be ten, eleven, or even twelve laps to the mile. In Oregon in late January, Smith avoided the banks by running a 60-yard race against Charlie Greene, Harry Jerome, and San Jose State teammate Bob Griffin. He was placed fourth, although all four runners were credited with 6.1. Lee moved up and ran 500 yards in 57.6, and then the two sprinters joined Shackelford and Talmadge to win an easy mile relay in 3:18. Later, in San Diego, Lee won a 600-yard dash in 1:12 and added a mile-relay leg in another San Jose State victory. These early-season results may cast doubt on the conclusion that Lee wasn't good at indoor running, but the proof was coming. At the LA Times, San Jose State won the mile relay, but the splits were 49.7 for Shackelford, 49.4 for Talmadge, 49.7 for Evans, and 47.9 for the anchoring Smith. On San Francisco's 160-yard track, another mile relay win brought splits of 49.7 for Shackelford and Talmadge, 48.2 for Evans, and a flying 46.5 for

Tommie Smith, one of the fastest legs ever achieved on so small a circuit. San Jose State's final time of 3:14.1 easily beat Morgan State's previous national record of 3:15.6 for 160-yard tracks.

If confirmation were needed that Lee was struggling to accommodate the indoor tracks, the confirmation came at Louisville, Kentucky's Mason-Dixon Games and then at the AAU meet. Mason-Dixon featured an unusually large 220-yard banked board track. Tommie used the track to run a scintillating world indoor record. The San Jose State sprinter followed Jim Kemp until the second backstretch and then, like a snake uncoiling and striking, took ten yards from him. No further advantage was taken, but none was needed. Upon first seeing the large track in Louisville, Tommie had predicted a time of at least 46.9. He actually ran 46.2, nearly a second faster than Theron Lewis's old standard. Lee did less well. He lost at 600 yards to Bill Bruckel of Cornell, 1:10.1 to 1:10.8. Later, at the AAU national meet, Lee again found himself suffering by comparison to his teammate. For starters, consider that the number one ranked quarter-miler in the world was scheduled to run the third leg on his university team, with the anchor reserved for someone else. In the spirit of the time, the proper reference might be to "something else," so remarkable were Tommie Smith's performances becoming. In the near future, Bud Winter would exhaust the available human descriptions and turn to the ethereal, and to comic books. Tommie would become like the Green Hornet, like Superman, a man from whom "beyondness" was expected but from whom a new result was being produced, "wayoutness."

:

The AAU Indoor National Track and Field Championship was hosted by Oakland, California, in 1967. In a meet that featured sprinter Billy Gaines, who defended his AAU 60-yard title by beating Jim Hines; Bob Seagren, who won the pole vault; Willie Davenport in the hurdles; and Art Walker in the triple jump, all of whom defended titles from the previous year, as well as a world indoor three-mile record by Tracy Smith, it was Tommie Smith who ignited the crowd of 8,199. The mile relay featured three teams, San Jose State, the 49er Track Club, and the Baltimore Olympic Club. Baltimore was notably dangerous because it included three members of the team from Trinidad-Tobago that had set a world record in the previous summer's British Empire and Commonwealth Games beating times earlier established by Arizona State and Southern University. The 49ers were dangerous because they opened with ever steady Jim Kemp, a compact, muscular man constructed to the exact specifications required for indoor running, and Dave Crook, formerly of Nebraska and a good closer. San Jose State of course had Lee and Tommie, as well as Ken Shackelford, but it lacked the usual services of Bob Talmadge, who was injured. John Bambury took Talmadge's second leg.

The race started with deceptive calm. Jim Kemp, who had won the 600-yard title earlier in the day, cruised 48.3, only to see Baltimore's second man, Kent Bernard, make up the deficit with his 48.2. Behind the two club teams, Shackelford and Bambury were, on this day, digging a bit of a hole for their teammates. Shackelford ran 50.2 from the line, and Bambury ran 50.0, performances that left Lee Evans with a deficit of perhaps twenty-five yards. He closed some of it by running 48.2 to the 49.1 and 49.4 legs of Don Payne for the 49ers and Nick Lee, the only non-Trinidadian for Baltimore, but he also tied up slightly as he came toward the exchange zone. Lee's distress forced Tommie to creep up a bit, to shorten Lee's leg and extend his own. The upshot was that Tommie was nearly fifteen yards behind Crook and Edwin Roberts when he finally set off. Edwin Roberts promised to be an especially difficult man to run down because he had not only run 44.8 on Trinidad's world-record relay, but he had also been runner-up in the 220 yards at that same Commonwealth Games. Viewed realistically, Tommie's situation was daunting. He was yards behind talented foes, on a track too small to permit him to unfurl his long, high-stepping stride, and he was sprinting around on banked curves likely to fling him off the upper lip if he attempted to gain speed or momentum. To make matters worse, Smith's first stride or two carried him into Payne, by then the detritus of the third leg rather than the sprinter he had been moments earlier. This bump required Smith to disentangle himself before he could even get a proper start. What a thrill went through the crowd. They stood as one to watch the race they had hoped to see. This was the great Tommie Smith, he of untapped and limitless potential, chasing good sprinters in a hopeless cause that he, of all people, might just accomplish.

Crook had three yards on Roberts and dashed away. In turn, the second-place Roberts had Crook in his foreground and Tommie Smith in his background, so he too ran desperately fast on the tight track. Smith, meanwhile, reached for his fastest gear. For once, he had to stretch, to reach into his reserves, with none of that gazellelike charm to take care of his problems. Strength would carry this day, and he no doubt knew it, even as he dived into the turn and went into the backstretch and around. Running on composition laid over boards, Tommie overtook Roberts by the gun lap and set off after Crook who was still strong. But Crook was alone, like prey separated from the pack, and Tommie's attention on him was complete. Roberts was gone and there was no sense paying the slightest attention to him. Crook meanwhile would sense what was happening behind him. If nothing else, the crowd's reaction would tell him. A preposterously tall and fast sprinter was at his back. He wasn't thinking of Edwin Roberts either. There was no room to worry about so distant a worry when the near one had terrible implications. But what can you do? Great long-sprinters never go away; they have to be forcibly removed from contention either by their own intemperance or by the conduct of an adversary. Being a great long-sprinter, the dead and forgotten Edwin Roberts surged back toward the front. Entering the final curve and coming out of it, he joined Crook and Smith for the short, indoor stretch run, the three of them flung carelessly off the banked turn.

Three abreast and with scant time and space left, Crook was on the inside, Smith was in the middle, and Roberts was on the outside. Measuring the effect of the bank and what it creates by way of momentum, Crook had the worst situation, Roberts the best, and Tommie was neither here nor there. The San Jose State anchor, however, was oblivious to advantage or disadvantage. He had a sightline. The finish line was just there. Why did these two men think they could survive him? Imperceptibly, his advantage grew, not as the others weakened appreciably, but by force of his own will and that mighty stride, now collapsed slightly, it must be said, but high yet, and ultimately high and strong enough. When the finish line finally arrived, it was Tommie Smith who reached it first, a half stride up on his two adversaries who finished evenly. Tommie had run his anchor leg in 46.5 on a 160-yard track, having taken the baton early in the exchange zone, after being bumped, and after running most of the race, indeed almost all of it, in the second lane. Roberts had run 47.6 and Crook 48.0, creditable times, but not otherworldly. Those were human performances. What Tommie did was considered something else.

Coach Winter admitted that he had not thought Tommie could win. The gap was too wide, and the sprinters in front of him too talented. But he had won. Even Tommie admitted the harshness of his task. "If they'd come at me hard, they could have had me," he said. "I had absolutely nothing left." Many months later teammate Shackelford recalled the event in decidedly human terms, bringing friend and teammate back to earth while adding stature to his performance. This race in Oakland, he said, was the only time he had seen his accomplished and serene friend heave.

:

Coach Winter played favorites. He favored Tommie Smith. He gave him more time. He spent more time, apparently, thinking about him. He made more outrageous statements in praise of him. He distinguished him more frequently in more ways from his predecessors or peers. He liked Smith and doted on him. If this sounds like criticism, it is only so in keeping with a coach's entirely natural inclination, an inclination that could be resisted but not overcome. Winter had a star at hand. He had that star with him two years before Lee Evans arrived at his doorstep. Lee Evans was good, a fine sprinter and a good and decent young man. But he was not yet, in Bud Winter's mind, what Tommie Smith was, nor would he ever be. Without surprise, one sees Lee described by his coach as an endurance runner, knowing that to a sprint coach those are,

inadvertently, words of disparagement, something akin to saying, I
have a Jaguar, and I have a truck. I value the truck, but I love the
Jaguar. The characterization is arguably overstrong, but the feel of
it is not unfair and not hard to understand. To the coach, there was
Tommie Smith, and there was the world. Lee Evans was in the
world. There was nothing to be done about that. Lee's first outdoor
season at San Jose State approached. Lee had not trained with
Tommie Smith. The coach tended to keep his sprinters apart. He
had not seen Tommie Smith sprint at full effort at practices. The
coach did not invite such spectacles. But he had seen Tommie under
competitive circumstances. And he still thought, "If Tommie Smith
runs against me in a quarter mile outdoors, I will beat him."

This is an engaging quality, characteristic of Lee. He could give
his teammate his entire due, push to his side of the table all the
earned credit in the world, and yet, still, think of surpassing
him. In the indoor season, Lee was in his training cycle. If he were
given a choice between running well in the indoor season and
running modestly, all other things being equal, he would rather
run well. But if he had to accept a disadvantage in the indoor
season rather than compromise his outdoor season, he would
accept the disadvantage. He would permit people to say he was not
a good indoor runner; he would permit people to say that Tommie
Smith was great and let them suggest by inference that he was not.
But he would not change his goals. He would maintain his
concentration on the outdoor meets, where championships of value
were handed out. He would deal with Tommie Smith then if
necessary, not at some thump-thump race up and around a board
track in an arena full of noise and smoke. In the outdoor season,
there would be Tommie Smith and there too, Lee Evans, and they
would settle the case. What is this? A hurricane party.

# .13

*Get this party started.*

Lee Evans had not been beaten in an open quarter or outrun in a relay leg at the distance since he was a junior in high school. The unblemished record is why he thought he could beat Tommie Smith at his chosen distance. The unfortunate fact is that Lee would get precisely one chance to run against Tommie in an important race over a quarter mile. Losing that, he would be left with the result forever. There would be no two-out-of-three, or six-out-of-ten. Regrettably, the showdown would occur before Lee was quite ready and in a circumstance that favored the older, swifter runner and worked to the disadvantage of the younger athlete who figured to be stronger. And even if Lee won, the result would not settle the question. People would still say, "It wouldn't have happened twice." Tommie's legion of fans would never believe that their man could be beaten in an even match. Fair or not, the tussle between Lee and Tommie over a single lap was going to happen, no matter how the principals felt about it. And it was certainly going to happen if Bud Winter had anything to do with it, and of course he had everything to do with it. The other element to consider about Bud's role is that he was a bit of a showman. He liked big events. He liked to set a runner against a world record, and tell a crowd, "Come see." He liked match races with advance notice and publicity, and he liked dual meets between putatively unfriendly schools. Showman that he was, Bud also knew the importance of a buildup, a tightening of pressure over days, weeks, and months in the nature of proof that genuine goods were on offer and that no one who stayed home would feel good about the decision. In the context of Lee and Tommie and the inevitable match between the two later in the spring of 1967, Bud Winter needed preliminary results of high quality. Fortunately, he had the team to deliver them.

:

In its vogue, the amalgam called Speed City was a collection of black sprinters, all of them preening and glowering in the requisite theater of racial politics, Lee and Tommie no less than the others. What this means, briefly, is that there was a lot of staring straight into the camera and wearing sunglasses, with the men standing or leaning into each other in a casual but alert posture that said, "I'm not fooling with you this time!" The image undoubtedly scared people who held authority, flushed them from cover, and made them do and say stupid things that revealed exactly the motive for the exercise. But that was a year away. In 1967, San Jose State was only fast, not fast and dangerous. In 1967, as in other years, the idea was to put the sprinters to work in the early-season relays and then separate them into individual events for the championship meets. In the relays, Lee Evans and Tommie Smith would carry the heavier load, but Ken Shackelford and Bob Talmadge were important cast members, whose job was to keep the team on goal pace or in contention. For success, every team member had to run to his capacity. In the culture of the relay, a slower runner who exceeds himself is more valuable than a faster runner who disappoints.

The Mt. San Antonio College Relays were held the weekend of April 28-29, 1967, in Walnut, California. After an unusually wet spring, the wind blew in gusts from five to twenty-five miles per hour. The wind assisted the discus throwers and some of the straight dashes but played havoc with the featured relays. Still, San Jose State won both the 880 and the mile relays with times of 1:24.6 and 3:09.0. Attentive fans noticed that in each case, Lee Evans ran faster than his accomplished teammate. In the 880, Lee split 20.1 to Tommie's 21.1, and in the mile relay, he finished his

*Lee Evans to Tommie Smith.*

leg in 46.3 to the 46.6 that Tommie contributed. Satisfying though these races might have been, they were mere tune-ups for the West Coast Relays two weeks later. At that 41-year-old meet in Fresno, Bud Winter was planning for world records.

The West Coast Relays had better weather than Mt. SAC had. The air was still, the temperature was neither too hot nor too cold, and the entire evening was characterized as balmy. The track was fast, and the crowd of 14,000 was sharpened and excited by the rumor that San Jose State was going to run for the records. What remained, of course, was for the San Jose State team to produce the anticipated performances. First up was the 880 relay, in which the goal was Abilene Christian's world record of 1:22.6, established in 1958 and tied by a second Abilene Christian team in 1961. The San Jose order of running was Shackelford to Talmadge to Evans to

Smith, a very traditional order with a good starter starting and then building momentum throughout. In fact, the only problem came on the second exchange, when Talmadge handed to Lee, and Lee got out so fast that he almost had to stop. Other than that, the race was an uneventful three legs of 21.1, 20.5, and 21.1, before an explosion on the anchor. On that anchor, Tommie Smith turned the jets on, as only he could, with knees high and stride supremely long, dashing his furlong in 19.4 seconds, which was the fastest 220 split ever recorded. The final San Jose State time for the 880 was 1:22.1, a half second faster than necessary for the new world record. A comparison of splits with Abilene Christian's 1958 run makes clear that Tommie was principally responsible for the record. Anchored by three-time Olympic gold medalist Bobby Morrow, ACC had run 20.1, 20.8, 21.2, 20.5. Thirty-five minutes after the 880 relay, with the stadium still buzzing, the same four San Jose State runners returned to the track for the mile relay. Of course, no one expected another world record, but they almost got one anyway. And this time it was Lee who had the jets on. After Talmadge's 47.5 and Shackelford's 46.4, Lee exploded with a 44.2 leg, the fastest 440 split ever run. With Tommie on anchor, a record was possible, but Tommie hesitated slightly as Lee approached, and then ran a solo 45.3. The final result was 3:03.5, a tenth of a second better than the old American record shared by Arizona State and Southern, but seven-tenths off Trinidad's world mark.

That is the situation, then. Lee had run faster than Tommie for both 220 and quarter splits at Mt. SAC. At the West Coast Relays, Tommie had run the fastest 220-yard split ever recorded, and Lee had done the same for his leg of the mile relay. As a result, both runners could feel confident about racing each other. And fans could rest assured that when Bud Winter said "y'all come," or words to that effect, he meant it.

# .14

*My, what high knee lift you have!*

On May 25, 1963, Adolph Plummer ran his last open race for the University of New Mexico. The occasion was the first conference championship meet for the Western Athletic Conference held in Tempe, Arizona. In the open quarter, his primary opposition figured to come from Ulis Williams, a talented runner in his own right, who one year later would be on the United States Olympic team at Tokyo, run the finals at 400 meters, and earn a gold medal as a member of the 1,600-meter relay. On this night, however, he could do nothing to stop Plummer from barging away from him. The 6-foot, 3-inch, 185-pound native of Brooklyn split 21.7 at the 220, repulsed Williams's surge coming into the homestretch, and ran unopposed into track history. His final time of 44.9 for yards smashed the record of 45.7 that Glenn Davis had established in 1958. Plummer was also credited with tying the 400-meter mark held jointly by Otis Davis and Carl Kaufmann during the 1960 Olympic Games. For all the good it did him, Ulis Williams broke Davis's record by running 45.6 in second. Notably, Plummer's run was the greatest single revision of the record since 1932, when Ben Eastman took a full second off his own previous world record. None of this impressed Bud Winter, Tommie Smith, or Lee Evans in 1967, however. Tommie good-naturedly referred to Plummer's record as humbug—a fluke, he said, everything coming together to produce a record. Even the normally quiet Lee Evans said Plummer's time did not seem worthy of a world record. For his part, Bud Winter saw Plummer's time and the future rending of it as a mere stop along the way. With Tommie scheduled to enter six weeks of ROTC service beginning on June 20, Winter had referred to the intervening time as a calendar of opportunities. The opportunities, it was said, were for Tommie to break every world record from the 100 to and including the 440.

These ambitions were the background for a talk Bud had with his star runners in early May. Speaking to them one at a time, he told them that they would race each other in the 440 on May 20 at the San Jose State Invitational. The Invitational would be the last one held on Spartan Stadium's cinder track, which was to be replaced. Something important should mark the day, a way of saying farewell to the great San Jose State runners of the past. Lee and Tommie understood what Bud was saying. For weeks, they had sensed his approach. The race on the old cinder track would not be man against man, not just Lee against Tommie, and not Tommie against Lee. Rather, the race would be man against man against clock, with Adolph on everyone's mind. If Plummer's world record was humbug, if it was not worthy of respect, the two young men from San Jose were expected to prove it.

When the news was released, everyone was excited, as Bud had expected. The two champions and friends would finally face off. For two weeks the track world churned. On the day, more than 4,000 people would overwhelm the 1,000 available seats, crowd four deep along the backstretch, stand on surrounding lawn, or climb poles or perch atop cars for a view. In reality, it was a bit of a rigged deal. If a person wanted a real race between the two San Jose State athletes, Tommie would run outside and Lee would run inside. That positioning would tempt Tommie to an early turn of speed, and let the strong runner key off him from the inside, thus predicting a homestretch battle of waning speed and gathering strength. If you wanted a world record more than you wanted a race, on the other hand, you put Lee on the outside and Tommie on the inside, thus giving the alternate assurance. With great speed hanging over his inside shoulder, the stronger runner would go out fast, the faster runner would relax in the wake, and then he would come through, in hot pursuit, for the win and the record. In other words, the placement of the runners in lanes, in this event as perhaps at no other ballyhooed equivalent, forecast the result.

When Bud Winter put Lee in lane four and Tommie in lane three, the decision was nearly a guarantee, on two accounts. Adolph Plummer's world record would fall, and it would fall to Tommie Smith. In his heart Lee knew this. He accepted the outside lane, as Coach Winter requested, because Tommie was a senior, and because he had no option, but, being Lee Evans, he also had a characteristic incendiary idea. He was going to run the legs off his good friend. If he was meant to make the pace, he would make it. He would extend Tommie from the gun, drive him down the backstretch, and make him push the second turn—take the high stride out of this fellow. He had, after all, run 44.2 for yards, equivalent of 43.9 for meters, on the relay at the West Coast Relays. He was ready. He could do this. If Bud wanted a record, he could have it. But Lee was going after that record for himself. He was Landy to no one's Bannister, no lamb out front looking over the wrong shoulder when the wolf leaped. All in all, despite the building pressure, Lee was happy to run against Tommie Smith.

Of course, Lee didn't know all the facts. A later recounting said that on the Wednesday before the race, Tommie ran a secret time trial of 34.5 for 352 yards. Secret from Lee, secret from a teammate? Would a coach have one athlete run a clandestine time trial to prepare him to beat a teammate? He might, if he had already picked a winner. Anyway, Lee had run no secret time trial. He just did what he had always done. He got ready to run.

:

The stands with 1,000 seats at San Jose State were in the homestretch alongside the eight-lane cinder track. Often used for warming up and cooling down, an open field was on the other side. The remaining border was occupied by the football stadium and by married-student housing. Three large redwood trees stood along the backstretch, just off the 250-yard mark. Some runners would have been tempted to run to the trees, as orientation. Lee was in the habit of running right past the trees without the slightest notice. When the entries in the 440 yard were called to the mark, the trees were only lightly swaying, and the temperature was a pleasant sixty-eight degrees. The weather was cause for celebration.

*Lee (right) leads Tommie Smith (left) from the blocks.*

No reason to pull the windbreaker along the fence line, the coach said. Never have I seen the wind so still at this time of day, he said. Ken Shackelford and Bob Talmadge settled in the two inside lanes; a young man named Dale Martin took an outside lane. Lee shook himself out and stood in lane four for the introductions, Tommie doing the same in lane three. To anyone, even Tommie, these introductions could be a burden. Coach Winter wrote them himself and enjoyed the drone of past accomplishments, especially in the case of Tommie Smith and his cascade of world records. To Lee, they could be infuriating, as if each word in praise of his friend diminished him by comparison. While the king lives, all are in bondage. Therefore the king must die. At the gun, Lee blew away from the starting line. He screamed past the 110-yard mark in 10.9 and the 220 in 21.5. Later he would acknowledge that he was out too fast, that if he had not been intent on the world record and the obligation he felt to provide it, he would have run a 220 split more like 22.1. But it was too late for reconsideration. In any event, regret was no part of Lee Evans, especially not in the middle of a race. He powered into the second turn.

Only at 280, near the trees he did not see, did Lee get the sense that the man on his inside was changing gears, that Tommie Smith was moving into the middle of his several jets. The sound of the cinder track, the rising attention of the crowd, and the inadvertent

*Tommie Smith on the homestretch.*

noise of accelerating effort, told him that Tommie's arrival, which had been anticipated, was imminent. Lee's task was to react by not reacting. He had to relax, to hold form, and to stave off this challenge. Lee had told a reporter before the race that the last 110 would make the difference. The winner would be determined there, and not with a quick start or a brutal backstretch. Lee had said that the pain in the last 100 would be etched on his face, but that he would withstand it. And now, as the two runners came around the turn and headed into the stretch, the pain was there, and it was etched on his face. Not only pain was evident, but also tension, the great burden of the long-sprinter and the bugbear against which Bud Winter coached. Tommie surely felt the tension, too, but he had been running in Lee's draft, a comforting position for a relatively untested quarter man and an additional benefit in that Lee was bound to suffer from doing the early work. As the race was run, Tommie was 0.1 behind Lee at the 110, 0.2 behind at the 220, and went past him in the critical third 110, 33.5 to 33.8 for 330. Turning for home, the initiative swung to Tommie. He glided smoothly through the final 110, this one in 11.3, and claimed what was

*Two champions, two friends.*

waiting for him at the finish line: two new world records. The result in the slightly shorter 400 meter was 44.5, thus removing Otis Davis and Carl Kaufmann from the books. The 440-yard time was a tenth better than Adolph Plummer's record, 44.8 to the prior 44.9. Lee tightened visibly in the stretch, yet ran well enough to set a personal best of 45.3 for yards and 45.0 for meters. Another year of experience, speed, and strength would have made a difference, but Lee didn't have a year. He had a single afternoon in San Jose.

After the race, of course, Coach Winter said what he was obliged to say. Lee had done the work. Lee was younger than Tommie. He was ahead of Tommie at this stage. But Bud was in love, well beyond the blush and into the throes, and about his love, a performer who would have been the love of any sprint coach, Winter was effusive. Tommie Smith, he said, could eventually run a quarter in low 43s or high 42s. He was talking about cinder tracks, he was talking about a sport in which money and professionalism had not taken hold, and he was speaking in a time before drugs mangled the sport. He was talking about a natural man doing what a natural man does, run one lap around the track and stop in the place where he begins.

:

Unadvised by a coach, the Australian John Landy decided that the only way to beat Roger Bannister of England in the mile at the 1954 British Empire and Commonwealth Games was to run the starch out of him. Landy also knew that the race between him and Roger, as the first two men to run a mile under four minutes, had excited sports fans generally and that this race might ignite interest in track and field. John Landy felt obligated to play his part. On a sunny day, he towed the field through a fast pace. He dislodged everyone but Bannister. Coming out of the last turn, Landy hoped he might have done the job entirely, but when he peeked Roger went past.

# .15

*Crossing Pattern*

The race between Tommie and Lee split friends into camps, some of them wishing that Lee would win and more that Tommie would, a product of Tommie's open nature, a talent that attracted fans in fair weather, which for him the weather often was, and his longer relationship with many of them. Lee understood. He had his own friends. Anyway, Linda was there, and she was a fierce competitor, a quality that Lee admired and for which he was thankful when times were tough. The loss to Tommie was a disappointment, of course, but Lee had his own rewards. He had a new personal record, the comfort of knowing that his time was the fifth fastest ever run, and the knowledge that he had done his best on the day. In any case, the race was early in his calendar. As a junior college transfer, Lee was not eligible for the NCAA meet, but he trained in preparation for the national AAU championship in June, where he expected to repeat his victory of the year before. Along the way, Lee's days were seamless and repeating. He had an old car and access to gas that hovered near 21 cents a gallon. He had an apartment that Bud helped him locate, for which he paid eighty dollars a month. He had a scholarship that paid tuition and books, and a stipend of eighty-five dollars for room, board, and incidentals. And there, of course, in the two numbers is the moment when math becomes reality. In financial terms, Lee's privileged life as a scholarship athlete was a scramble. He sometimes joked that he, and Tommie too, would use a dollar for gas and a dollar for bait and they would fish for dinner, but this is a joke that is no joke. The fishing was an occasional accommodation to tight times, as were the other opportunities to supplement the family's income, catch as catch can. If it happened that Lee could, especially in Europe in a summer, find the chance to pick up a few dollars, he did it without remorse or conscience. The rules of amateur competition were no match for the needs of his family. Whatever happened, Lee and his wife were up to the task. Lee rose at six o'clock and the family was in motion, getting prepared for the day. Out the door, Linda drove Lee to campus and then took the baby to his grandmother's. She then doubled back to the university for her own classes.

Lee's classes were usually in the morning because track practice was at 1:30. Lee rarely ate a substantial lunch because he couldn't (or didn't want to) afford it, and because he didn't like to eat so close to the workouts. When the time for practice arrived, Lee got a ride the two miles to the locker room, changed, and then walked over to the old track, where his teammates and Bud Winter waited. Arriving, the runners fell into a routine so strongly emphasized that it could almost be called ritual. They ran an easy mile, then stretched before running a regimented lap, consisting of 100 meters slow, 100 meters medium, 100 meters medium, and 100 meters concentrating on high knee lift and short strides. Next, the runners did Bud's drills, of which he was an early advocate and in some cases the innovator. In pairs, the athletes worked back and forth over a 30-meter distance, working on lifting the knees high, reaching with the foreleg, swinging the arms correctly, running tall, running relaxed, and bounding with a push from the ankle. At the end of all this, Bud would discuss the workouts themselves. In their first days as teammates, Tommie and Lee ran together, but the pairing did not take. Tommie liked to lead, Lee liked to lead, and the result was predictable and not good for either person. Also, Tommie was a pure sprinter. More particularly, he was a pure sprinter with a history of breakdowns. Sportswriters referred to Tommie's lean body as a fine instrument, efficient but fragile. Even teammates suggested that if Tommie ran the workouts they did, he would falter, his legs would go flat. So, because the two men competed in workouts and because they required different workouts to meet their strengths and frailties, Bud quickly separated them.

Over time, Lee did workouts assigned by Bud or taken from his previous coaches Dowell and Baker. Teammates occasionally joined Lee for all or part of one of his workouts, but more often he ran by himself. That didn't matter to him because he led every interval, even if someone was doing the workout with him. At the end of every practice, Bud gave his charges one lap of killer-dillers. The runners sprinted 50, jogged 50, sprinted 50, and repeated to the end of the lap, then warmed down gently. The workout ended a little after three o'clock, and Lee usually got a ride home. There, he took his turn with his son, spent time with his wife if she was not working or at classes, and he studied. In the progress of every day, the married couple was in a social world that was growing more conscious of indignity and unfairness. Each was growing angry, although righteous is perhaps a better word, and began to spend time and energy working toward social justice, although others might have called it agitation, a code word applied by people who held power and resented competing claims to it. What is responsible for the agitation, the unmoving stone or the water running over it? The initial forum for Lee's interest was the United Black Students for Action. This campus group addressed issues specific to San Jose State University but present too in the greater culture. The group included Professor Harry Edwards, who lived close to campus, Tommie Smith, and a young man named Ken Noel, among others. Noel was a San Jose State half-miler, Lee's friend, a fishing companion, and a person he trusted. If Ken called Lee and said, "Come to a meeting," Lee usually went. If Harry called, Lee might or might not go, depending on the circumstance. No matter who called, the important work of the UBSA was heightened by the fact that many, if not most, of the black students at San Jose State were athletes. Therefore, the athletes were expected to lead.

:

When Tommie went back to the 220, he took the media and the publicity with him. Lee was left to do his own work. In the run-up to the AAU, he won the California Relays quarter in 45.6, finishing against a strong wind and ahead of Felix Johnson and Elbert

Stinson, and then added the Compton title in 45.8. At Sacramento, he ran a 220 in 20.7, losing to Tommie and to surging Willie Turner of Oregon State, and a winning quarter in 45.7, a one-day double inferior only to the 20.6 and 45.6 Adolph Plummer had run at the 1963 Compton meet. With these performances, Lee wasn't much worried about anyone else, not even Vince Matthews of Johnson C. Smith University in North Carolina, a young sprinter who was dramatically improving. Matthews anchored his team's 880-relay team to a win over favored Rice at the Penn Relays and then ran a mile-relay leg of 44.9 in a nonwinning effort. Matthews also moved to sixth all time in the open quarter by winning the NAIA national title in 45.4 over Thurman Boggess's 45.6 and four runners from Arkansas AM&N who occupied third through sixth: Stinson, 45.9; Harold Francis, 46.0; Henry Smothers, 46.0; and Walter Smith, 47.0. So remote was Vince Matthews from Lee Evans that Lee might have been slightly more concerned about Jim Kemp, who was also running well and promised to challenge at the AAU meet scheduled for Bakersfield, California, on the weekend of June 22–23.

With artificial surfaces not yet generally available, this AAU meet was conducted on crushed brick, clay, and volcanic ash. The highlight, once more, was Jim Ryun, who ran a solo 3:51.1 and, sentimentally, Gerry Lindgren, who won the three mile. Perhaps, too, Tommie Smith was a highlight, given that he was now on active military duty at Fort Lewis, Washington, had blisters on his feet from combat boots, had not trained since before the NCAA, and was beset by Jim Hines, the Texas Southern athlete who had won the 100 in this meet over archrival Charlie Greene and had beaten Tommie himself at Compton, 20.5 to 20.6. Many people thought the victory over Tommie Smith was surprising, but not Hines, "If we ran ten times," Hines said, "then, I'd beat him ten times." But Jimmie Hines didn't beat Tommie Smith for the national championship at Bakersfield. Smith ran the turn with more vigor than usual, unwilling to let a "cat" like Jim Hines have too much head start, and then easily overcame the single yard he had given up. Smith's winning time was 20.4, Hines followed in 20.6, and in third came John Carlos, previously of East Texas State

*Vincent Matthews of Johnson C. Smith University.*

University and now running for the Houston Striders. Observers felt that Carlos had actually gained on Hines in the stretch.

As for Lee, he qualified for the finals and then had to deal with Jim Kemp. Hanging out all alone in lane eight, Kemp dashed through a 21.5 opening 220. Matthews also went out fast, with 21.7, but Lee ran the pace he might have run against Tommie, were it not for his worries about the world record. He split 22.1. Off the second turn and into the stretch, Kemp held a five-yard lead on Elbert Stinson running in lane seven, seven yards on Vince Matthews, and a full eight yards on Lee, who was finally starting to move, and who was prepared to take what he considered his own. The work had been done throughout the long fall and winter and into the early season. Lee had done his cross country season; he had let himself be dismissed and minimized by people who still worried about his motion. He had run his long intervals. He had sharpened his speed in 220s he was bound to lose; he had done his killer-dillers and his drills, the reach with the foreleg, the slight turn of the wrist to keep his arms under control. He had pranced through the endless high knee-lift exercises, the deep breathing, the relaxation techniques, and his alternating 50s.

He had been beaten by Tommie in the glare of publicity; he had run too fast too early and paid a high price, which he was prepared never to pay again. Those many years ago, he had picked his trays of grapes and taken cotton from the field; he had bent his back and done his work and seen his mother sick and his father tired. He had worn old clothes, sat in the back row, and loved his wife and his boy. He had nursed their grievances as his own, and vowed and promised that things would change, and now, in a moment of becoming, the wholeness of it was fuel for the fire that was driving him along the homestretch in pursuit of Jim Kemp, Elbert Stinson, and Vincent Matthews. He was simply in no mood nor had he ever been, not for the waiting and certainly not for the losing. He didn't care what anyone else's dreams were; he cared nothing for their pain or their privations, their work, the risks they took, or the accomplishments they might bring to bear. He didn't care what they wanted or needed. He wanted them all and every one out of his way.

The changing of a race, when one man takes charge and the other does not, when one man prepares to win and another to lose, seems like a bare instant, but it is a lifetime in the making. In a stride or two of new effort, Lee was immediately past Matthews and making his way to Stinson and Kemp to finish the job, to take in these two men who were fading finally, only that Matthews would not let go, and Lee had to tow him down the long stretch, and past and past and upon, until the line was near and it was Lee or Vince to win, and the crowd was waiting for the two men to distinguish themselves, one from the other, and to define a champion, which Lee thereafter did. In the meters upon which he made special claim, the last ones, that is, Lee surged and made a final shrug toward the line, dipping and driving himself along the surface and into the finish. Vincent Matthews could do nothing to stop the thing from taking place. Lee Evans was for the second time the champion of the United States in his event. His winning time was 45.3, a meet record, and 0.34 better than Vince Matthews's.

# .16

*The trouble with Vincent*

Vincent Matthews eventually defined himself in a single image, much as Tommie Smith and John Carlos would do. But while Tommie and John left no doubt about their purpose in 1968, what Vince did in 1972 was mystifying. He was photographed passing the time on an Olympic dais, with his shirttail out and his manner distracted. How was he to know that people would say he had crossed a line and that they would give him the boot, along with his friend Wayne Collett? How was he to know that his departure from the Olympics would be peremptory, and that his leaving would disappoint teammates, friends, and fans who had looked forward to the next event, the 1,600-meter relay, an event his team was destined to win but would never run? How was he to know that his conduct would be viewed through the prism of genuine terrorism, and that anything that even sniffed of political action would draw an exaggerated response?

But all that experience was unknowable in 1967 for the younger Vince Matthews. In 1967 he was unmarked and unadorned. He was also a fine runner. Like his contemporary, Lee Evans, Matthews was not a sprinter moving up to the quarter, nor a half-miler dropping down. For his event, he was the pure blend of speed and strength. Like Lee, he protected his balance. He had the speed and would sharpen it as required, but he did not neglect the hard work that made his speed functional. He trained with the cross country team in the fall, he ran a few miles on many mornings, and he worked intensely in the afternoon interval workouts. Also like Lee, he paid attention to what he was doing. Although he had a good relationship with his college coach, Kenneth Powell, he did not defer to him absolutely, but rather worked with him to establish the daily schedules, adjusting as necessary for his reactions on the day. If he was to run 5 x 300 and was tired or perhaps tight after three, he stopped and warmed down. If he felt good, he might add an extra repeat. All in all, Vince Matthews was determined to be as good as he could be, and this simple attitude, surprisingly, is often what separates champions from also-rans. In Vince's case, his talent made it apparent that he might be, with work and good fortune, the best in the world. This ambition was a prescription for conflict with the fellow out in San Jose. Put two marks on the map. Draw a line between North Carolina and California. As Vince Matthew's ambition grew in pace with his achievements, he became increasingly unhappy in his relationship with Lee Evans. What made him unhappy was that, time after time, Lee beat him.

The problem started at the AAU meet in 1966, which Lee won, and in which Vince was an afterthought, a full 0.8 seconds behind in fourth. The situation wasn't made any better when Vince was left off the 1,600-meter relay team at the LA Times meet in favor of Bob Frey and Tommie Smith. Frey had beaten him at the AAU, so he could accept that. But Tommie Smith? Tommie had been injured and run nothing at the AAU meet. Matthews understood that Smith was unique, as Henry Carr had been at Tokyo, but it still hurt to be odd man out when the records were being distributed. The 1967 season had been more of the same. Even after running the relay leg of 44.9 at Penn and securing his credentials, he had come up short at the AAU. Evans had dipped to the line in front of him. And it wasn't so much that Evans had won, but the way he had won, as if the Californian intentionally delayed his arrival to the last second. Matthews was determined to respond. He was asking friends and competitors, "How do I beat Lee Evans?" Hang in there, they were saying. Lean at the tape, they were saying. Don't stand so tall coming in, they were saying, relax. Easy does it! That is good advice, but hard to follow when a man is being chased down the homestretch by the most consistent, most competitive quarter-miler in history.

A couple of weeks after his loss to Lee at the national meet, the scenario repeated itself despite all the good and kind advice Vince had received in the meantime. Running in the dual meet between the United States and the British Commonwealth, he went out hard, led Lee by eight yards at the head of the stretch, and seemed to have the victory at hand. And he should have had because Lee was fighting a cold and running a desultory race. But the homestretch went wrong when Vince stopped running before the finish line, having apparently mistaken one line for the other, and Lee sailed past him for another win. Although Vince subsequently led off the 1,600-meter relay team with the fastest opening leg in history, 44.9, while Lee struggled with the anchor, the comfort was slight, the result only emphasizing that Vince had squandered an opportunity in the individual event. A couple of weeks later, Lee returned to full vigor and promptly beat Vince at the trials for the Pan American Games. That both athletes ran 45.8 emphasized the problem. Lee was winning every single close race. Could that be explained by reference only to speed and strength, or to such niceties as lean or technique generally, or was something else going on, something more sinister for an athlete? Had Lee beaten Vince so often, by such close margins, that Vince could no longer, really, imagine anything but losing? No, that would not be true. Vince Matthews was an extraordinary competitor. If he could find a way to win, he would win. But at this stage of his career, Vince Matthews was up against a young man who had a lot of tricks up his sleeve, but whose last, best trick was that he ran all-out the entire distance. Too often, Vince did not. The one time in LA he stopped in error. Occasionally he tightened, and his head went back. Other times he seemed to relax a stride or two in front of the finish line, or maybe that was the impression left when he did not lean to the tape. In any evaluation, Vince was making his mistake exactly when Lee Evans was most dangerous.

:

The Pan American Games in Winnipeg, Ontario, Canada, were held July 29-August 5, 1967, in an atmosphere of pronounced

119

courtesy and friendship. The track events were held on tartan, the first artificial surface Lee had experienced. As events proved, he found the surface fast. In fact, Lee's performance was so quick and felt so right to him, that he later took the race as a model and used two words to forecast its repetition in big races: Winnipeg Tip. The two words were meant to call to mind a special lightness in technique, high on the toes, smooth acceleration, and relaxation. On the day of the 400-meter final, Lee had lane eight and Vince lane seven. Vince ran marginally faster than Lee for the first 100, but Lee closed along the backstretch. As ever, he was racing according to his pattern: the fast first 100 meters, the second 100 meters in which he deliberately extended the reach of his arms and therefore his stride, the third a somewhat shorter but quicker stride to carry him into a favorable position coming off the turn, and the last 100 meters to pick up whomever might be leading or to run for the line himself, if he was leading. In this race, the two men were even off the last turn, so all Lee had to do was open up his stride and run relaxed. He won 44.9 to 45.1, with Lee's winning time a tenth faster than he had run in the match race against Tommie and equal to the world record as it had existed before Tommie beat it. As to Vince, he had another narrow loss. In a later recounting of the race, he referred to a thunderstorm that delayed the start by twenty minutes. The delay, he said, was just long enough for him to lose 0.2 of sharpness while thinking about Lee. This, it has to be said, is not an acknowledgment that Vince was psyched by Lee; only that he was ready too soon and lost an edge.

In a way that neither runner could have predicted, the rest of the 1967 season went Vince's way, after all. In the Americas versus Europe meet held in Montreal on July 9-10, Vince stormed the first 200 meters of the 400 in 20.8 and got away from Lee. While he closed six meters in the last 100 meters, Lee lost by one. The final times for the two runners were 45.0 and 45.1. Thereafter, Lee felt the effects of a year that was serious too early, with the race in May against Tommie, and lasted too long. In August, he suffered a hamstring injury and absorbed losses against Vince in Germany and England before calling off the rest of the season. He went back home to San Jose. By the time he got there Lee's old life, the one to

*Vince Matthews wins this one, in Germany.*

which he was accustomed and which he thought he controlled, was almost over. An old friend was making a difference. Tommie Smith was in Tokyo completing his own season. In the ordinary course, a reporter casually asked Tommie Smith a question. Just as casually Tommie Smith gave the answer that changed everything, not only for himself, but for Lee Evans.

# .17

*This little chapter should stand apart.*
*It divides.*

On September 3, 1967, Tommie Smith was in Tokyo competing in the World University Games. A Japanese reporter asked him a direct question: "In the United States, are the Negroes now equal to the whites in the way they are treated?" The answer being no, the follow-up came: "What about the possibility of Negroes boycotting the 1968 Olympics?" The question is notable because uncertainty is built into it. Even an affirmative answer speaks only of possibility, not of inevitability, not even of a tentative decision that might later be changed. Tommie therefore answered in a way that responded to the form of the question. "Yes," he said, "depending upon the situation, you cannot rule out the possibility that we Negro athletes might boycott the Olympic Games." The answer includes the initial reservation, and then adds another. The possibility cannot be ruled out. Nonetheless the equivocal answer to the equivocating question was sufficient to set off a controversy. Questions followed questions, answers required new questions and new responses and then more questions. So long as Tommie refused to say, without qualification, that Negroes would not boycott the Olympic Games, the issue was live. Along the way, Tommie Smith was converted in the public perception from a soft-spoken, ROTC-attending, well-mannered, college class–attending American sprinter into a Negro who might cause trouble in the future and, in fact, was threatening to do so. Almost instantly, Lee Evans stood with him. Cursory investigation revealed that the two athletes had been involved in social activity at San Jose State intended to win rights and privileges for black students, and otherwise had views consistent with an unhappy state of mind. The question was why. The answer was in the newspapers, of course, if you went in for that kind of thing. Otherwise, the answer was everywhere. The Irish poet Yeats had forecast the day when things would fall apart, the center not hold, and mere anarchy would be loosed upon the world. Because the quotation from Yeats is forced to serve whenever order fails, the old poem from which it comes is tired and worn, but it was less so in 1967. In that year, on matters of race, the center could not hold, indeed had collapsed already, and let loose a terrible harm. The viciousness of the events was disturbing. Yet more disturbing was the fact that many people could not decide which was more vicious, the cause or the effect.

# .18

*Two trains coming, but neither going my way.*
*A blues song.*

Granted, no social history is wholly good or wholly evil. Complexity is beneath the surface. A library could be filled, for instance, with stories of kindness and courage in the face of the holocaust that enveloped European Jewry in the period between 1932 and 1945. But nothing in the library would make the holocaust go away, or return to life, much less to dignity, the tens of millions of people who were its victims. Similarly, American history includes examples of kindness directed to people of African descent; courage too can be found. The Freedom Summer is proof, just as surely as the doffed hat or the opened door, the little courtesies and manners that indicate civility and regard, but that were acts of bravery in an Old South. The examples—the kindness, the courtesies, and the courage—are inadequate to change the dominant reality. Black is still black. White is still white. And insufficient progress has been made to blur the distinctions, even yet. But, then again, this is not the summer of 1967. For that, at least a measure of thanks can be given. In 1967, the United States was on fire. More often, the country was described as at war with itself. Vietnam was in ferment, there and here, but prominently there, in Asia somewhere in the area of Japan. The closer war was in U.S. cities, where black people were in revolt. In July 1967, a cab driver was arrested for a traffic offense in Newark, New Jersey. When the cab driver was taken to a police station across the street from a housing project, a crowd gathered. The crowd was predisposed to be angry, and rumors fed a fire, "The cab driver was dead. The police had killed the poor man."

He wasn't dead, and the police had not killed him, it naturally follows, but the fact did not catch up with the rumor, and so off it went, a terrible energy of looting and burning. Before exhaustion stopped the riot, Newark had suffered 21 deaths, more than 1,000 people injured, and 1,600 arrests. Detroit followed. This was lava from a twin cone, identical in its source to Newark, creating a confused nighttime scene in day or night. Before this one was over—occasioned, people said, by a police raid on a speakeasy— Detroit had experienced ten deaths, 2,250 injuries, and 4,000 arrests, seen its streets filled with National Guard troops, lost countless properties, and incurred immense economic damage. Entire blocks in the city were simply gone. Some shops survived, the few with signs that said "soul brother," or "Afro all the way," or, as one did, "very, very, very, very black." And of course there were the snipers shooting at police officers and firemen and there were the whites pulled from cars and there was the terror and there was the feeling that nothing would ever be right in the city of Detroit again.

Nor did Detroit and Newark writhe alone. Around the country, demagogues and preachers of hate came out of cover to spread a frightening message. Where they went they said, "Burn it." American citizens of African descent rioted in so many cities and put the torch to so many properties, that the map of the country was pockmarked: Toledo, Cincinnati, Cleveland, South Bend, Memphis, Milwaukee, East Harlem, even Waukegan, Grand Rapids, Rochester, and Mount Vernon. There seemed to be no place to hide. "Thunderously," said one white columnist, "the black citizenry has proved its equality with white citizenry in the capacity for senseless cruelty and mindless demagoguery." Under these explosions, many Americans detected a disturbing element. Account after account described the riots as joyous, as marked by gaiety and celebration. What a puzzlement this was, and what a surprise, that it was possible to bottle people up, to drive them from one low rung to another low rung, to scramble their chances for advancement, to send them into atrocious disregarded houses and apartments, to deprive them of jobs and education, to rob them of respect and accord, as well as the honest and full rights of citizenship, and then to find them anxious for the chance to get a bit of their own back! "Racists," said the commentators. "These people are calling for a black America, a separate country of their own. The streets ring with the cry," they said.

Meanwhile, out in the country, away from the fires, removed from the cries for power and revenge, deep in the fields, not in the cities of the North or the East, things were getting even worse for black people. There was a backlash, as it happens, even to the lawful grant of slow-carried, long-delayed, recently acknowledged civil rights. Not surprisingly, the lash was down south.

:

Short as the history of civil rights was, it was too long for the South. The reactionaries were reacting. When a woman named Mary, for example, a scion of her family's fortune, sold the agricultural fields while retaining the mansion house, she spoke for the region, "I wept bitterly when I sold the land," she said, "and all my nigras wept. But I couldn't keep 'em—they wouldn't work a lick. Ever since they got that civil rights bill they all figure the government will take care of them. I'll tell you one thing. If I was head of the Ku Klux, there'd be some eliminating." A southern planter spoke less sentimentally, "The niggers is got to go. It's like the deer. We got a lotta trouble with the deer eatin' our soybeans. We just wanta thin 'em out. It's the same thing with the niggers. We don't want 'em all to leave—we just wanta thin 'em out so we can live with 'em." Mechanization, too, provided excuse for decisions based on race. "When we got rid of our niggers," said one farmer, "we found out what money was." To which a black observer said, "Them white folks got a lot more interested in machinery after the civil rights bill passed." Events swirling around them, rural Americans of African descent in the South were often isolated and often alone, living where they had always lived in the hills and on the plains, with little or no education. Many were hoping to do the work they had always done, but seeing even that opportunity shrink. As it inevitably would, the terrible poverty came but worse now. Throughout the agricultural South, the children soon appeared.

Hollowed out, with distended stomachs and blank eyes, running sores, and listless manners, the children were a kind of cry, to match that coming from the city. Or, to catch the tradition of the South, the children were a lantern on the levee, lighted to show the danger and to show what fairness required. Predictably, many people did not want to see the lantern and not the light. They turned away.

# .19

*Tommie and Lee are bad boys,*
*no doubt about that whatsoever.*

When Tommie was answering questions in Tokyo, and when he was subsequently asked to clarify his views, or more accurately, to recant and retract, in effect to retrace his steps and to remove the boycott as a cloud on the Olympic horizon, he would not and neither would Lee Evans when given the chance. They were young men with brief life experience to instruct them, but they had hardship. They had been insulted and aggrieved often enough to know that resistance was necessary, and courage its requisite. The tradition behind those principles was long, and in many respects it belonged to the churches from which Tommie and Lee had come and which, in early years, helped form them into people of conscience. If Martin Luther had once said, on matters of religious belief, "Here I stand; I can do no other," that expression captures also the youthful insistence of Tommie Smith and Lee Evans that something was seriously wrong in the country they loved, and they would not say otherwise or stop trying to improve it. In the trying times of 1967, a prominent black leader had said that a black man could be either a radical or he could be an Uncle Tom. There was no third way and no middle ground. That softer way, that ground, he intimated, had collapsed under the feet of black people time and again, and no one could trust it again. Of course, it was always true that black men and women leading quiet, obscure, private lives could avoid the categories and be neither radical nor accommodating, neither Panther nor Tom. But the heart, even in such people, would move. In any event, Tommie and Lee were not private people. They were public people. Making the choice, the young college students were quick and together. Picking between two alternatives, they became radicals.

The irony is that Tommie and Lee did not make radical statements. In long interviews, the two claimed for themselves, and for other people of African descent, the rights enjoyed by white Americans. The trouble came when they took the next step and said that they would join a boycott if fellow black Olympians decided that the action was necessary or helpful in order to dramatize the plight of black people in the United States. The two men did not say that they had decided to boycott and that they were leading an effort to organize such a boycott, although this was a frequent misapprehension. It was the Olympics that caused the furor, without question. The reference to the Olympic Games took a personal decision and made it an aspect of patriotism, as if the two young sprinters had desecrated the American flag. Few people noted that the emotional reaction was proof that the Olympics had been political long before Lee Evans and Tommie Smith came along. If the Games had not been used in the past to hoist the flag, they could not be used to lower it now. But of course the Games had been used for such purposes.

:

Avery Brundage was the face of the Olympics in 1967. Formerly the head of the American Olympic Committee (later the USOC), he had been elected to the International Olympic Committee in 1936 and been made president in 1952, a position he maintained. In his years, Brundage built a record consistent with the characterization of him as an anti-Semite, an isolationist, a bigot, an elitist, and a person with a chronic inability to understand the opinions of other people or to credit them appropriately. He also had a propensity to put his foot in his mouth. These traits apparently were considered splendid qualifications for high office. Brundage maintained in his long career that the Olympics were an ideal and that they should be unsullied by politics. But he admired, and in fact participated in, the effort of the United States to make

*Avery Brundage*

an exhibition of the early games in order to glorify its own achievements, and he had no qualms about the national uniforms, the parade of nations to highlight the very big and the very little, the mighty United States marching every four years in its hundreds on the track with the single Mongol, for example, wearing a fur cap, the weak and the powerful arrayed for easy comparison, the separate flags, the playing of anthems, the counting of medals, the jingoistic funding of participation, and the wild scrambles for host status, every one a fight that was intrinsically political. Indeed, the entire Olympic spectacle was political, right down to the customary dancing girls—in native costume—at the opening ceremonies.

Brundage's most extraordinary performance as president of the American Olympic Committee was his anticipation of Neville Chamberlain's famous appeasement. It will be recalled that in a time of heightened international tension, when concerned statesmen actually feared that Nazi Germany might invade a (rather, another) neighboring country, England's prime minister received personal assurances from Chancellor Hitler that no such invasion would occur. Waving a signed piece of paper in London in 1938, he proclaimed peace in our time, a false hope as it happened. Chamberlain is distinguished from Brundage only in one particular. Chamberlain may actually have been deceived. In his act of appeasement, Brundage almost certainly was not. When he was faced with a proposed United States boycott of the 1936 Olympic Games in Berlin, Brundage went to Germany to see for himself. He wanted the minimal assurance that Jewish athletes would not be foreclosed from participation as members of the German team. Finding that, he went home. He was happy to say to the press:

*I was given positive assurance in writing by Tschamme und Osten, Germany's official Olympic representatives, that there will be no discrimination against Jews. You can't ask more than that and I think the guarantee will be fulfilled.*

The guarantee was not fulfilled. Only a man with his head in a very deep hole could have thought it would be. The other possibility is that Brundage did not have his head in a hole, but shared Germany's antipathy for the Jews and winked at the outrages committed against them before the war. The word and deed of the man support the alternative, even if they cannot prove it. As an isolationist who resisted the United State's entry into the war and expended his capital railing against Roosevelt, Brundage wrote that "one of the cleverest tricks of the Communists and Jews in 1939 was the smearing of 'America First' [an isolationist organization] as pro-Nazi." More generally, Brundage condemned the "stupid, dishonest, and criminal" politics of those who risked war against Germany. In a famous and well-reported speech in Madison Square Garden on October 4, 1936, Brundage addressed the German-American Bund, in these words, "We can learn much from Germany. We, too, if we wish to preserve our institutions, must stamp out communism. We, too, must take steps to arrest the decline of patriotism." Later, when Leni Riefenstahl's documentary film, Olympia, a lyrical homage to the Berlin Olympic Games, excited a storm of criticism leading to doubt that it would be distributed in the United States, Brundage explained the matter by saying that "unfortunately the theaters and moving picture companies are almost all owned by Jews." The fact that the talented Ms. Riefenstahl had produced another film, The Triumph of the Will, that was the finest specimen of Nazi propaganda in a regime famous for the art made no impression on Mr. Brundage, nor did he credit that, beautiful as the Olympic film was, it too was propaganda. He showed Olympia privately. Brundage's personal letters referred often to the materialism of Jews and to their supposed inability to conduct themselves by the rules of fair play and sportsmanship.

To add action to words, Brundage maintained memberships in private clubs that excluded both blacks and Jews. In fact, he owned one such club. The memberships became controversial in 1967 and 1968 when busybodies argued that someone of color should be represented on the USOC. Because Brundage had sufficient influence to remedy the situation, the lack of diversity suggested that the problem was in the man himself and thus opened the question of his exclusive memberships. On even this prickly matter, Brundage was unapologetic. He said that if a club chose "to accept only red-haired barbers for members, I think it's their right." Perhaps that is correct, from the perspective of the red-headed barber. As to the inclusion of a black person on the USOC, Mr. Brundage was agreeable. He thought that Jesse Owens was a "fine boy" who might be considered. At the time of the statement,

Mr. Owens was in his fifties, but he was special to Brundage not only for what he was but also for what he wasn't. The hero of the Berlin Olympics, Jesse Owens was vintage, not like the new generation of black people who seemed always to have a complaint. But a "boy"? Was Jesse Owens in his fifties yet a boy to Mr. Brundage? If so, one can only conclude that Mr. Owens's race made it so, for no other factor appears to explain the result. Further, if Mr. Owens was a boy to Mr. Brundage and race made it so, were there any men, so far as Mr. Brundage could see, in that race? In the vernacular of the day, were there any Negro men? If not, what made that so? Did other people see the men in the race, and Mr. Brundage not? This was the web Mr. Brundage spun for himself every day, but he never, in any pronouncement or moment of recorded introspection, seemed to see it. Perhaps seeing the result of his words, seeing the words themselves in context, comprehending finally what the words meant, he would be required to take responsibility for them. If he did that, he could not remain president of the International Olympic Committee. He should not have, in any event, but it is the nature of power to endure, self-sustaining and existing for that central purpose, if for none other, and Brundage remained year after year and decade after decade.

Books written about Mr. Brundage give a rounded view of the man. Possibly, other readers will find virtue in him, people whose views accord with his on critical matters. This sketch is designed only to introduce the man who became bete noire to Tommie and Lee as they spoke their minds and made their decisions and to highlight features in him that increased the tension of an already hot social climate. In the contest between the principals, and the views they espoused, the remarkable Mr. Brundage appeared always to claim for himself a moral high ground. Tommie and Lee were the aggressors; they were the transgressors. They were the ones who attempted to blight the Olympic ideal. Mr. Brundage portrayed the Olympic Games as a force for good and for harmony in the relationship between differing peoples. Those were goals toward which he professed to work. But those Olympian goals turn in on Mr. Brundage. They mock him and subject him to one more charge. The charge is hypocrisy. And it didn't take 40 years of time passing for Lee Evans and Tommie Smith to notice. Had a man other than Avery Brundage served as IOC president in 1968, it is entirely possible that only a track fan would know the names of either Smith or Carlos, as another man would have taken steps to make protest unnecessary, or at least he would have refrained from making himself, personally, a natural target for demonstration and objection.

# .20

*I have a friend whose name*
*is Harry.*

The primary styles of leadership are institutional and charismatic. Avery Brundage was an institutional leader. Take away the institution and Avery Brundage is a gray man in an expensive suit. Harry Edwards, who was destined to become a thorn in Brundage's side, was a charismatic leader. Lacking institutional structure, he made use of his personal skills and the manner of his presentation to move people and influence events. The holder of a master's degree in sociology from Cornell University and on the faculty at San Jose State while pursuing his doctorate, Edwards regularly involved himself in matters of importance to the relatively few black students on campus. From time to time, he lifted his efforts to national significance, as he did in the fall of 1967 when his planned protest of the football game between San Jose State and the University of Texas at El Paso forced the cancellation of the event. Had the game been played, Edwards later said, he and his group would have burned the San Jose State football stadium down. As a former basketball player, Edwards was particularly sensitive to the interaction between sport and race, and conscious of the extent to which black athletes had been exploited. More specifically in the context the Olympic Games, Edwards monitored the IOC's decision making with regard to South Africa. When South Africa's participation in the Games was suspended in 1963, the condition for readmission was narrowly drawn to the makeup of the teams and the fairness of competition, rather than to a change to the apartheid structure that had caused the problem in the first place. Edwards and others insisted that South Africa remain out of the Games until apartheid was gone.

Tommie and Lee knew Harry Edwards as a teacher, as a confidant, and as a participant in the United Black Students for Action. They agreed with him about South Africa. Both had been furious the previous season when South African sprinter Paul Nash had been permitted to compete against them in the United States, while they would have been denied that opportunity in Nash's country. When the boycott controversy broke, the two Americans grew closer to Edwards. Inevitably, they heard that the young teacher was another demagogue, another man using popular prejudices and false charges to gain power, and that he was exploiting them for his own purposes. In contrast, what they heard and saw for themselves, at least initially, was a man saying true things to people who did not want to listen. This was something they had in common. Most people didn't listen to Lee and Tommie either. When Tommie said that the boycott, if it occurred, would be just another step in a series of movements designed to promote racial equality, these people heard "Olympics." When Lee said that the whole idea was to encourage freedom for all Americans, these people also heard "Olympics." They could not be shaken from the idea that a protest involving the Olympics was directed against the Olympics. That being the case, they asked, "Why would black athletes protest against an athletic competition that by its own rules prohibits discrimination based on race?"

Harry Edwards knew the answer of course, as did Tommie and Lee. Sometimes the protest is made where the injustice is, like the lunch counters in Wilmington or the bus routes in Montgomery. Other times, the protest is directed specifically toward the media. In this case, both options were open. The media was preoccupied with the Olympics. The Olympics were therefore a natural pressure point, as the interest created by Tommie's remark proved. If South Africa was a specific Olympic sensitivity, the challenges to apartheid went beyond the Olympics. And if Tommie and Lee were talking generally about equal rights and liberty, those issues transcended the Olympic Games, a fact that did not eliminate the Olympics as a vehicle for expression. A person interested in civil rights could work, therefore, out from the Olympics, or in toward them, and carry the same message. Be that as it may, the boycott was a difficult sell for the actual athletes. They had almost a year to think about it because no decision could be made until the Trials were complete and a team chosen.

The amount of work each athlete would do during that year, and the sacrifices they would make, argued strongly against a decision not to compete. Furthermore, the proposed Olympic boycott was abstract, even with South Africa in the equation. If you have a problem at home, a boycott whose principal effect was in a foreign country and directed against an event that had little responsibility for the grievance was confusing. "Tell me again, why are we boycotting the Olympics just because Tommie can't find an apartment in San Jose?" And inevitably there was the personal cost. Already, many of the athletes knew that Tommie and Lee were receiving regular death threats by mail and phone and that the two men had families, as they did. The question of retaliation and consequence was especially strong for the southern athletes who tended to be less strident, less aggressive, and less militant than the athletes coming from the coasts. This different tone might have been because violence directed toward black people in the South was no fairytale or bogeyman, no highly unlikely "thing" that might happen. For these athletes, such violence was a fact of life, handed down from generation to generation on both sides of the social divide. Taken together, the factors led realistically to the conclusion that the boycott, which Tommie and Lee had described in terms of consensus if not unanimity, would not happen. But no one could say so. Therefore, the controversy continued, something like a smoldering grass fire that occasionally bursts into flames.

On the positive side, this meant that the press continued to talk about the boycott and to examine the causes and implications. On the negative side, at least so far as the two students were concerned, Tommie and Lee were now joined in the public mind with Harry Edwards, who took the lead in orchestrating events. If the professor needed to make the rhetoric more inflammatory, to make additional or more serious threats, to glower, to appear less friendly, to sport Black Panther regalia, to stop wearing sports jackets, to make his image darker and sharper, to promise danger in order to hold the media's attention, and to make that grass fire burn, he would carry Tommie Smith and Lee Evans with him. The two might be at the track or with their families or fishing or attending a class or doing any number of guileless activities, but the public would be watching Harry and thinking of them. In sum, Harry was reconfiguring Lee and Tommie in the public perception every time he opened his mouth or had his photograph taken.

Of course, the two men would say that the controversy was not about them. It was about principle. What was needed was a further definition of the principle. An initial step toward that end was to develop names to which people could rally or refer. At a meeting at Harry Edwards's house on October 7, a sympathetic group formed the Olympic Committee for Human Rights and designated the boycott to be part of the Olympic Project for Human Rights. In a few well-chosen words, both names connected the Olympic protest to an end result that was beyond dispute. Who would argue against human rights? Another step was to have a preliminary meeting to talk about the issues in a directed way. On Thanksgiving Day in 1967, Harry Edwards chaired a meeting at the Second Baptist Church in Los Angeles. Approximately 200 athletes attended for the give-and-take session, but of them, only five were considered world class: Lee and Tommie, high-jumper Otis Burrell, hurdler Ron Copeland, and basketball star Lew Alcindor (Kareem Abdul Jabbar, in his future). Tommie was at the meeting only because Lee persuaded him to be there. Otherwise, Tommie's reticence would have kept him home, no less committed to the cause of justice but not quite as visible. He need not have worried; Harry Edwards was in his element and would do the talking. The temper of Harry is in his words:

For years, we have participated in the Olympic Games, carrying the U.S. on our backs with our victories, and race relations are worse now than ever. Now they are even shooting people in the streets. We're not trying to lose the Olympics for the Americans. What happens to them is immaterial. If they finish first, that's beautiful. If they finish 14th, that's beautiful, too. But it's time for the black

*people to stand up as men and women and refuse to be utilized as*
*performing animals for a little extra dog food. You see, this may be*
*our last opportunity to settle this mess short of violence.*

The rhetoric is classic: the "us" and the "them," the broadening of
the conflict by relating the unrelated, in this case, athletic events
being attached to violence in the streets, the hyperbole regarding
degradation, the dog food, and the implicit threat of violence. Or, as
author James Baldwin famously phrased it, "the fire next time."

After the meeting, the 200 attendees screamed in unison for a
boycott. The chorus was only a gesture, however, coming too early
in the game, with the wrong people in attendance, save the five.
When Harry told the press that the meeting confirmed the call for
a boycott, his statement was a mere stirring of the pot. Even
Tommie was forced to deny that any binding decision had been
made. But the meeting did establish a public embarkation much
more appropriate than the offhand remark Tommie Smith made
half a world away. The meeting also produced tangible results. The
attendees agreed that the boycott should be linked to the future
Olympic participation of South Africa and Rhodesia; if those
countries came back in, everyone understood that the boycott
would be a virtual certainty. This issue tied the knot closer between
the Olympic Games and a generalized bias against people of color.
There was also agreement that the New York Athletic Club would
be the first organization to feel the burden of a black boycott
because it allegedly barred blacks and Jews from membership.

Several weeks after the Thanksgiving Day meeting, Edwards
expanded the protest. In a speech delivered at the Greater Los
Angeles Press Club, he listed the comprehensive objectives: a
boycott of all NYAC events, a demand for the exclusion of South
Africa and Rhodesia from Olympic competition, the restoration of
Muhammad Ali's heavyweight boxing championship, and the
desegregation of the United States Olympic Committee
administrative and coaching staffs. The next day in New York,
Edwards added one more. He wanted Avery Brundage removed
from the IOC because he was a "devout anti-Semitic and anti-
Black personality," one aspect of which was his ownership of the

Montecito Country Club, which barred blacks and Jews from membership. A cry for justice would be abstract without a list of grievances, of course, and this one from Harry was unsurprising, even if insubstantial compared with the central questions of opportunity, education, housing, and freedom of movement and association. Nonetheless, the committee was on its way. The next important events were in February when the NYAC would host its big indoor meet and when the unrepentant Mr. Brundage would attempt to bring South Africa back into the Olympic Games, almost literally putting a stick in the eye of Harry Edwards. The professor could tend to that when the time came. Tommie and Lee had other work to do and other forces with which to contend.

# .21

*Not a Day Goes By*

Some people were so impressed by what Tommie and Lee said and did that they took pen in hand and wrote letters of opinion and advice to various newspapers and magazines. You have to read between the lines to get the meaning of the correspondents.

*All the talk of boycott*

*that goddamn nigger*
*should just get on the*

*boat* *and that goes for his jigaboo friend*
*the congo*

*better*

*too.*

:

Tommie and Lee knew that the reaction to the proposed boycott would be harsh. They knew that the reporting of their words would draw from cover the racists and the haters, who would write their letters and express their opinions and their threats, and that they would draw as well the petrified who thought any gain by Americans of African descent would mean less for them, and they had little enough as it was. Talk of a boycott would anger the privileged, too, who built their stability on the collective pain suffered by all the others, and it would rouse the many more who had an instinct for bias buried deep in the bones, the lessons forgotten and the memories obscure, but the result unshaken if unacknowledged. Finally, the talk would alarm even some people of color, who would fear the loss of hard-bought gain. Still, Tommie and Lee moved forward, permitting Harry to increase the demands, to broaden the dispute, to make more controversial the stand, and to bring up the heat. Obviously, the circumstances would have been difficult for anyone. For two runners who had spent competitive lifetimes dreaming of Olympic glory, visualizing the result, and then imagining the ceremony—the walk past cheering throngs to the dais, the energetic climb to the top rung, the moment of quiet, the dignity, the heaviness of the time and the approaching joy, the weight of the medal around their necks and the feel of it in their hands, and the bashful first look at the symbols and the etched figures—the possibility of boycott was especially difficult. Literally they were being asked, or they were offering, depending on the dynamics, to push that dream away. And yet, despite the talk and the bravado, they had not definitely said that they would stay away from the Games. They still wanted to be Olympic champions. So they would work for it. Throughout the controversy that raged, Tommie and Lee continued to train. For one thing, the ordeal would be meaningless if they did not first make the Olympic team. But something else was going on as well, less tangible than some of the other issues but no less real. Even if the two young men from San Jose withstood the pressure now placed upon them, even if they eventually made the U.S. Olympic team, decided to compete in Mexico City, and then won their respective events, a valuable property had already been taken, or been given up. Their gold medals would not glitter. The pleasure of victory, of relief and celebration at the conclusion of prolonged effort, would not be pure. The emotions stirred by the boycott would intrude. There would be sadness and regret, and there might be the weight of new responsibility depending on how things turned out. But that was the die they had cast, and it was fine. Lee and Tommie would do their part. Others, outside the realm of athletics, would do even more, as the coming year proved.

:

When the world rankings for 1967 were announced, Lee was once again the top man. He had gotten past Vince, who was second, because he had beaten him in the important championships. He outranked Tommie, who was third, because he had run more races than Tommie had.

*In this event we had a major problem: where do we rank Tommie Smith? He was undefeated and set a new world record. But he ran this distance only twice and never in any major meet. We finally decided that first place was to go to either EVANS or MATTHEWS who together were clearly the class of this event throughout the season. Since there was no clear-cut third to these two, we decided to insert Smith at that spot. We must add that in our personal opinion, Smith is the greatest quarter-miler ever, but that is not what world ranking is about. Returning to first place, a close analysis revealed that Evans had a slight but perceptible edge in each of our major categories and so he was first.*

Thus said *Track and Field News*, leaving Lee hanging. He was a "perceptible" step ahead of Vince, but both deferred to the higher glory of Mr. Smith. Actually, Lee didn't mind the attention Tommie had gotten. Better than anyone, Lee knew what Tommie could do on a track. Besides, Lee wasn't going to waste much time looking at the lists unless they helped him plan the future.

Casting an eye up and down the rankings and projecting, Lee knew that Vince would continue to be a problem in the Olympic year. Matthews was young, he was improving, he was gaining confidence from having beaten Lee three times, and he appeared to be correcting his mistakes. As Dick Bank reported from the

European tour, "Vince Matthews was tremendous, and the way in which he can produce 45- after 45-second races really impresses. Now that he is not tying up at the end with head and chest thrown back, he is going to be very hard to beat."

Thurman Boggess of Prairie View was also attracting favorable notice. When he ran 45.6 for yards, the 6-foot, 190-pound Boggess had beaten the frosh record held jointly by Ulis Williams and Lee. He also had recorded a relay leg of 44.8 and had run numerous fast times in both open and relay events against SWAC and NAIA opposition. Boggess missed the AAU meet with a pulled muscle, a major disappointment because he had finished a close second to Vince Matthews at the NAIA national meet and had hoped for another chance. As to his ambition, Boggess described his preoccupation with running, "I live, eat, love, and die track, day in and day out." He was said to train four or five hours a day, nine months of the year, and of course, he wanted to be Olympic champion. The young Boggess was sixth in the world in 1967. Other Americans in the top-ten world rankings for the year were Jim Kemp in seventh, Elbert Stinson in eighth, and Emmett Taylor in ninth. Lee figured he would beat any of these athletes, but they were dangerous runners. If he faltered even a little, they would go past him. And these known challengers were not the extent of the risk. As ever, mile-relay teams were the launch pad for other quarter men who might threaten Lee.

Taking into account performances from 1967, the experts suggested that seven schools from the Gulf Coast alone, with one excursion up to Arkansas, could field teams faster than 3:10 and a few of them considerably faster. Prairie View had Jesse Ball, Finnis Taylor, Felix Johnson, and Boggess and calculated out to a possible 3:01.9. Southern with Webster Johnson, Oliver Ford, Robert Johnson, and Anthony Gates appeared capable of 3:03.9; Arkansas AM&N with Walter Smith, Harold Francis, Will Thompson, and Henry Smothers projected somewhere between 3:05.8 and 3:04.4, with Rice countering at near the same time with Mike Casey, Fred Cloud, Dale Bernauer, and Conley Brown. Even Lamar Tech of Beaumont, Texas, not previously considered a contender for national honors, could run something like 3:05 or 3:06. Tech expected to run Waverly Thomas, Mike Favazza, Henry Harrison, and Randy Clewis. The University of Texas at Austin and University of Texas at El Paso rounded out the list; each of the two schools would go under 3:10. UT in particular had a runner of note; prep sensation Dave Morton expected to improve. Likewise, Villanova had promising people to introduce in the forthcoming season, including Larry James, the former high school hurdler, triple-jumper, sprinter, now being reconfigured for the long dashes and a person likely to make his first, strong impression in the relays. Finally, as 1968 opened, one man was like no other.

Martin McGrady had emerged from the obscurity of Central Ohio to run a world best of 1:09 for the 600-yard dash on Louisville's oversized track in 1966. In subsequent indoor performances he had proved unbeatable at the distance, leading people to wonder at his best event. Should he step up or down? To observers, a favorable result seemed certain no matter what event McGrady selected. Lee had a peculiar interest in McGrady. In the first place, no one really knew what McGrady could do because he had been injured for most of 1967. In the second place, McGrady had reacted to Central Ohio's decision to reduce its commitment to track and field, which was miniscule to begin with, by transferring to San Jose State. In California, the enigmatic man would wait out a year of ineligibility, work a job, and train as opportunity and inclination permitted.

In finding his way to San Jose, McGrady was part of a trend. In the near future, San Jose would become known as Speed City. First among equals was Tommie Smith, and a close second was Lee Evans. Tommie was the best all-around sprinter in the world, and Lee, entering his junior year at the university, had two AAU quarter titles to his credit, two years as the best in the world, and countless fast times. McGrady's arrival was intriguing, but McGrady was relatively unaccomplished outdoors. More so were Bill Gaines and John Carlos, two other arrivals. Like McGrady, Gaines was something of an indoor specialist—a 60-yard-dash man perpetually in search of an extra 40 yards—but he was undeniably sensational. As a 17-year-old high school sophomore, the 5-foot, 5-inch sprinter won the AAU indoor title over 60 yards. After equaling the world record of 5.9 in the heats, he won the

*Chairman of the Boards: Martin McGrady.*

championship with 6.0 over second-place Richmond Flowers of the University of Tennessee, who shared the same time. Outdoors, Gaines was fifth in the AAU 100 before returning for a second indoor 60 title as a junior in high school. Coming now to San Jose, Gaines was enrolled in a local high school but competing for the Santa Clara Youth Village. Also competing for the Village was John Carlos. The native New Yorker had grown weary of college life at East Texas State University, weary, really, of being called a "nigger" or a "nigra" or any other thing that might occur to people down there. California was calling, loudly.

In 1964, the 6-foot, 4-inch, 190-pound Carlos was a promising 9.7, 21.3 high school senior, then had his first open success a year later at the AAU meet. Running for the New York Pioneer Club, Carlos was fifth in the 100 and fourth in the 220, recording times of 9.5 and 20.7. After an unsuccessful 1966 season, he accepted the opportunity to run for East Texas, where the social climate horrified him, but his sprint fortunes improved. Indoors he ran 60 yards in 6.1 and 300 yards in 30.4, the latter a world best. Outdoors he thrust himself into the first rank with a 9.2 wind-aided 100 yards and a frosh record 20.3 for the 220 on the curve, as well as quarter legs of 45.7 and 46.4. Close losses to Charlie Greene and Jim Hines at Drake showed his competitive ability, as did a third-place finish in the AAU 220 in 20.6. Later, Carlos ran 20.4 for the United States against a team from the Commonwealth while losing to Tommie Smith and Hines, and won the Pan American Games 220 in 20.5. He then followed up with an impressive European season and a number three ranking in the world for the 200 meters/220 yards. Street-smart, street-bred, Carlos was said to be a natural comedian, a man who ran like a "big farmer," and a vast, untapped talent. While Tommie was reserved, and Lee was quiet, John Carlos talked as fast as he ran and appeared to thrive on conflict. If there was no conflict at hand, he was likely to provoke one, pushing an issue, cajoling a friend, issuing a challenge, or climbing out of the stands, cold drink in hand, to run 100 yards on a dare at a big meet. If Carlos was comedic, if his high school education was inadequate, if East Texas did him no better, and if at San Jose he was an athlete set apart by personality, he nonetheless had the last virtue. John Carlos was his own man, take it or leave it.

Before the migration was complete, the San Jose area, consisting of San Jose State University, San Jose City College, and the Youth Village also included Kirk Clayton as a transfer from Grambling, 9.3; Jerry Williams, 9.4; Bob Griffin, 9.5; Frank Slaton, 9.5; Sam Davis, 9.4; and Ronnie Ray Smith, 9.4 and 20.9. For several of these men, including Gaines and Carlos as well as Jerry Williams, the man who made their relocation to San Jose possible was Art

Simburg, a student at the university with an abiding interest in track and field, a gift for persuasion, and an eye for talent. Carlos says that Art even rode the bus with him from New York to Texas at the beginning of one school term. By the time the two men got to ETSU, the sprinter had decided to transfer. After a short rest in the dorm, he went over to the track coach's office and said, "Ahem," or words to that effect. Then, it was off to San Jose. With regard to Jerry Williams, Art knew him as a fine high school sprinter who was not enrolled anywhere. Art went by, talked with Jerry, and then helped him make the necessary arrangements. Art even had a hand in Lee's presence on the San Jose State campus. When Lee was at the City College, Art had made his pitch in a good-hearted conversation that Lee found preposterous. Forecasting great relay teams if only Lee moved over to the university, Art referred to Tommie's fast quarter, and then added, "and with your 46.9." A reference that made Lee jump, "46.9! Is that what Art thinks I will run next year?" By the end of the year, Lee would be AAU champion, of course, proving that Art's view had been conservative, but nothing in the meeting colored the ongoing relationship between the two young men. Lee and Art got along fine. How could they not, with Lee's interests and Art's in agreement, and Art willing to put time, energy, money, and considerable skill into tasks that worked to Lee's benefit? As Art continued his work, putting Speed City together sprinter by sprinter, his success was no surprise to Lee Evans.

This, then, is the developing picture. Speed City was gathering force. The boycott controversy was bubbling. The quarter men were circling. And Lee was in the middle. Looking ahead, there is the temptation to accept what came from all this—the various triumphs and defeats, what happened to Lee—as inevitable, but that would be a mistake. The possibilities were numerous.

# .22

*Start here to get there.*

For Lee, the mix of new people, new talent, and new ambition was interesting but not central. He had his own work to do. Nineteen sixty-eight would be a demanding year, not merely because the social issues loomed so large, not even because it was an Olympic year, but more specifically because the Mexico City Olympics were scheduled for October. That made for a very long season, indeed. To prepare for it, Lee would need a deep foundation, a careful management of his speed and strength work, and a willingness to reassess and adjust as necessary, including, in all likelihood, a rebuilding in the middle of the season, as if the calendar were broken into two pieces even though it looked like one. One change was immediate. Lee could not run with the cross country team in the fall of 1967 because he had a class conflict. So he would have to do a lot of his running alone, or catching partners along the way for occasional practices. As ever, in doing the workouts and in preparing them, as well as appraising them, Lee benefited from a methodical nature. He kept a daily log from which a sampling is taken. The efforts started slowly and sporadically and then built toward the indoor season.

*September 18, 1967: Ran slow for half hour. Surprised that I didn't get too tired. 15 V-ups, 20 push-ups, and 20 sit-ups.*

*September 19: Ran slower today so Jerry Williams could keep up.* [Williams was beginning his comeback after a layoff.] *I didn't get time at all. 15 V-ups, 20 push-ups, 20 sit-ups.*

*September 20: Today is very hot, 96 degrees, so running was difficult. I also ran faster today. 15 V-ups, 20 push-ups, 20 sit-ups.* [From this point, Lee records that he is doing 20 push-ups, V-ups, and sit-ups every day.]

*September 21: Attended rallies for United Black Students for Action.*

*September 22: Attended executive meeting for UBSA.*

*September 23: Gave speech at Overfelt High School.*

*September 24, Sunday: Just striding.*

*September 25: Today I ran about 6 miles and then a lot of stretching with Coach Winters.*

*September 26: Ran slow for 5 miles. Lot of smog today and was it hot! Coach Dowell came over also.*

*September 27: Ran about 6 miles today. Art ran with me. I was surprised he could keep up. Today Coach Winter told me Chris Papanicolaou will compete in Balkan Games this Saturday. I hope he <u>wins</u>.* [Papanicolaou was the European record holder in the pole vault at 17′ 4 3/4″, the winner of the Little Olympics at Mexico City, and a student at SJSU. Near the end of a season that left him number three in the world, he had no height at the Balkan Games on October 1, 1967.]

The work changed in October as Lee continued to run longer but introduced sessions on the track:

*October 19, 1967: Ran 8 miles for time. I ran faster than anyone else with a time of 55:09.*

*October 20: Ran three miles faster than ever before. I tried to catch up with* [other teammates] *who had started about 1 1/2 miles ahead of me.*

*October 21: I worked at the football game, and we won over UNM, 52–4.*

*October 22:* [Bill] *Gaines and his wife came today.*

*October 23: Today I ran 10 x 220. Ran the last one fast. I don't think I will run intervals anymore. It's too early. I'm going to start running with the cross country team. Gaines and Tommie ran today for the first time.*

*October 24: The time the cross country team works out will keep me from training with them. Coach Banks says he will give me a schedule to do. Today, sprint form—4 straightaways—couldn't finish the workout because Dr. Brozan* [a faculty member] *called all the Bloods in for a meeting.*

*October 25: Ran sprint form—4 straightaways—10 x 110. Ran the last one hard. Felt good.*

*October 26: Ran sprint form—4 straightaways. 3 x 660s. I really felt bad today. Found Gaines a house today.*

*October 27: The Coach calls this Free-Play Day. We played keep-away with the medicine ball. I was really tired afterward. Next we had to run 5 x 220s. I took it easy. Chris Papanic. was my running partner.*

*October 28: Went to work at the football game.*

With the first meet approaching, the tempo increased:

*December 27, 1967: Ran 8 x 220 with 2-minute rest in between. Averaged 28.2. McGrady ran with me.*

*December 28: 2 x 660 with maximum rest in between. 1:26.0, 1:25.1. Bambury [teammate, John] and McGrady ran with me.*

*December 29: Tired from last two days of workouts. Ran 6 x 150.*

*December 30: Rest.*

*December 31: Ran 2 x 330 and 4 x 110 with no time, but ran pretty hard.*

*January 1, 1968: Did not run because tomorrow we have time trials for our mile relay.*

*January 2: Ran off for mile relay. Perez [teammate] did not come back from New York. We really need him on our team. It was cold and a strong wind was blowing. 1.) Lee (me), 48.8; 2.) Talmadge, 49.7; 3.) Bambury, 50.4; 4.) Peo 50.6; 5.) Walls 51.8.*

*January 3: Ran 352 yards very fast with no time and 4 x 110. We practiced relay passes also.*

*January 4: The day before the meet. Took pictures, we practiced baton passes, and that was it for Thursday.*

*January 5: San Francisco Indoor Meet. I was very nervous for this meet, more so than any other during the last year.*

The San Francisco Examiner All-American Games, for which Lee was nervous, was his first appearance as a "radical," the first time people could be expected to stare at him not because he was a fabulous runner, but because he was stirring things up. But that didn't happen in gentle San Francisco where the audience cheered Lee when he beat Jim Kemp, 48.5 to 48.9. In other respects, too, the meet was dedicated to sport rather than politics and to the foul-ups that occasionally made indoor running in the old, cramped arenas special. What do you make, after all, of a 60-yard dash field that included football star O.J. Simpson, Bill Gaines, Jim Hines, Charlie Greene, Kirk Clayton, and ever ready Mel Pender?

Bud Winter knew what to make of it. He said that the race could almost be the finals of the Olympic Trials. Hines had been ranked number one in the world at 100 meters for the previous outdoor season. Charlie Greene figured that he was the fastest man in the world in the short sprint, and meant to prove it to Hines at every opportunity. Gaines was an overaged high school student recently relocated from the East to the West Coast having a difficult time finding a high school that would admit him, not least because he was married and wore a mustache. Pender was a compact, muscular sprinter with an explosive start and an excellent chance to make the 1968 Olympic team. Kirk Clayton had both Grambling and Speed City in his resume, and O.J. Simpson, while a modest 9.4 100 man, was a USC football star only four days removed from the Rose Bowl. As for the race itself, Gaines got out fast and Charlie Greene chased him narrowly across the line; immediately afterward the entire field smashed into a restraining rope that was intended to protect them from a wall at the end of a corridor. Gaines went down, bleeding from the forehead and was soon embraced in the arms of his worried wife. Clayton was unconscious. Greene fell to the floor. Pender and Hines fell over them, and only O.J. remained upright. The accident aside, the highlight was Greene, who was good for a quote. "I ended last season with a beef about Hines beating me at the AAU meet," he said. "Don't tell me I have to start the year with another beef."

Actually, Charlie was not absolutely required to start the year with a beef. But it was right and proper that he do so, in order to give the upcoming season a proper orientation. From this day on the first weekend in January, let us have controversy and complaint about the reading of the photo or the calculation by the clock. Let us have complaint about lane assignments, the number of spikes on a shoe, the Olympic Trials that selects no team members, and the protection of people of special interest and the discredit of others. Let us shake this hand and not that one, run against people from this country and not the other one. Let us celebrate in a single way, the way of our fathers, or not at all. Let us designate the price for disobedience and say who shall pay it. In all respects, in every way, let track and field and its wonderful athletes join the hope-filled, terrible, onrushing year. Let it be 1968.

# .23

*The two days in February.*

At the Los Angeles Invitational meet, several weeks after the opening session in San Francisco, Lee and Tommie got a look at a real beast. This particular beast, the one to concern Tommie and Lee, was conservative. He did not like change, unless the change was back to an earlier time and earlier condition. The beast did not listen to complaints about unfairness; in reality, he could not abide the sound of the word "justice" on lips other than his own. The beast did not like anyone to suggest that his status was supported by inbred privilege. He was righteous and quick to anger, and, needless to say, he hated people like Lee Evans and Tommie Smith. The beast was the one who sent Tommie and Lee racist mail with no return address. On the day in Los Angeles, Lee was not running but watching as a spectator. He was there when Tommie was introduced, and he heard the boos and the cries come down. The noise was the beast in full throat. Figuratively, the two friends raised their heads a bit, to react the way one does to a rustling in nearby bushes or to birds leaving the treetops at once, or—more to the point—to the sound, deep in the Delta, of an approaching car with the lights off and the wind-blown voices of men who have detected discontent and mean to put an end to it. But the two runners did not break or depart a step from what they were doing.

:

Without exaggeration, a person would have to be a fool to pluck at the issue of South Africa's participation in the 1968 Olympic Games. The country had to stay out, as it had been required to do when suspended in 1963. No change of consequence had occurred. Apartheid ruled. White Africans ruled. They decided who, what, when, where, and how much, and there was no way to pull a single issue or a single endeavor, like athletics, out of the mix and say "here we are good while otherwise, and comprehensively, we are quite bad and unapologetic to boot." Only a person like Avery Brundage could see it otherwise. But of course, if you were South African, you had every reason to think that Avery Brundage would see it differently. You would remember that on behalf of a force like South Africa, Brundage had done it before. Knowingly, he had danced with the devil. He had permitted the National Socialist Party in Germany, known to almost everyone as Nazis but to Brundage as Olympians, to put a negligible fig leaf on the discrimination practiced against Jews, and then he had used every influence at his disposal to overcome American displeasure. Principally, he was responsible for sending the large United States team to Berlin in 1936, and he was therefore responsible for the worldwide propaganda that Hitler enjoyed from the unprotested and unboycotted Olympic Games. Let us speculate. How much more cautious would the leader of the National Socialist Party in Germany have been, short years later, when he was deciding whether to march his troops into the Rhineland or to take Czechoslovakia piece by piece if the mightiest country in the world had refused to come to his Olympic Games because of his Nazi Party's attitude toward the Jewish people?

:

The South African issue remained active after 1963 because the IOC, led by Avery Brundage, raised no objection to apartheid itself. The IOC objected only to the fact that the implementation of apartheid impinged, narrowly, on the selection of athletes to represent South Africa at an Olympic Games and the manner in which those athletes were housed, fed, and trained. An accommodation on those issues would open the door to participation, despite the fact that the condition that fostered them, indeed caused them, remained. In other words, what Avery Brundage wanted was a minor accommodation to South Africa's racial policy. The accommodation would be directed to the Olympic principle that forbade discrimination based on race, religion, or political preference. This hurdle could be low or high, depending on how the rule was interpreted. For Brundage and the people he influenced, the successful approach was a tiny hop. On February 15, 1968, the IOC secretary general, Col. John Westeroff, announced at a news conference in Grenoble, France, that an absolute majority of the seventy-one member nations had voted by mailed ballot to approve South Africa's reentry into the IOC, and South Africa was free to send a team to the summer Olympics in Mexico City. Westeroff suggested that South Africa had made valuable concessions in order to achieve the result:

*While South Africa in the past put forward separate, racially divided teams, it would now be an integrated team marching under one flag at opening and closing ceremonies.

*The South African team would travel together, live together in the same quarters, and wear identical uniforms.

*While previously, whites and nonwhites could not compete against each other, now they would be permitted to do so at the Olympics and at other international [but not domestic] meetings.

These accommodations were akin to changing the wallpaper in a house with a collapsed foundation. Even a cursory analysis betrayed the insubstantiality of South Africa's promises. A glaring problem was that the "integrated" team would not be selected in a domestic meeting, at which black athletes and white athletes competed for slots, because South African law did not permit such meetings. More seriously, the majority of people who might have Olympic ambitions would suffer a lifetime of deprivation before going to the starting line, hefting a shot, picking up a pole, or aspiring to toss a javelin, much less swimming in a modern pool,

8888888888d

playing basketball, riding equestrian, or wrestling in a Greco-Roman style. In effect, South Africa, having dug a deep hole for its majority population, was willing on selection day to pretend that there was no hole and that everybody would compete evenly and to let the best man win. Stiff upper lip, and all that, being the attitude, one presumes.

The IOC was acting in an absurd way, never mind that later reports said that approximately forty of the seventy-one member states had agreed to the readmission. The fact remained that no country wanted to be associated publicly with the decision. Asked how the United States voted, Douglas Roby, the president of the United States Olympic Committee and an IOC member, said that the ballot was secret, that no one knew how he voted, and that he did not know how anyone else voted either. Without a denial, everyone knew how Roby voted, or thought they did. Roby voted the way Brundage told him to vote. Here is what Robert Lipsyte of the *New York Times* said about Mr. Roby's reticence on the very day of the vote:

*Since Roby and the American Olympic effort are said to be representative of all Americans, perhaps he has no right to keep his vote a secret. The American Olympic teams are presumably supported by contributions solicited from the public. The public has the right to know whether its representative has, indeed, voted for or against the admission of a country whose legal policies—not customs, now, or manner of living but legislated standards of conduct—require the separation of the races and the suppression of free speech.*

Other IOC member countries reacted more forcefully. On February 16, Ethiopia and Algeria voted not to send teams to Mexico City. Gone, then, were Abebe Bikila, Mamo Wolde, and the undiscovered talents that Ethiopia might reveal in Mexico City's altitude, and gone too were the successors to Allain Mimoun, Zatopek's magnificent rival. In short order, gone too, or on the way out, were thirty-two other African nations, and hanging by a thread was the participation of the Soviet Union, which was trying to establish a position of influence in Africa and could not afford to allow the Olympics to create disharmony. Soon, the other Eastern bloc nations were also talking boycott, and the countries of Asia, including India, Malaysia, Pakistan, and others from the Middle East were reconsidering participation. Mexico City itself, the host nation, was aghast and angry. Brundage, a spokesman said, was a dictator, a person who had double-crossed them. Mexico City had spent an approximated $84 million on the Games and now faced the prospect that no one would come to the party.

Despite the furor that he needlessly provoked, thick-headed, woolly, 80-year-old Avery Brundage continued to feel that the problems could be handled and that an "apolitical" Olympic Games might go off exactly as he intended—that they could be purged and fumigated of all unbecoming talk and threat, and that the countries of his choosing could nestle side by loving side. For this to happen, however, Brundage had more work to do in his own country and more problems to overcome. A jibe in the newspaper was one thing, but another matter altogether was an in-the-flesh person bent on making capital at his expense. By coincidence Professor Harry Edwards was in New York City, the media capital of the world, on the exact day Avery Brundage let loose his South African salvo. In fact, Harry was doing so well that his picture was in the *Times*, joined in the shot by a couple of other notables: H. Rap Brown of the Student Nonviolent Coordinating Committee and Omar Abu Ahmed of the Black Power Coalition. The three men were in town to help the New York Athletic Club celebrate its 100th anniversary.

:

The story of the NYAC Invitational indoor track meet in 1968 was one with several beginnings and a bad ending. One beginning was conventional, with men making arrangements for the hall, setting the date, seeing to the availability of equipment, recruiting volunteers and hiring professional staff, encouraging participation by teams and individuals, informing the press as the fields built, negotiating during the year for a team of five Russians to compete, setting the price for admission, and making sure that the track was set up and ready for the pounding it would take, watchful always for the dead spots that would buckle a lead runner's leg and take a record away. But this, unfortunately, was a beginning that had little, if anything, to do with the notoriety of the event in 1968, so the second beginning is the place from which to start the analysis. The second beginning was the moment Harry Edwards spoke of the proposed Olympic boycott and then gestured east toward New York and the New York Athletic Club and said, "You, too."

And then came the third beginning, the beginning that featured phone calls. These were the phone calls made to Mike Goodrich, an Indiana University sprinter and a black man, who withdrew from the NYAC meet after an anonymous caller warned him that acid would be thrown in his face if he ran. These were the phone calls made to John Thomas, a high-jumper with an Olympic medal to his name and world records and a favorite of the eastern press, who received threatening calls at his home. And, further, these were the calls to Jim Hines and to high-jumper John Hartfield in Houston that promised physical danger. And then, of course, there were the phone calls and the personal messages passed from person to person to build a crowd outside the Garden on the cold night in February. Y'all come to picket and to foreclose, to hear Harry Edwards's message and to plumb its meaning. "Any black athlete who does cross this picket line," Harry had said in the morning's *New York Times*, "could find himself in trouble, and I, nor any member of this committee, would not be personally responsible for anything that happens." Was that a threat? Was that a promise? Was it a warning? Was it a disclaimer? No one could reliably know, but an athlete who had received one of the phone calls would understand it, surely. And just as surely, a motivated person in the crowd would understand text and subtext, because the times were hot, and the people were angry.

On the evening, a picketing crowd of almost 2,000 people gathered. "Militants lose 7th Avenue scuffle" said the next morning's headline, with detail added:

*Civil rights demonstrators tried to storm the Seventh Avenue*

*Harry Edwards in prime time.*

*entrance to Madison Square Garden last night but were repelled by the police after a furious scuffle.*

*At 7:20 p.m., a group of Negro militants waving a black, green and red banner, tried to invade the main entrance area. They bowled over a policeman and battled other policemen for a few minutes before they were shoved back into the street.*

*The police made three separate charges into the crowd during the demonstration, arresting five persons. During one clash, several policemen used nightsticks to push the demonstrators back.*

Otherwise, reports were typical of attempts to report a shifting disorder in orderly terms. A bomb threat was called in to the Garden at 8:00 in the evening. A bomb would go off in an hour, the caller said, but no bomb was found. The Russians canceled. Jim Hines and John Hartfield stayed away, as did John Thomas, and so too did Mike Goodrich. Bob Beamon from Texas El Paso, appeared and did jump, but just once. Black sprinter James Dennis of the Air Force was roughed up and his glasses were broken. The teams from

Providence and Holy Cross were chased by chanting and screaming demonstrators into Penn Station, from which they were later escorted by railway officers into a safe area behind police barricades. Later, the demonstrators milled from the Seventh Avenue entrance to the main entrance looking for opportunity to break the police lines; at one point a speaker with a bullhorn yelled to the enthusiastic crowd that they should "break into twos and threes and go in and tear that goddammed building down." And Harry Edwards said to the crowd...and Harry Edwards said to the crowd?

Well, Harry said this and that. Having participated in taking the crowd to the edge, he pulled it back. Identifying the choice as either to continue to circle the complex or to rush the entrances, he said that if the crowd wanted to go in, they had his endorsement. But, as for him, he would prefer to let the thing rot. That was the end of it. The demonstration dissolved at about nine o'clock. Meanwhile, inside the Garden, a track meet had been run. Attendance was down, many white athletes refrained from competing, and only nine black American men participated. The two mile was good, though. George Young ran 8:38.8 to win.

:

The New York experience was new for the world of track and field. The simplest of athletic competitions had been thrust into social significance. The confusion attending the demonstration could be described as inherent in the leadership of Harry Edwards, a man whose influences included H. Rap Brown, Malcolm X, and Stokely Carmichael, three names that cumulatively meant, in the general view, a call to arms against a white majority. To make the matter certain, Edwards stated his opinion that violence was natural and desirable, and that no black man should die of natural causes. The country must change radically, he said, or "we will destroy it." To this end, Harry Edwards demanded unity from Americans of African descent, about which Edwards said, "I will use whatever tool, political or otherwise, to bring about unity within the black race." These are, of course, the printed words, flat, colorful only against plain paper, and not much like the effect when pronounced from Harry Edwards's lofty height of 6 feet, 8 inches and spoken in earnest, if not in agitation, by a man who claimed that as a child he had pulled his rotten teeth out with his own hands, such was his poverty, and stayed in school primarily to have access to a shower.

Live or recorded, heard or read, the words put people on notice. The principles governing Harry Edwards were illimitable, and no one was removed from him, not black man or white. Predictably, many whites reacted instantly to what they heard from and saw of Harry Edwards. Contemporary stories gave prominence to Richmond Flowers Jr., a hurdler, sprinter, and football star at the University of Tennessee, whose father had been attorney general of Alabama. In that capacity the senior Flowers had often crossed swords with George Wallace on matters related to race; as a result Richmond became accustomed to being taunted as a "nigger lover." Like father like son, his opinions were sympathetic toward people against whom prejudice was practiced systematically. But Richmond Flowers did not like Harry Edwards's approach, and not that of H. Rap Brown:

*When I found out that Rap Brown and Harry Edwards were running the boycott, my conscience [in deciding to compete at the NYAC meet, where he won the hurdles] didn't bother me. I put them in a class with George Wallace, whose views I hate, but as long as you've got Wallace on one side and Brown and Edwards on the other, the views of the middle man won't be heard. And I consider myself a middle man, even though in Alabama they consider me all the way over the other way. But you can't disagree with a Harry Edwards. If you do, then he says it's because he's a Negro.*

To similar effect was a remark attributed to Oregon miler Roscoe Divine, who said that if the white athletes had been asked to stay out, they would have been receptive, but "the only people who talked to us were the black-power guys. They threatened us with stuff like 'Don't run or else.' Nobody's going to take that stuff." A recent commentator has written that reactions like those of Roscoe Divine and Richmond Flowers reflect a cultural phenomenon in

165

which fearful white Americans failed to evaluate the politics and actions of the protesters. That many Americans reacted emotionally to Harry Edwards is undeniable; that Edwards intended an emotional reaction is equally undeniable, but to say that the controlling emotion was fear, and to conclude further that the fear clouded appropriate analysis, are conclusions worth looking at, especially because they have implication to the developing career of Lee Evans. The difficulty, as ever, is to separate fear from loathing.

More difficult yet is to speak of regret, of failed opportunity, of the boycott that was not.

# .24

*When is a boycott not a boycott?*

The mischief of the beast is the creation of people like Harry Edwards, pushed by anger not to radicalism, which is only an argument for change, but toward violence, or at least the threat of violence. If Americans of African origin had previously basked in an innocence beyond individual virtue as a result of being universally victimized, and if people of conscience—of all races— had sympathized with them, and even worked to the common good, many of these same people were frozen into inactivity by Harry Edwards and the black leaders with whom he was associated. Before, there had been one correct view and one incorrect view, with no moral ambiguity. Now there was polarity, a militant left attached by word and deed to violence and disorder, and a reactionary right, which above all else promised to restore and preserve order. It was all very confusing, more so in this case because the course Lee Evans and Tommie Smith set, and the path that Harry Edwards originally announced, was based on a traditional remedy of nonviolent resistance. A favored weapon of Gandhi and Martin Luther King Jr., the boycott worked because individuals made sacrifices, precisely as Tommie and Lee proposed to do, and because the moral and ethical issues emerged naturally from the conflict, leaving the innocence of the victim undisturbed and the messages clear. But the boycott was a difficult weapon to learn, and more difficult yet to maintain, in large part because of its passivity. The boycott promises that an action will not occur, that a product will not be purchased, that an establishment will not be patronized, and that a race will not be run, to name a few examples, the pressure in the situations building over time and operating on both parties uniformly. Boycott leaders are anxious to avoid violence, not because they are less angry than those who advocate it, not less impatient, nor less watchful of the passage of time and the progressive, harmful effect of discrimination on future generations, but because the threat of violence releases the pressure, leaving the alleged aggressor on an even keel with the putative victim. Furthermore, any change achieved by violence is short lived, for if force produces the change, force can reverse it with no loss, relatively, of moral definition in the act. The very caution inherent in the boycott, the balance necessary for its success, demands a particular kind of leader, beginning with a steady temperament, but requiring in no lesser degree a respect for words, the misuse of which can easily undermine the entire venture.

Harry Edwards was not the right person to lead a boycott movement. The young professor did not discipline his words or his emotions in a way consistent with the task. Within weeks of the demonstration outside the Madison Square Garden—the near-riot over which Harry Edwards had presided—Martin Luther King Jr., a winner of the Nobel Peace Prize and a man popularly associated with nonviolent resistance and the boycotting of goods and services, would be dead. Harry Edwards did not kill him, of course, nor did any of the others with whom he was allied. In the phrasing of the day, a "white man" killed him. But all the leaders who permitted themselves to be wooed by violence as an instrument of social gain, who spoke of result without process, who sought to incite the end by any means necessary, as if all means to an end were equally valid and defensible, as well as sustainable, had deadened the Reverend King years before his death. If the Reverend hurried to catch up near the end of his days, his was a heavy and despondent chase behind people who had traded the future for the present and marked the present with the illusion of control.

How had Harry Edwards in particular done this? He had said the wrong things, to the wrong people, in the wrong way, at the wrong time. Seeking an emotional foothold, he pushed first one way and then the other, encouraging one result and then backing away from that result, leaving uncertainty in a situation that demanded sureness. Edwards did this, for example, in New York, and he did it later. Whipsawing his audiences, Edwards should have known, indeed he must have known, that a mild statement does not cure the effect of a harsh one. Even as the crowd disperses, the hard language reverberates while the soft language slips away, no comfort to anyone. And who was the target?

Edwards was unlikely to excite sympathy from whites, the reaction of Richmond Flowers being characteristic. More credibly, Harry wanted black people to change. He called the goal unity. After New York, less generous people would call it conformity. In either case, the pages on the calendar turned and the man kept on talking. He taunted white people and threatened black people with equal enthusiasm. White people were dismissed as crackers, whitey, or honkies. Police officers were "pigs in blue." Lyndon Baines Johnson was "Lynchin' Baines Johnson." For balance, black people who still referred to themselves as Negroes or opposed the Olympic boycott could find themselves defined as traitors. Harry Edwards reportedly kept a poster in his office to identify prominent people who fit the bill, including at various times Willie Mays, Rafer Johnson, and Jesse Owens. On occasion, Edwards defined the people on whose shoulders he stood as the "Uncle Jesse Owens generation." And black athletes who preferred to compete in Mexico City were not only disparaged, they were at risk:

*I don't think any black athlete will go to the Olympics. If they do go, I don't think they'll come back. I am not threatening. I am not encouraging violence. I am assessing reality. I know the demeanor of the black people. They see a black man back from the Olympics, and they'll say, 'Look at the devil, with his medal around his neck.' Some of them are going to have accidents. You can't live with the crackers and come back to Harlem. The athlete who goes will face ostracism and harassment. People are fed up with those shufflin' niggers. The black athlete who goes will be a traitor to his race, and will be treated as such.*

There is Harry Edwards again playing both sides against the

middle, issuing his threats against black athletes while denying them. With statements like this, Edwards hopelessly blurred the distinction between nonviolence and violence. To say, as one might, that Harry Edwards had moved on, that he was interested in "black power," and therefore had no need to account for the remedies of the past, and no reason to adhere to the principles that governed them, depends on a specific definition of that phrase to include the possibility of violence. But is that proper? In the long continuity of resistance to oppression, many tools have been used. If "black power" is historically related to an emphasis on esteem and self-regard, to a pride in African heritage, with economic independence, if it is associated with a willingness to separate from the surrounding culture or on the other hand to assimilate into it, if it is associated too with the use of violence, all these qualities and approaches had been tried before. At one time or the other, each methodology was in either ascent or descent. The genuine misfortune is that the phrase "black power," as it was used in the '60s, cut the black community in half, the separation being between those who would and those who would not endorse the last answer to injustice. This happened because angry people acted as if they had created a new world. In that new world, they were the only brave men.

For purposes of consideration, it might be well to reject the '60s definition of black power and put the community back together—to answer the question "What is black power?" in a way that acknowledges the many roads to freedom. Was it black power, for example, that won black people the right to vote and the right to travel freely, that brought the National Guard to Ole Miss to protect James Meredith? Was it black power that was forcibly removing prohibitions against miscegenation or cohabitation between races, black power that employed the interstate commerce clause of the United States Constitution to require restaurants in the Deep South to open their doors to people of African descent, and black power that created political constituencies and lobbying efforts and coalitions of the powerful and the powerless? Was it black power that marched on Washington to shame a country, or black power that placed Marian Anderson at the foot of Lincoln? Yes, beyond doubt, black power did these things, just as black power compelled Tommie Smith in September of 1967 to say, in answer to a casual question, that yes, he might boycott, and it was black power for Lee to stand with him through the torrent of abuse, and black power, as well, for both of them to conduct themselves with a reproaching dignity and respect, and to threaten the life of no man and no woman. But it was black power also for Tommie and Lee to claim the right to respond to individual abuses with force if necessary.

If they put the dogs on Tommie, they would get the dogs right back, Tommie said. For him, the limit had been reached. Just as definitely, a person who approached Lee with a malignant heart would make a serious mistake. How tightly was the anger coiled within the young Evans? And how fierce would be the release? Lee Evans would beat you to the ground to avenge an insult based on race. And, it has to be said, when he discovered that a white runner from Cal-Berkeley ran at the NYAC meet, Lee brought the matter to his attention. "I hope," he addressed the young man at the start of a race later in the spring, "that you run faster than you did in New York." And then Lee blew him away.

In matters of public concern, the two San Jose men would refrain from participating in an activity whose central function was to exploit them; in every way, they would seek the opportunity to present grievances in powerful and forthright ways. In the melding of responses, Tommie and Lee were modern and complex, but there was a limit, a step they would not take. This was the step that threatened to burn down buildings, and it was the step that forecast harm for people with different opinions and values. This, too, they would not do. In haste one adds that Tommie, and maybe more so Lee, could grow angry, could argue and grow restive, could shun the counsel of people who had placed security above integrity. When riled, Lee could say that an athlete who walked a different course was a "Tom." But Lee would take no action based upon that judgment. He owned the right to say the words only. Much the same could be said of his remarks to the Cal runner. But would these limitations matter, these distinctions between Lee and Tommie and Harry, now that Harry had hit his stride and increased his rhetorical reach? Had Tommy and Lee, no less than others before them, chosen to dance with the devil? If this was a devil created by oppression, was he less dangerous? Was he less divisive? Was the consequence of the attachment less enduring? This is not about Harry Edwards as a person. By contemporary accounts he could be a charming fellow, perhaps not as threatening in person as he was in print or behind a bullhorn, popular with students, defended by university administrators, and lighter, in tone, when journalists peeked behind the curtain to find the real Harry. But this is about the public person who sought influence over other people as they made critical decisions. This is about a man who put events in motion, and then stood back to watch.

Now, at the end of the discourse, the mind should wander, as it doubtless does. But here, let it go to Mexico City and to the victory ceremony for the 200-meter dash. The scene is familiar, even iconic, so it gives away nothing to refer to it, but see the occasion, this time, through the eyes of Avery Brundage, as he viewed the victory ceremony firsthand or saw it on television. Who did the IOC president see on the dais prepared to receive the gold and the bronze medals? Did he see Tommie Smith and John Carlos, or did he see Harry Edwards? And there in the stands, where a slight scuffle revealed the intense interest of Lee Evans, who did Avery Brundage imagine was sitting in Lee Evans's seat? Was it the man himself, or was it Harry Edwards? You will know, soon enough, that Harry Edwards was not even in Mexico City on the day, but his specter was, and the question is raised. Who did Avery Brundage maneuver to remove from the Olympic Village? Was it Harry Edwards that he sought to ouster? The dictate of conscience is here. The conscience of Avery Brundage is beyond serious consideration, for this man who once made a hobby of collecting right-wing literature, who thought Franklin Roosevelt was an enemy of the people, and who considered Dwight Eisenhower a liberal, the man who had two sons in California by a woman not his wife, the secret life he kept unlisted on the IOC biography. But the conscience of Tommie and, specifically, of Lee Evans is real, and live. To whose values and whose judgments would the conscience of the two men respond? In Mexico City, to whom would they answer? Were they required to answer to Harry Edwards, or were there other possibilities?

# .25

*The greatest indoor race ever run.*

Many years later, Harry Edwards would acknowledge that he had increased the force of his rhetoric and adjusted his wardrobe from suits and ties to African robes and to ensembles of black slacks, black shirts, black sweaters, black sunglasses, and black berets, effectively, that he had become less civil, less compromising, more militant, and therefore more aggressive in his posturing, purposely to inflame the media, to make the grass fire burn, to return to the earlier analogy. These were dangerous decisions because there was no way to control the impact of what he was doing. A graduate of an Ivy League school and a university professor, Harry was responsible for the consequences reasonably related to his actions. In addition to the praise some people gave him for manipulating the media, Harry was responsible for the increased tension that accompanied his pronouncements, for the temper of the new audiences that received his messages, and for the calls made to coerce black athletes into compliance. He was responsible for the confusion, for the uncertainty, and for the wakeful nights of athletes trying to decide what to do. Harry was responsible, in sum, for the whirlwind his words and images created, a whirlwind that eventually broke against the backs of Tommie and Lee in Mexico City. But all that is to one side now as the chronology rejoins Lee in the early winter of 1968.

When Avery Brundage blundered again into the South African question, Lee added his signature to a petition circulated by the American Committee on Africa. Along with sixty-four other

175

prominent athletes, including Arthur Ashe, Jackie Robinson, Len Wilkens, and John Carlos, he affirmed support for the boycott movement. He and the others also asked the USOC to pressure the IOC to reverse the decision to readmit South Africa. Whatever the consequence, Lee was spending his youth with such signatures. Decision by decision, action by action, he was becoming a greater part of the social revolution in his country. That point made yet again, Lee returned to raising a family, studying, training, and racing.

Gauging the challenge on the track, Lee was aware that the United States had forty sprinters who had run a quarter mile in 46.5 or faster, but two of them were making a notable impression in the early indoor season. One was Villanova sophomore Larry James, who won two fast 500s in the New York indoor season and was making the transition from versatile prep to collegiate star. The other man, unavoidably, was Martin McGrady, the winner of sixteen successive 600-yard races indoors dating back to 1965 and the indoor world-record holder for the distance. Recently returned from a triumphant race in Moscow, the new resident of San Jose was nonetheless reserved, even a little gloomy in the winter of 1968. So many things had gone wrong: the first tiny college and its small budget, the difficult training and travel, the battle for respect, the injuries, and always the added features of his own personality, the shying away some athletes detected, the diffidence. All of this affected the way people viewed McGrady.

When people spoke of his potential, as they inevitably did in the indoor seasons, McGrady often demurred. Maybe someday, he said, he would do what people said he should be able to do, maybe when he was eligible to run for a college, didn't have to work, had trained more consistently, and when he had an outdoor event to call his own, rather than dividing time between the quarter, the intermediates, and the half. When Bud Winter said he could run a half in 1:44 and own all the records, McGrady understood that these were predictions, not accomplishments. He had run no such races outdoors and owned no such records. In truth, he must have wondered whether he ever would. If the press wanted real champions, they had only to look nearby. Several champions were training on the same track as he was. Lee Evans was there, for example, quietly putting together his own indoor season. Evans ran and won a series of early-season 440s, 500s, and 600s, before narrowly missing the world record for 500 yards while running 55.6 on the eleven-lap track in Seattle. That done, he set his sights on the AAU meet scheduled in nearby Oakland. At nationals, Lee decided to see what Martin had to offer at 600 yards. Maybe he could snap the winning streak that Martin was dragging behind him like an old blanket. If the streak were a burden to Martin, as it seemed to be, it was a temptation to Lee.

:

Ron Whitney was a wrong-footed, fifteen-step intermediate-hurdler who was the number one ranked man in the world for 1967. As a quarter-miler, Jim Kemp was tenth in the world in 1966 and seventh in 1967, but third in the AAU outdoor championships. Martin McGrady was the "chairman of the boards," and Lee Evans was the top man outdoors in his event and a two-time AAU champion. All of them would be featured in the Olympic year. Lee's interest was obvious, whether he boycotted or not, Ron's equally so, Kemp's somewhat more hedged, and McGrady's an illusion, held most fondly by his fans. By year's end, Whitney would be obsolete, made so by an Englishman who revolutionized his event; Kemp would be forgotten, the way a man is who draws the inside lane in the Olympic Trials; McGrady would still be an indoor specialist, and nobody would be talking about his future. As to Lee, he would be neither kith nor kin to many people who called him friend on this night. None of this they knew, of course. They knew only that the 600-yard race in Oakland was the start. The boards would be high and the turns tight. One of them would rush into the lead. The others would follow, but alertly, each runner watching for the opportunity to sweep past and grab a precious yard. Acting against each other in this way, they would all run too fast for the conditions. All of them would burn and all be left coughing in the dry interior air. The four experienced men would also know that if they made a mistake they would probably lose, and if they made a mistake in the last lap they would lose absolutely. For that matter, two of the men were lucky even to be on the starting line. Jim and Lee had dawdled in the qualifier and had had to sprint the last bit to stay ahead of an upstart Canadian they had left with ginger in his legs. But they made it, blew a sigh of relief, and then waited for the other two, who advanced more quietly.

On the evening of the final, the warm-ups were finished. The crowd was uneasily settled, ready to jump up at the gun. The competitors were on the line. All eyes searched for Martin McGrady, the man who was the thinnest of the runners, the one who seemed the least forceful, the least aggressive, the least likely. Still, the streak was his. If someone wanted to win, they had to get past McGrady.

:

Martin was troubled by a virus he had caught in Moscow. Lee was wishing the race was a 440. Kemp was looking like a guy who knew how to run indoors and understood the value of a lead on tight turns. And Whitney was overmatched, his only hope, really, the dismal possibility that the other three runners would collapse in front of him, the victims of ambition, and there he would come to take armor and weaponry off corpses littering the field, a ghoulish and attractive prospect. But this is enough. Fire the gun.

Quick and strong, Jim Kemp broke for the lead and took it. McGrady settled in second, knowing that Lee Evans was behind him but not likely to stay there. As a matter of fact, he expected to see Lee soon because Lee, he thought, was too impulsive to sit for long. McGrady was running the race front and back, an eye for Jim and another for Lee, and neither he nor Lee was looking to Whitney, who trailed. Even less interested in Whitney was Kemp who had the race by the scruff of the neck. This was what Kemp did. He ran from the front, he ran aggressively, he fought hard, and most of the time he won.

Kemp's aptitude aside, this part of the race was for observation. The fans looked to see who was pretty, who was rough, who looked mean, and who looked soft; they looked for the pushers and the pullers and the drivers. Many thought they could predict who would win, who would run tough but lose, and who would pull back when pressed. To the 9,000 of them, McGrady looked smooth, certainly compared to the sturdy, scooting Kemp, and even more obviously when compared to the strongly built, kinetic Evans, who was barely contained by this small eleven-laps-to-the-mile track. Smoothness is good indoors, being a way to smother the curves.

Through the first laps, the three leading men ran in an orderly row. The static quality of the formation, the one-two-three of the men and then the interval back to Ron, served only to build the tension, because the rule for any truly interesting indoor race is that the field must eventually shuffle, the first become last, the last first, the middle move up or back, and the devil take the hindmost. The noise was growing louder, too, a product of the banked turns, the reverberating air under them, the deadened straights, and the crowds sitting and now standing close to the scene, so near at times to give the impression that one of them could reach out and pull an athlete back by the strap of his singlet, and the athletes on the infield, many with a rooting interest for a teammate or a friend, and the building itself that prevented the release of sound to breeze and open air. All this created a loudness that would have been unusual outdoors. There was nothing for the runners to do. It was impossible not to hear the noise, but they could not listen. They ran by. The four of them were not late; they only seemed to be, hurrying and sweeping past the cries of encouragement and disparagement, the taunts and the trash, the misguided advice, past the hopes and wishes, and the imploring. The distance was dwindling as the runners spun and the nature of their opportunity too was changing.

The opportunity was narrowing and becoming proscribed. A tactic that might have been possible was no longer so, and new approaches were becoming necessary. In the gathering of time and distance, with each foot-falling and space-taken and second-passing, the swell from the crowd was growing louder still, and somebody had to make a decision. Somebody had to do something. Only the announcer kept his drone: Kemp, McGrady, and Evans, and then, Kemp, McGrady, Evans, and Whitney, with the three leaders on schedule for a world record, as everyone knew they would be. Still, McGrady was sitting and Kemp was sprinting and Lee was waiting, against the odds that said he would leave early, that he would create disorder where order was. But Lee remained calm, and if not calm, steady. In any event, he remained. He was waiting until instinct and experience told him that it was safe to go, indeed that he must go, for to delay was to take the chance that McGrady would rip past Kemp and leave him a lifeless third with nothing but the possibility of clawing past Jim for second place and a closer view of Martin's victory. So, no, Lee had to accelerate. He had to get past Martin and get up to Jim, and he had to get past Jim as fast as he could, to leave Martin, for once, in an isolation from which he could not possibly emerge. Let Martin be the one with the hopeless last-lap chase.

But when? When should he move? Time, time, time, always time passing, and then—as if inevitable—time and place fell in together, and the bell finally came, and Lee Evans threw himself into the uproar and flashed past McGrady. McGrady had delayed; he had waited too long. As a result, McGrady was third. More to the point, he was behind Lee, a new positioning that might have resolved the question of victory or defeat but for Jim Kemp, who would not yield the lead despite the momentum Evans had gathered and applied, not at Lee's first strike, not on his second on the second-to-last turn, and not down the backstraight. Lee had hoped to end the race, but he had merely changed it. The three leaders were still hustling along in a line, and Whitney yet trailed. In the circumstance, everybody knew that Lee had to make another decision. Should he complete his lunge, go past the leader at all cost, grab the inside lane and fight his way to the line, meanwhile exposing himself to late charges from Jim, coming back at him, or Martin, resurgent? Or should he fall back into the pole, save a few inches, and then kick the homestretch? The killer detail was Martin. He wasn't gone; he had given sway to Lee but not away to him. He was right there on Lee's heels.

If Lee stayed high on the turn, Martin could come through under him and have the best chance to outkick Jim Kemp, but if he moved in too soon or too late, McGrady could move up, impede him, and get a clear run to the tape. Maybe, in fact, Lee had no choice after all, maybe there was a place on the track that he needed to be, and he needed to get to that place at an exact moment. Or he could be seeing this wrong, and the best thing would be to stay and wait and kick from here, forgetting McGrady, who would be dealt with only if he appeared, which he might not. What? This was why the crowd was standing.

This race was all about position and what to do with it. Jim had his lead, Lee had his decision, and Martin had a problem and an opportunity, and all of them were closing in on the end. Of course, Lee in the circumstance was not the chairman of the boards, he did not have a vaunted winning streak, and his tactics were not watched and studied by indoor aficionados. But he did know a thing or two about running. Most particularly, he knew that he had a right to take what was his, and he knew that the rules governing possession were various. Which is to say, a foul outdoors is not a foul indoors. Every experienced runner knows it, and each is careless or careful to his own ends, and Lee, who had a full stride up there on the bend, either did not see Martin and acted in his own interest in chopping down toward the inside lane, or he did see Martin and intentionally moved down, to close the gap and foreclose the danger of Martin's decision to drive through it. In either event, one to Lee's credit and the other equally so in the dubious ethic of indoor running, Lee moved in precisely when Martin moved up, and he gave Martin a little bump. Just a little bump, it was, but the bump was given about 50 meters from the finish line, in a race being run at full speed, against two men dashing for the line, while the remaining runner was lodged permanently in fourth, disappointed to realize that the field would be littered tonight with his own dignity, that his own armor would rust in tomorrow's hot sun, the result of being beaten in this way. And with the bump, not a stumble or a fall but a critical check of his momentum, McGrady, too, would have his place in the field, his own armor destined to lay beside Ron's, his own bones to bleach, with the streak ended and the race to be decided between Kemp and Evans. Oh, yes!

Kemp, that scoundrel, was still charging for the line. No doubt, he was happy to think how wise he had been to get out of trouble from the start, to leave the bumping and jostling to the other two. Kemp of course could hear Lee and Martin entangled behind him; he could hear the inarticulate surprise of the crowd and the echoes and reverberations from all over the arena. The sounds came to him from a distance, far removed from the beating of his own heart. His own heart was throbbing at the temples, as if to make escape, to do or die. He was a sprinting man enclosed totally within himself from effort and lack of care, and from caring. The finish line was so very close that victory must surely be his. The noise was for him now, the cheers. Yes, for him, for Jim Kemp. Leave McGrady and Evans to the scramble. They deserve each other, and he, the man from Kentucky State now running for the Army, would win. He would be the champion.

The Army! The words were emblazoned across his chest, an easily countable four letters plain enough to see. But this was a different era, when sensation caved in on words and letters, and these four letters were peculiarly subject to the phenomenon. A-R-M-Y was instantly converted in the trick of the eye to a new word entirely, with a wholly different sound and a fuller meaning: V-I-E-T-N-A-M. The war was a fact of American life, as was the draft. Before the year was out many more athletes would be forced into uniform and a few would volunteer. Just as well, then, to start the year with a triumph in this uniform, with these words, and this hellish prospect. Next stop, Vietnam, the song said. One, two, three, four. What is the rest? Of that song? What are the next words?In the hurry toward the finish, there is a moment of sweet contemplation, a pause in the midst of chaos. Twenty meters from the line, there are the runners, this is the occasion, and here is the moment.

You get in a fight, not often, but sometimes, and you knock a man down. You figure, well, that is the end of that, and you start to walk away, and you hear behind you the sound of the man rising, and you sigh and go back, and you knock the man down again, and you walk away again, and you think to yourself that the deed is done, an unfortunate necessity, the need to hit the guy twice so very hard, but he brought it on himself and is responsible for the harm. And then, unaccountably, the man is up yet again, with your back still turned, your thoughts languid, moving on to something else, maybe lunch, or class, or an assignment, or a girlfriend and firelight, or—and he hits you. He hits you just the once, but hard and suddenly, maybe from just the right angle at just the right place on the back of your head, a soft spot, or maybe a spot where your brain has a little crease in it, or something odd anyway, something that makes you a tiny degree more vulnerable than you ought to be or thought you were. And down you go.

McGrady surged, coming now from the extreme outside, off Lee's right shoulder, Lee being one removed from Jim Kemp who still held the inside lane. In that instant it was too late to react, and both Lee and Jim knew the awful truth. McGrady had not stayed down. Arms swinging wide, eyes gleaming, for all the world a man screaming across a green-grassed field, acceleration remarkable, spirit magnificent, the supreme indoor runner was in flight, and the crowd, and each of them, rose up, open mouthed, astonished, some lifting their arms in surprise and amazement, all in disbelief. McGrady was the champion after all! He was across the line as fast as that. Forget the running man and the green grass. McGrady looked the way he would at heaven's gate, as if the hard times were forever ended. Lee was leaning when it happened. He was leaning toward the finish line of course, toward completion but hopelessly so, and Jim Kemp was grimacing, turning his body slightly to the infield, a torque and away from the presence of McGrady.

All three men first across the line were hand timed in 1:09.2, two-tenths slower than Martin had run on the oversized track at Louisville, so not the fastest 600 ever run indoors, but the fastest on an eleven-lap track. Whitney ran well, too, as it happened, but not well enough to have a place in memory with the top three, from whom he had separated. When the results were calculated at greater leisure and the electronic clock consulted, Lee lost a tenth and Kemp two. But by hand or electronic result, the order of finish was the same: McGrady, Evans, Kemp, Whitney. McGrady was still the winner, and Lee was just tired and thinking of leaving the building. He was fine, really. He had lost this race, but he had other dreams in front of him. Martin McGrady, who had beaten him tonight, was not part of those dreams. He was not even part of Lee's nightmares, the ones that had him losing the races he cherished. Martin would never trouble Lee outdoors. From the effect of other obligations or for reasons known only to him, Martin would never train hard enough to be a world-class half-miler, and he would always lack the speed necessary for the quarter. But it was impossible to take from him what was his. Martin owned the 600. In the coming years, Lee might beat him at that distance. Indeed, he would. But the odd result would not change the general flow. So give each athlete his due, and leave Martin McGrady indoors. Leave him with his own dream. Leave him with the dream in which he sprints past the world's best quarter-miler, and the throng cries one name only.

# .26

*The Iceman Cometh (all will be made clear)*

Rather remarkably, the AAU and the NCAA were still squabbling as the indoor season of 1968 made its way. As customary, the athletes were in the middle. The latest threat was from the AAU. Referring to the USTFF-sponsored Madison Square Garden Invitational, the AAU said that if even one athlete competed without the proper sanction, everyone at the meet would be suspended. In an Olympic year, the AAU's hammer was especially heavy. The hammer was too heavy, as it turned out, and swung incautiously. In response to the AAU announcement, the USTFF flew prominent track and field athletes from all over the country to Chicago for a meeting. After hearing the USTFF view and reviewing the situation, a representative cross section of the best America had to offer simply said no. What they said specifically was that if the AAU suspended anyone for participating in the USTFF meet, they would consider that they, too, were suspended. And so went Ralph Boston, George Young, Jim Ryun, and Gerry Lindgren, along with Richmond Flowers, Lee Evans, Charlie Greene, Ed Caruthers, Wade Bell, and Tommie Smith. Incidentally, the USTFF promised to sue the AAU, the United States House and Senate expressed concern about the situation, and Avery Brundage added a bizarre note. Referring to the interest of the House and the Senate, Brundage said that government interference with the Olympic movement would not be tolerated and could lead to the barring of the United States from the Games entirely. Brundage's statement was so confusing that Don Hull of the AAU had to clarify. What Mr. Brundage actually meant, he indicated, was that any governmental action would be a problem unless the AAU agreed with the governmental action, in which case everything would be absolutely fine. Of course, the whole affair was both serious and silly but mostly silly in this instance. Few people believed that the AAU would disenfranchise the heart of the United States Olympic team, that the House and Senate would invoke authority, or that Avery Brundage would do anything at all. In due course, the AAU backed down, the NCAA simmered, and the athletes went back to work.

One person missing from Chicago, among others, was the new star of the eastern indoor season. Larry James was missing. If Larry was not yet as accomplished as the Chicago attendees were, he was fast becoming more famous than most of them, in part because the circumstances were favorable. New York was the center of the world. Philadelphia was a short train ride away from New York. Villanova was located along Philadelphia's Main Line. The Main Line was associated with old money. Villanova was Jesuitical, and that too was old. Furthermore, except for the occasional wild Irishman let loose in the world and in the city, the Villanova men caused little disturbance. They worked hard, studied some, lived by the clock, and won the races they were supposed to win. With particular reference to Larry James, Villanova also provided a bloodline that included Ed Collymore, Charlie Jenkins, Paul Drayton, and Frank Budd. Jenkins of course was an Olympic champion in 1956, and the other three were great sprinters. This year, too, the team was stocked with talent. To go along with the emerging Larry James, Villanova had Dave Patrick, the tough-minded miler who led by example; the freshman Marty Liquori, America's third high schooler to dip under four minutes for the mile; Charlie Messenger, a reliable relayist with a wonderful name; Frank Murphy, a Celtic import with an even better name; and Irv Hall, a versatile hurdler and sprinter. Supporting the entire Villanova team was a patina, a sheen, derived from association with a single man whose name in the program in prior times had put people in the seats. He was his own Notre Dame with his own subway fans and fans in the American middle and far west, too, who peeked at the results to see how he did, of a night, especially on the indoor circuit where he ran a streak to make Martin McGrady blush. The patina came from Ron Delaney, and it was an old, green, golden reputation from a man now returned to Ireland as an Olympic champion, and how many of those did Dublin sport? The upshot of all this was that when Larry James brought his silken stride into the Madison Square Garden, people were prepared to notice. They did notice when he won the Millrose Games 500-yard dash in early January, and they noticed again a couple of weeks later when he upstaged even Jim Ryun's 3:57.5 mile at the controversial USTFF meet by running an eased-off 56.0 in another 500-yard event. On that occasion, the press said that the world best would have fallen if Larry had not slowed. A fast mile-relay leg of 47.0 added to the smart talk about how fast James could have run, if he had wanted.

A couple of weeks later, James showed his range while helping Villanova win a ninth Intercollegiate Association of Amateur Athletes of America (IC4A) title in eleven years. Running again in Madison Square Garden, James beat David Hemery of Great Britain and Boston University in the 600-yard dash, 1:10.2 to 1:10.8, and then stayed one step ahead of Mark Young from Yale to win the mile relay. After the five New York races in the three meets, Larry James was no longer an obscure young man on a team of more accomplished seniors and juniors. He was one race away from the Olympic pressure that had already settled on Patrick and Liquori. The new sensation needed a nickname, though, or at least he ought to have one to break him free from the crowded field of American athletes. This was a shy young man. He was new to the game. He could get lost without the addition of color, an element to make him sizzle on the page as well as the track. In their good time, his teammates and friends did the job. The Burner, they came to believe, would suit, or more to the point, the Mighty Burner.

:

They say they do, they may even think they do, but they do not. No natural person kicks at the end of a hard quarter. But they do compete. More specifically, they compete in the final yards and meters of the lap if they are suited by style and temperament to do so. They compete if they have a stride that can change to meet a need, if they are capable of surges and suitable to being roused, and if they grow fierce when challenged. Of course, the surge is mythical, being more resistance to fatigue, fighting it off, than anything. Done well, the last surge has a rattle and a tremor, something like a death throe in fact. Do not go gentle into that good night, is what it is, for such men. They rage.

Another style and temperament does not compete at the end of a quarter, and it certainly does not kick. This other style and temperament pours its energy over the entire quarter with style and dignity, and to unkind effect. The man in this model considers, at the last steps, that the job is done and come what will. He may duck his head at the end, but this is a concluding gesture, as if to say the deed is done. It is decidedly not a lunge. A lunge would suggest that the race had been miscalculated from the inception— that the energy had been misallocated. The maneuver should not be necessary and is not often done, not by such a man who does not die with each race, but merely exhausts himself. Unavoidably, there is something in the description of the hypothetical men, the assigning of temperament, the suggestion of versatility, the ascribing of ferocity, that foreshadows preference, but the foreshadowing is unreliable. Try to follow Larry James over the course of a quarter in 1968, try to withstand the brutal pace he will lay down, and then ask yourself whether you care that he ducked his head for one purpose or the other. You will not be close enough to see. And there it is, then, the surprise released early in the story, the fact that Lee is one and Larry the other, and the further fact that the conflict between them was built in, and drawing nearer.

:

A time of 47.0 is modest today. Even indoors, the athletes run on tuned tracks and take the advantage from doing so. In 1968, however, no one tuned the eleven-lap-to-the-mile board track at Detroit's Cobo Arena, the traditional site for the NCAA Indoor

*The new star, Larry James, on the left, with Jesse Owens in the center and Bob Beamon on the right.*

Championships. They just hammered the sections together and opened the doors. In the casual circumstance, even fellow competitors were stunned when Larry James slashed a world-record 47.0 to win the quarter. He had dived into the lead and kept on going, Old Man River, except younger and less black and with fewer jetties and swirls and no meandering at all. Upon completion of the event, this is what the new man said:

*I wanted to be sure to get the lead from him* [Tom Randolph of Western Michigan who had run the fastest qualifier] *right away. I have trouble if I can't take charge in a race, because I don't have a strong kick. If he had taken the lead, I was afraid I wouldn't be able to make it up.*

Indoors or out, the question for Larry James was never about kicks and surges, no matter what he said, but about the application of force over a distance. The smooth, unfurling stride dictated the tactic because it made changes of pace and rhythm more difficult. In any event, at this NCAA meet, Larry James was a sensation.

Not only had he beaten Theron Lewis's old record for the quarter on an eleven-lap track by eight-tenths, but he also had added a 46.6 anchor to Villanova's winning mile-relay team. The victory in the mile relay confirmed the Wildcats team championship over favored University of Southern California. Earlier in the season, the experts had looked at Larry James's sturdiness, his long stride, his calm demeanor, and they had remembered his stint as a high school performer in the 180 low hurdles. All this had led to speculation that he would run the 400 intermediate hurdles in outdoor season. After the NCAA, that talk stopped. Now the talk was that the kid from Villanova could beat Lee Evans at the open distance. Shut him down! Shut him down! Or not, as the case may be, but let us see.

This was however the spring of 1968, you recall, the cauldrons bubbling, the gyres spinning, events out of control, and a time when even the most ardent fans occasionally stopped caring about runners, jumpers, and throwers. Move on to Memphis. That is the next stop.

# .27

*Carry that weight your own way.*

What was needed after April 4, 1968, was an acknowledgment that something had happened beyond the death of one man. That Martin Luther King Jr. had died, that he had been shot to death by James Earl Ray on the balcony of the Lorraine Motel in Memphis, Tennessee, was plain. The man was gone, and with him the voice to still the impatient violence. Dr. King's death was not an occasion for mourning. Mourning is a process of accommodating loss. This loss was permanent, for which no accommodation was possible. It would never get better. "I learned of King being shot last night," said Lee in his diary, and indeed there was not much more to be said. Eventually an image would be created. Often misunderstood, the image would stand where Martin Luther King Jr. might have stood, had he the occasion, head bowed in sadness and regret, with reproach the only hint of anger. Meanwhile, ready or not, there was a track season to be run. If the activity measured against the calamity seems insubstantial, even insulting, so also did everything else in the country except for the expression of shame.

The day after the killing, Lee and his San Jose State teammates traveled to Arizona for a meet against Arizona State and Brigham Young University. On the other side of the country, Larry James and his Villanova team flew to Knoxville, Tennessee, to run a dual meet against the University of Tennessee. Lee's trip was quiet. He was met at the hotel by his friend Ron Freeman, and then beat him the next day, 46.3 to 46.8. He also added a 220 in 20.9 and a 46.2 relay leg. Amid the confusion and the anger of the first days, when the country was on fire, the trip and the meet were an acute distraction, a place and event not wholly at peace but a step removed from the absolute troubles. The Villanova trip to Tennessee, in which Larry James participated, was different.

:

The Wildcats had taken a vote whether to cancel or not. The vote being split, they went down to Tennessee to see what they could see, to hear what they could hear, and to do what they could do. You remember. They were on the other side of the mountain. On the day of the meet, Larry James was running, idly. He was running across the campus to the track on April 6, 1968, in the very state where Dr. King had been killed, a state that from border to border should have been silent as the tomb, but it was not. A man in a van drove past Larry James and shouted to him, "Run, nigger, run!" The words were a jolt. It was not that a person could not have predicted them, but only that no one did. The sophomore athlete immediately stopped and started to walk. He had been given an instruction, which he refused, from instinct one presumes, or instantly from a willingness to draw a line, no matter the consequence.

In that attitude, stop where Larry stopped, before he started to walk. Comprehend the meaning of the three spoken words: Run, nigger, run. Wouldn't it be fair in the circumstance to think of mortality, to think of the recent events in the state of Tennessee, and to think of the exact instant the possibility of death draws near, to the time when it loses remoteness? Wouldn't it be reasonable for a person in Larry James's situation to think that his entire future was at risk, including the wife he never married, the children he never knew, the career he never entered, and the long, shaded grayness of middle and advancing age, which he would never experience? Might he have considered that life in all its diversity was imperiled? All or any of that is for Larry James to say. But the meaning here is more general. He could have thought such things, and that is sufficient to remind ourselves of a day in the unreconstructed South. And if the imagined rumination seems exaggerated, recall that this South was the land of strange fruit, of Emmitt Till, of children killed by bombs set off in churches, of civil rights workers buried in levees, and of James Meredith shot on the side of the road. This South was the land where Jim Crow made his stand, and where hatred based on race was rapidly being hidden inside the Republican Party's new Southern Strategy, as Lyndon Johnson had supposed it would be. There's a Trojan horse for you! If Tennessee might once have wished to stand apart from Alabama and Mississippi, the state was drawn near by the killing of Dr. King in Memphis, however much the killing there had been a coincidence. Tennessee was a border state no longer, not in the world of pickups and vans and speeding white Mustangs. Rather this was a Dixie state where men in pickup trucks yelled grand threats to black men. In sum, the atmosphere was charged with violence. On this day, though, the man drove away, leaving only his memory and the occasion to remember old happenings.

Shortly after beginning to walk, Larry James came to the stadium. He completed his warm-up, and then he ran the quarter for Villanova in 45.2, a time equal to number three on the all-time world list. He was behind only Tommie Smith. Notably, his time was faster than any time Lee Evans had ever recorded. To add emphasis, James returned to anchor the mile relay in 45.4. In April 1968, on the day in Knoxville, Larry James was not as old as two-time national champion and social activist Lee Evans was—not in years and not in experience. But in more ways than one he was getting there. In three weeks he would run at the Penn Relays. Challenged by Rice University's outstanding runners, he would blaze an anchor leg of the mile relay in 43.9 and spread his name in newspaper headlines from coast to coast. In the honored American way, the time would have arrived to go west, where the fair weather would be general, destiny manifest, and the prospect good. In any case, Lee Evans was west, and Lee Evans was the man Larry James needed to meet. Gentle, though, the approach would need to be, just a relay first, an exploration in force, at the West Coast Relays in Fresno, California.

This is where we started. Lee had been informed. A new man was come to make him obsolete. Lee had been told that his demise was imminent. He did not believe this. He had worked the race through in his imagination, and then he had seen three legs run, and he had been stirred and lifted by the crowd when his time arrived. He had but one lap to run. He was the anchor.

# .28

*Circle back.*

Running on the shoulder of Larry James, coming off the second turn in Fresno, California, at the West Coast Relays, Lee Evans was a man at peace with himself. He had heard the stories and steeled himself. Taking off with a deficit in the mile relay, he had closed it. Now, he had collected himself and was in total control. Like a jeweler who sees a flaw in a diamond others pass as faultless, Lee had seen something he liked in Larry James. He had seen an aspect in the challenger that the press reports had not told him was there, and something that Billy Gaines and John Carlos had not mentioned. While the experts were impressed by the 45.2 in Knoxville and the 43.9 relay leg three weeks later at Penn, and everyone talked about the man's scary nickname, Lee had detected vulnerability, which he intended to exploit. The hard running behind him, he was now in position to do just that, but there is a pause, you know, a hesitation, a flicker like that from unease.

To the crowd, the hesitation was a signal that the race hung in the balance, that Lee might or might not get past. For Lee, however, the hanging was on purpose. For the moment, he just liked being where he was. He liked the sound the crowd was making. He liked that he could release the tension whenever he wanted to do it. He liked the fact that after so many hours of hearing about this race and so much thinking, he was going to win. His team was going to win. So, he stayed where he was. He stayed until he went past. One hundred yards from the end, Lee surged, in his characteristically energetic tumble of arms and legs. Larry did not slow and, likely,

Lee did not appreciably accelerate, but this was a matter of will, and it swept Lee Evans across the line. Years later, when Lee was asked to name a favorite race, this was the one he named. They carried him off the track in triumph. In his own hometown, outside of which he had picked cotton and grapes and where he had lived quietly with his family, of which he was proud, his friends and neighbors carried him off the track. Hundreds of athletes, coaches, and fans, many of them wearing the badge proclaiming allegiance to the Olympic Project for Human Rights, swarmed the finish line as he arrived. They joined Lee where he stopped. In their grip, they quickly had him as one of their own. In the darkness of the night, in the shadow of the lights, they carried him in a joyful procession. Lee had relayed 44.9 to Larry's 45.6. To the sound of Dionne Warwick and the way to San Jose, "put a hundred down and buy a car," there went Lee, unsteady but aloft. In the arms of these others, Lee was truly and magnificently happy. That the emotion could not last is no offense against the time itself, and no qualification. "We chaired him through the marketplace," the poet said of an athlete dying young. Soon enough Lee Evans would learn that death is not an isolated sadness and is not the only way to die. But that story is common; indeed it is nearly universal, and there is no reason to spoil the happy story by telling the sad, at least not now.

:

Lee says he saw a flaw, a vulnerability, in Larry James? Is he the one now reading history backward, proceeding from the result to the cause? Did he see anything of significance at all, anything to dispose of the matter between the two of them? Perhaps only the skill of his own performance cast Larry in poor comparison. Imagine the reverse, to see the issue clearly. What if Lee had slumbered? What if he had lost his concentration on the backstretch, or grown discouraged and not run hard at all? What if Lee had cantered the first 200 yards and then finished with a rush, a yard behind, but heroic in his failed effort? Was there a flaw in Larry James's race that Lee, after all, saw and tucked away on the night in Fresno? If so, the quality he would have identified is the obvious one, the want of a gear, the difficulty of shifting from such a smooth stride, but would a shift have been necessary if Lee had been run off his feet? Maybe all that happened in Fresno is that Larry James was tired or disinclined or off his best. James had traveled across the country, he was sleeping in a bed not his own, and he was eating meals not prepared specifically for him. He was running against an experienced man who had been the number one ranked quarter-miler in the world for the last two years, he was in the man's hometown, and he had been the beneficiary of uninvited publicity, all of which Lee Evans could have viewed as diminishing him.

Doubtless, Larry intended to do his best. He had always done his best, and his teammates expected a full effort this evening, maybe something that could be described as explosive, but he was in reality a lesser figure, a man who had only recently lowered his personal best below 47.0, and had been completely unranked, indeed unlisted, in the previous year's result. With the great distance between Larry and his opponent, maybe Larry had tried to hold a little back, taking comfort from his lead, coasting with it, rather than using it as a stake to drive into Lee's beating heart? Lee thought he saw a flaw? The solution for Larry James was obvious. Run faster. Lee Evans might be a man who could adjust on the move, a man who could jump the last meters, but what would happen if, time after experimental time, Larry added a bit more fuel to the fire? Would there come a time when Lee Evans, for all his homestretch mastery, would fold? And if Lee grew concerned, or restless, or was provoked beyond his patience by something that happened on or off the track, if he were the one who burned the first turn and sledge-hammered the backstretch, could he survive as well as Larry had? There was a world in front of Larry James that night in Fresno. Lee Evans was in it. He was held high, it is true, by friends and family in a happy celebration at his expense. But Lee Evans did not own the world that Larry embraced the first night in Fresno. He only thought he did. For the time being, Lee had something Larry wanted. He had the highest regard. Larry's task was to seize that prize from Lee, one way or the other, in successive races in the long season that awaited.

# .29

*Left leaning*

Lawson Robertson in 1932 sent Bill Carr out from Philadelphia to humble Ben Eastman and his troublesome coach, Dink Templeton. Bill had done it, three times as it happened, ending with the world record and the Olympic title. Poor Dink had suffered harm. In 1968, Jim Elliott sent Larry James from Philadelphia to the coast to deal with Bud Winter and his man, Lee Evans. The test in Fresno had not gone well, but there were other races ahead and training to be done. They had seen Lee. They could adjust. Meanwhile, just a little more information will be added about Lee and the West Coast Relays before the event is abandoned in our consideration. Lee had been injured. Two weeks before the race with Larry, he strained a muscle behind the knee. For the next several days, he recorded his worries in the diary: sore, leg still sore, leg sore. Finally, on May 4, Lee decided to race the pain away. He lined up to run his indoor foe Martin McGrady in an open quarter. Running cautiously through the first 220 in 22.3, he finished in 45.7 to win by 0.4. He then added a strong relay carry and felt better about the condition of his leg. The next week, the one preceding Fresno, his training improved. On the Monday before the race, he ran 24 x 110. The next day, he did 1 x 550 in 67.2, coming through the 440 in 52.3, and then he practiced 880-relay exchanges. On Wednesday he ran step-down 220s with Martin: 26.6, 24.2, 24.0, 23.8, and 23.1. Finally, on Thursday he worked easily on exchanges for both the mile and 880 relays. With the showdown approaching, he noted for his diary, "Really looking forward to running Larry James." On all the days, of course, Lee was doing his drills and stretching and his specialized stride-outs, concentrating always on relaxation, and he was doing sit-ups, push-ups, and V-ups, the mention of which defines the difference between Lee's day and the day of the modern sprinter, with weight rooms and supplements. Fortunately, on a day that mattered, Lee succeeded, but he did not make too much of the result or, indeed, of anything that had happened so far in the year. The most that could be said was that he had done all that could be done. So far, he had beaten Ron Freeman, he had popped the Martin McGrady bubble, and he had cooled the Burner.

:

Vince Matthews was quiet in North Carolina, tempered by the nation's social unrest. Thurman Boggess was working through an injury and getting pressure from teammate Felix Johnson. Theron Lewis was active again. Jim Kemp was, too. The NCAA champion from the year before, Emmett Taylor, was still in school. Ron Freeman was improving. Larry James was the new star. Close behind him were even younger runners. Dave Morton of Texas, Wayne Collett of UCLA, Fred Newhouse of Prairie View, and Curtis Mills of Texas A&M appeared on national lists as freshmen. Even some of the 200 men looked like they could move up, chief among them Oliver Ford of Southern. In their variety, all these men were the same to Lee, at least to the extent that he intended to treat them all in exactly the same way. He intended to beat them so often that each race predicted the result of the next race until all of them came, at once and universally, to the conclusion that he was unbeatable, that no matter how you ran him, Lee Evans would find a way to win. In truth, and along this line, Lee did not want any of his opponents to even think that they could beat him, not when they were honest with themselves. Should they get to the verge of accomplishing the result, he wanted them to hesitate, the way one spontaneously does at the sight of lightning, when the only safe course is to duck for cover. This is a difficult thing to do with world-class runners, but it can be done because most people cannot help but learn from experience. Yet, this process, for all its effect, was relatively unimportant.

More important was how Lee was preparing himself and how he set his own expectations. He was reminding himself, constantly, both on the track and off it, that he did not have the luxury of time and therefore, of error. In events even as short as the half mile, a person might miss a step, move left when right is the choice, follow when leading is preferred, let an eye stray to the infield, or permit a fluttered recollection of wife or son to distract, and still have time to make it up, to readjust the load, and to get the balance back. With only one lap to run, Lee could make no mistakes. Perhaps this fact was more obvious in the 100 and 200, but it was also true in the 400. If other men felt different about the issue—if they thought they had room for error—so much the better. When Lee aimed to be perfect, and they did not, the conclusion was foregone. From time to time in these days in 1968, Lee's face went blank, as if he had picked up and gone somewhere else, a previous smile gone, an ongoing conversation dangling. He could be reading and lose the meaning of a word. He could walk suddenly away. At such times, the man was thinking in dreams, which to him were plans. In each vision of himself, he was becoming Lee Evans. He was becoming, again and again and again, the winner.

:

Lee was the undercard in the spring of 1968 in the three major California meets that followed Fresno. At the California Relays, the Champions Meet in San Diego, and the Coliseum-Compton Invitational, the aggregate star was Speed City, of which Lee was, nominally and naturally a part, but from which he was momentarily distanced because he was running for San Jose State and not on the Santa Clara Youth Village (SCYV) with Tommie Smith, John Carlos, Kirk Clayton, Jerry Williams, and Billy Gaines. Also, he was of less interest because he was not Tommie Smith, and he was not the one staving off an unexpected challenge from Jimmy Hines.

* At the California Relays, Hines anchored his Houston Strider team to a 4 x 1 victory over the SCYV team that Tommie anchored; then Hines won the 200 meters, although Smith did not run.

201

* In the Champions meet, Hines took an early lead from Tommie in the 200 and held him off, with both leaders in 20.3 and Carlos in third. Hines reacted as if this were a perfectly natural result, while others gasped.

* At Coliseum-Compton, Tommie and his teammates finally pulled things together. Carlos beat Hines in a disputed 100 meters; Smith beat Hines in a 200, and the Santa Clara team consisting of Gaines, Clayton, Williams, and Smith beat not only Hines's Striders but also an outstanding University of Southern California team composed of Fred Kuller, hurdler Earl McCullouch, O.J. Simpson, and the Jamaican Lennox Miller.

With the last series of performances, Speed City had actuality and not just promise, a fact that cheered Lee even as he stood slightly apart. In California, he had anchored his San Jose State team to an 880-relay victory over an Army team from Ft. McArthur anchored by Jim Kemp, and then he had run a cleanup leg in the mile relay, occasioned by a teammate's inexplicable split of 50.0 that had left SJS well behind the winning effort of Prairie View. The SWAC school used legs by four outstanding individuals—Fred Newhouse, Jesse Ball, Felix Johnson, and Thurman Boggess—to run 3:07.7. Anchored by Dave Morton, the University of Texas was second. Three days later, Lee again found himself in a vain mile-relay chase, as Cal beat San Jose State at the Pacific AAU meet despite Lee's 45.9 anchor. The relays were, thankfully, only preparation for Lee's return to open racing where he could begin to set the pieces in place. At the Champions meet, he overtook Ron Freeman in the homestretch to win in 45.8, Ron's time as well, with Vince Matthews closing for third in 45.9. At Coliseum-Compton on June 7, Lee won again, this time over Wayne Collett, who had gone out at world-record pace before Lee tracked him down. Both Evans and Collett shared 45.8 but not the victory, which went to Lee. Matthews was third again, this time in 46.2.

Lee Evans had two good wins, then, to start his season, but both were close and could conceivably have gone the other way, or at least it appeared that they could have. Lee also knew that Larry

James was still a problem. James had been beaten at Fresno, and it would have been nice to think that he had dragged ashamedly back to Pennsylvania never to show his face again. But that would be fantasy. For all the talk of Larry James and his featherlight stride, the young man's resilience is slighted. At the Intercollegiate Association of Amateur Athletes of America (IC4A) on the weekend of May 31, James ran seven races for Villanova to help his university win its ninth team title in twelve years. He anchored the Wildcats to a win in the 4 x 1, and twenty minutes later won the open quarter in 45.5. He then added a 45.9 leg in the mile relay, not as fast perhaps as he could have run, but enough to provide a comfortable margin over Yale's Mark Young, who ran 46.1. In all, the IC4A was a decent way for Jim Elliott and his young charge to give notice that Fresno had changed nothing substantially. Lee Evans was still on top, and Larry James was still coming at him, a scenario that would play out as both men ran their first outdoor NCAA championship the weekend of June 13-15 in Berkeley, California.

# .30

*Where Lee went and what Lee did,
then a short pause.*

The University of California at Berkeley was a special kind of place in 1968. Years past, Cal had sent young professor Robert Oppenheimer out to supervise the building of the first atomic bomb, the most morally ambiguous achievement in the history of the world. More recently, Cal had a claim to Robert McNamara, who had done his undergraduate work there. From 1961 through February 1968, McNamara was the secretary of defense for the United States. Understanding his job to be wheedling, lying, manipulating, and smothering the facts about Vietnam, he had eventually been honored by a retitling of the entire conflict, which was often called McNamara's War. Cal Berkeley was home, too, to ardent and early opposition to the war and to an embrace for every love and peace idea that came down Telegraph Avenue, with a particular affection for free speech. If the perception of the place in 1968 was crafted by the publicized events and figures—Oppenheimer, McNamara, the war, and free speech—the emotional reality was smaller and tighter, being constructed from the collected experience of the people who were walking the lanes on campus or cutting the tangents heading from class to class, haunting the libraries, maintaining the dorms and dining halls, operating the administrative offices, and, not least, perpetuating the university as an athletic power. On Saturdays in the fall, the students, or at least a fair portion of them, would follow the band into the great stadium to watch the Golden Bears recreate—well, play football, to be precise. All of this is where the energy came from, the complex drift and swing, the sawing back and forth, of the mammoth academic community, to include but not be dominated by politics and certainly not by what old grads and old professors had done.

Drawing the circle tighter and closing on the topic at hand, the University of California at Berkeley had an illustrious history in track and field. Don Bowden, the first American to run faster than four minutes for the mile, had been a Cal man, for example. Sprinter Hal Davis, coached in junior college by Bud Winter, later ran track for California, as had Grover Klemmer, one of the all-time great quarter-milers, whose career was cut short by World War II. Often, the team placed high in the national championships. Much of what was good about Cal track and field, of course, was the work of someone who came to Berkeley from somewhere else, in the great California tradition. As to the track and field teams, the man was Brutus Hamilton, a native Missourian and a graduate of the University of Missouri, who coached at Cal for thirty-three years, beginning in 1932. Coach Hamilton had been off the job three years by the time Lee and Larry came to campus for the NCAA outdoor championship in 1968, but his lifetime achievement was part of the weekend.

:

The track at Edwards Stadium was cinder. On the weekend of the national championship, the weather was warm, turning to hot. On successive days, 5,000, then 9,000, and then 17,000 fans came out to enjoy an event expertly produced by Cal's track and field coach, Sam Bell, and sports publicist Bob Steiner. Lee Evans was running two events. The first was the 400-meter dash, and the second was anchor leg of the 440 relay. In the first heat of the 400, Lee qualified easily ahead of Ben Ollison of the University of Kansas, who was permitted by Coach Timmons to run the meet only after he agreed to shave his goatee. Surprisingly, fine runners like Dave Morton, Curtis Mills, and Mark Young did not advance. The revelation in the heats was Tommie Turner of Murray State, who was both talented and aggressive. Larry James also moved along without difficulty. In the semifinal on Friday, Lee was a little surprised to find himself joined by cofavorite Larry James and by Ron Freeman, whose 45.8 had been the fastest run of the heats, but only a little. Away with the gun, Lee ran a hard 200, eased, let Larry and Ron run on ahead, and then surged—gently surged, it has to be said—to third, and a place in the final. For his lackadaisical effort, he got the outside lane for the last race.

With Lee in lane eight, Larry James in seven, and Ron Freeman in four, with Hardee McAlhaney of Tennessee, Tommie Turner, and Mike Mondane of Iowa also inside, the final had at least the possibility of an upset. The upset was imaginable if Lee waited to run until he could see the entire field in front of him, if Larry keyed exclusively on Lee and let the other runners climb up his back, and if Freeman, et al. used their sightlines to advantage. For Lee, then, the job was easy to define. He had to get himself in gear a little earlier, or he had to be prepared to drive the homestretch, or he had to do both. Approaching the final on Saturday afternoon, Lee was nervous, of course, and edgy, as he would be for any big race, but he was also accustomed to his own race-day reactions. Typically, he remained nervous until the second command, the one that asked the competitors to "set," and then he relaxed. "I'm going to win this race," he would say to himself. This was a comforting routine, with the last words carrying the greatest promise: The last thought of any runner before the gun goes off often being the most important.

On this day, McAlhaney took off quickly, Tommie Turner gave chase, and Mike Mondane moved strongly into the lead at the top of the stretch. In the next sequence, Mondane gave way to Ron Freeman, and Ron Freeman then invited challenge from Larry James, who closed on him. Through these parts of the race, Lee was biding his time. He was biding his time so well that he was fifth entering the homestretch, a fact that most fans would have thought was going a bit too far with the biding. But at least Lee could finally see where he was in the field, see the distance yet to be traveled, and he could run freely. Just as clearly, it was time to run, and fast, before the time and distance expired together. This was not "push-button" running, with a barely detectable purring of energy, a soft patter, the smooth, loose motion of a dancer. This was Lee Evans again, a sight not easily forgotten once seen, the obvious struggle to get arms and legs coordinated, to keep himself moving straight ahead, to prevent his ambition from throwing him off the track sideways. This was Lee, who let everybody get a look at how hard it was to run well, how much work was involved, how the pinpricks of fatigue pressed into his legs and arms, how they burned. His face made everything plain. Be that as it may, the hunter was in motion now and the game ahead. In fact, he was sprinting strongly. One by one the other runners came back to him until, in the dwindling of the time and distance, he had won. He had tracked them down, every single one until at the last he reached Larry James, and then he had taken him too. By Lee's standards, the margin of victory was luxurious. He ran a meet-record 45.0, only a tenth slower than his best, while Larry had 45.4 in second and Ron the same time in third. A newly crowned national champion in his individual event, all that remained was the final of the 440 relay, for which his San Jose State team had also qualified. With the short leg, Lee could not catch Lennox Miller of USC, but he did bring SJS to second place and All-American status. He was joined by teammates Sam Davis, Frank Slaton, and Bob Griffin.

:

Does the bell in the campanile ring? Does the tower on the campus of the University of California issue an actual toll—to call people to celebrate or grieve or merely to notice? If so, now is the time to ring it. Ring it as a reminder that it is possible to mourn the death of a stranger. At 12:24 a.m. on April 28, 1968, a private plane returning from the Drake Relays crashed less than a mile from the airport in Beaumont, Texas. On board were the pilot, Winston McCall; Lamar Tech track coach Ty Terrell; John Richardson, a 1:50 half-miler for the college; and all four members of one of the nation's fastest mile-relay teams: Don Delaune, Mike Favazza, Waverly Thomas, and Randy Clewis. By right, these young men should have been in Edwards Stadium with their coach for the NCAA. They should have been thinking of handoffs and splits and speed. They should have been hoping for medals. There was a war; it took many lives. These several died by accident.

# .31

*Lee is the peak. Others climb.*

Likely as not, Vince Matthews would beat Lee Evans in the 400 at the AAU. He could wake up on the morning and say of the evening, "I will beat Lee Evans." He could take a short nap at midafternoon and rouse with the knowledge that, tonight, he would beat Lee Evans. He would warm up. He would say to himself while stretching or striding out, "Tonight, I will beat Lee Evans." Approaching Lee, he of all people would not see lightning and hesitate. He had beaten the man before, several times, after many efforts. There was peril though, and Vince would see it. Beating Lee Evans was like climbing a steep, icy mountain. Once on top there was a view, no doubt, and satisfaction, but there was also the possibility of sliding off and going down, down, down, and landing. Lee was the mountain. He stood while others fell around him. Such was Lee's confidence, and such was the reality of a man who seemed never, even at such a young age, to lose a big race. So, Vince had beaten him late last year. Lee had been injured. So, Vince had beaten him late last year. Lee had been at the end of an exhausting summer. So, Vince had beaten him late last year. Lee was the defending and two-time AAU champion, Lee was the AAU meet record holder, Lee was twice and currently the number one ranked quarter-miler in the world, Lee was the new NCAA champion, and Lee was running in his home state where he would feel supported and comfortable. Naturally, all this made Lee the favorite and Vince the challenger. On the other hand, this was a new night and a new year, and Vince Matthews was no Larry James. He was not a young man making his first foray into national competition and running a new event in the bargain. This was Vincent Matthews, originally of New York City, the leader of his college team, a social conscience in his own right. Most important, he was a man equipped with power and speed to match his adversary. Maybe, then, Vince was right in his confidence. It was hopeless, really, all this back and forth about who would beat whom. A fan could marshal the facts, complete the analysis, pry the conclusion loose, and let it be Lee, but quickly, almost immediately, the idea would follow that Vince Matthews might confound the prognostication. All he had to do was run through the tape and not leave Lee Evans the last lunge. One fact in any case was unavoidable. If Lee wanted to win, he had to bring all his force to bear. Larry James had been a threat. Vince Matthews was a real and present danger.

The nights in Sacramento were warm. Each evening the temperature started at ninety. The crowds were large. The two nights brought 23,000 people through the gates and many more simply appeared as athletes or coaches or trainers or even as friends. These people did not count in the calculations, but they added their voices to the din when it came, as it did most notably in the 100 meters and the 200 meters. In the 100, seven different men ran 10.0 or faster before Charlie Greene edged Jim Hines for the title. In the 200, San Jose ruled supreme, as Tommie Smith, John Carlos, and Ronnie Ray Smith swept the first three slots. And in the 400, too, the noise came, but building, first in the heats and then into the semifinals, as the runners eliminated themselves or moved along, in their time. The notable absence as the 400 began was Larry James. He had returned home after the NCAA. He would fight a later day in the long Olympic season. Otherwise, the field was full. And as Larry James was missing, Emmett Taylor entered to take his place. Taylor had won the NCAA 440 in 1967 and then dropped down to win the 200 in 1968. With that kind of speed, he made a tantalizing addition to the already strong field. In the heats, the casualty was Thurman Boggess who had never recovered from injury. In the semis, the casualty was Ron Freeman. Lee however was safely through, as was Vince. Lee was unhappy, though. He had drawn lane eight in the semifinal, and he drew it again for the final with Vince just to his inside shoulder in seven. If the race were between the two men, Vince had the edge, and Lee had another tactical decision to make.

Fortunately, Lee started his visualization drill days before a big race. He did not wait for a lane assignment. Serially, he took himself through the race in lane one, then lane two, then lane three, and worked his way to the outside. In lane eight, then, on this evening, Lee was still angry, "I'm getting suspicious about getting lane eight all the time," his diary said, but he was ready. Relaxing at the second command, he went out fast with the gun. He drove the first fifty meters, hurried through the first turn, lengthened his stride on the backstretch, relaxed as Bud advised, and entered the final curve with a lead. In the appearances of the race, however, Lee had accomplished nothing with his front-running. Vince remained on his inside shoulder with 100 meters to run, and Vince was the one making the energetic motions. In fact, he was moving up. With fifty meters to go, Vince grabbed the lead, and Lee was second. The race would have been over for anyone but Lee, who lifted one more time. With the distance collapsing under the two men as they ran, with the finish hurtling toward them, with no difference between them except that one was lean and gliding and the other not, the crowd stood and roared. They wanted to see the upset, despite Lee's California ties, a different result, a little tempering for the man who always won. Or perhaps that is wrong. Maybe Lee's crowd was making the noise and it was the upset they feared, and the last lunge, the one he owned and that Vince could not permit, that they wished, finally, to see. For all of that, the moment belonged to Vince. He had the lead. Lee had only the burden of his first decision, the one that impelled him to take the pace out fast, from which he now suffered. Would that it were false, but there was a man in front of Lee, and he was moving away, a shade or a shadow along the surface, an inch or a part of one, and that is all it takes to lose a race or to win one, and this race was Vincent's, or at least it should have been.

To be sure, Vince's lead was not a trick of the light, not an aspect of the shadow or the shade. The lead was no trick at all, not even the most likely of illusions, that of one body sweeping past another

*Of course, lean on me! Lee is left and Vince is right.*

and distorting the images. Lee was actually losing, and he would continue to do so absent a response so spectacular as to be pathological. A healthy person, surely, would stop, put the hands up, wait for a clear day, maybe even recant the ambition and be satisfied. But that was not Lee's world. Even the thought would have changed him forever. In short order, Lee did what needed to be done. In the last strides of the race he forced himself past Vince Matthews and leaned. The photograph of the finish is particularly nice. Both of Lee's arms are sweeping down and away behind him. He is tilted forward. He is showing his lower teeth, in a kind of grimace. His eyebrows are lifted, and his eyes are wide open. Lee is looking with his wide-open eyes at the tape. The tape is hitting him across the chest. The tape is not hitting Vince across the chest. Directly to the left of Lee, Vince is holding himself straight up. His hands are clenched. His arms are high. His eyes give the appearance of being closed, as if they too are clenched. He is not looking at the tape, and he is not looking at Lee Evans. Vince is looking at nothing. Or maybe, through the slits of his eyes, he is looking at the ground on the infield side.

Whatever Vince is looking at, or even if he is looking at nothing, he is trapped in a nightmare. In the nightmare, which is imputed to him from the body of his experiences, Vince is running down a dirt path toward a finish line. He is tired from his effort and is tightening up. He is running next to a man who must also be tired and certainly just as tight, but as the finish line comes up, the other man is leaning. In the awful dream, Vince tries to do the same. He knows how to do it, he has even practiced doing it, but his torso remains upright. Time and surroundings are passing in a blur, and he is struggling and punching the air as if tangled in a sheet, or likely a shroud, and still he fights—and then it is over. The other man wins. He has snatched away the well-earned prize with a suddenness that is stunning. Afterward, when he has lost, friends ask Vince, "Why didn't you lean, man?" The question has no civil answer. At the AAU meet in 1968, Vince shares a meet-record time of 45.0 with Lee. But he does not share the victory. The victory belongs to Lee alone. The other finalists trail across the line, every one a champion, but not tonight: 3 Wayne Collett, 4 Mike Mondane, 5 Jim Burnett, 6 Jim Kemp, 7 Emmett Taylor, 8 Dave Morton, 9 Hardee McAlhaney.

# .32

*Last call.*

The prospect of an Olympic boycott by American athletes remained through the spring of 1968 and into the championship season. In some quarters, the talk cooled, however, as Avery Brundage was forced to acknowledge that he could not have things his own way. South Africa went out of the Games in a wave of protest that the IOC official dismissed as political even as he bowed to it. The boycott also faded when individual athletes insisted on the right to make individual decisions, thus depriving the movement of consensus. Nevertheless, the idea of protest was still discussed. Harry Edwards in particular was keeping the fire burning. He appeared in May in a feature in the *New York Times* Sunday magazine. In the article, Edwards darted in and out, but the overriding impression was threatening. To this extent, his presentation did not express perfectly the attitude of the people whose association gave him any voice to begin with: Tommie Smith and Lee Evans. But too much can be made even of this important matter. To suggest that Harry Edwards went one way and Tommie and Lee went the other, if only in degree, is to cast Harry in too dark a light and to discolor Tommie and Lee as well. When Harry went too far, they could have walked away or even have rebuked him, especially when it was clear that other black athletes were being coerced and intimidated. Of record, they did not do that. Furthermore, Tommie and Lee let Edwards do what amounts to the heavy lifting. Conceivably, every black person in the United States in 1968 could feel, or at least acknowledge the possibility of feeling hate, resentment, and a hard resistance that admitted no compromise, recognized no courtesy, no law, and no forgiveness, in which a person was either part of the solution or part of the problem, in which the vaunted middle ground was so thoroughly and completely obsolete that a person claiming to stand on it was a coward and an enemy. In this regard, it might help to shrink the scene—to create a stage for the theater this was. On the stage, two actors are in the foreground speaking softly but with emotion. They speak from the heart, but the heart is hidden, because it is only half expressed. In the near background, to the side, another man stands in lower light. In a pause, he steps forward. The light is richer now and he claims it. He speaks darkly into the silence while the two men in the foreground listen. This is dramatic, as it is intended to be, a little play between three people allocated space on the stage, and the business of responsibility. Harry used Tommie and Lee. He loaded them down with symbols and words. But they stayed on stage. They decided to do that. If people watching the two men remembered most the voice of the third man, who could say that that had not been the intention all along? Let us assume that Tommie and Lee, now, years later, with the maturity of years and experience that they lacked then, would sort the matter out and say yes to this and no to that. The exercise would have no value. It is too late. What was is all there is.

:

The talk of boycott rumbled through the AAU meet in Sacramento and continued a week later when the United State's leading track and field athletes convened in Los Angeles for a meet originally described as the Olympic Trials, but which quickly devolved into farce. The meet was farcical because the organizers could not get straight what was happening. At various times organizers said that the meet would select the Olympic track and field team for men, that only the winner of each event would absolutely make the team, that even the winner would not make the team unless he subsequently maintained a degree of excellence, or to put a finer point on it, unless he demonstrated "his competitive excellence in the finals to the satisfaction of the track and field committee and if he demonstrated his ability to perform at altitude." Soon enough the athletes and fans got the idea. Nothing was happening in Los Angeles. There were balloons, though, and pigeons and flags and sky divers. And there were victory ceremonies, but only on the first day. On the second, the dais was carried away and the ceremonies canceled because the black athletes had decided, or somebody started the rumor that they had decided, not to climb up on the steps. Generally, the meet in Los Angeles was an angry affair. The black athletes who were sympathetic to the boycott were angry with those who were not; the black athletes who were not sympathetic to the boycott were angry to be pressured and angry that the more militant athletes were angry with them. Meanwhile, the white athletes might not have been angry, exactly, though some probably were, but others were tired of the whole affair and anxious to get back to sport, or at the very least were weary of being cast as villainous—the great anvil against which black hope and ambition had been dashed for years. Who, me? And then, to close a circle, add the selected white athletes who cast their lot with the black ones. If the prominent badge—the one that proclaimed allegiance to the Olympic Project for Human Rights— was honest, if human rights were all that the people wanted, this was a goal easily embraced. But there was always the question of gamesmanship, characterized in this instance by the use of the two words as a substitute for many and varied words. And this was the difficulty. No one knew precisely what the "human rights" in question were and how they were distinguished from prerogative or privilege or even earned advance. People were poking around in the argument looking for a place to put the concept of "merit," especially as they defined themselves to have it and others to lack it. All in all, the meet in Los Angeles, with all this roiling and backstory and controversy and confusion, was what the British would call a cock-up, a total mess, except for the performances. Those, at times, were quite good.

Harry Edwards was in Los Angeles, of course. He and others who joined him were sitting up in general admission looking for the chance to raise hell. Or they were hanging around talking among themselves and with the athletes, to the same effect. The contemporaneous report said that the professor was dressed in a camouflage jacket over a brown T-shirt, that his pants were short and tight, that his headgear was a black beret, and that he wore dark glasses, no doubt to shield his eyes from the sun. The reports also suggested that violence was beneath the surface of what was going on. A national magazine reported:

*There was mounting evidence that the boycott movement, if conceived in righteousness, is now passing into a virulent stage that—by grim paradox—bodes ill for those it is supposed to be serving. If the signs are accurate, compassion has given way to coercion. At the athlete's training quarters at Cal Poly in Pomona and in hotel lobbies in Los Angeles there were whispers of black lives being threatened by black hands.*

The grim paradox of course was not new. In February, New York had been the first test of the boycott. The little unity that had been achieved there had been coerced. So, if the boycott had a virulent stage, the stage was first, last, and constant. In especial danger was Coach Stan Wright, a black man and a member of the Olympic staff. Coach Wright did not support the boycott, said so, and for his candor received death threats by mail. He trailed around Los Angeles with bodyguards and with talk about his four children who could lose a father. Coach Wright was also a critical figure in the most explosive incident of the weekend. Once upon a time in a well-respected movie, an angry man opened his window and yelled to his neighbors, "I'm mad as hell, and I'm not going to take it anymore." In this instance, the angry man was John Carlos, and the angry man had an angry friend, Tommie Smith. John was upset because meet officials would not let him run the 100 meters, allegedly because he had run poorly at the AAU, and because he drew lane one in the only event left to him, the 200 meters. Tommie Smith had lane eight in the final of the 200, which was not a bad lane for a person occasionally troubled by tight turns, but the look of the assignment—its symmetry, with him on the extreme outside and John on the extreme inside—was suspicious.

*A gathering of symbols. Harry Edwards makes his point.*

What's more, if anyone had the right to open a window and start shouting, it was Tommie Smith. The young man had suffered through months of reaction to his initial support of the boycott. The threats against his life were bad; maybe worse were the patronizing letters that filled newspapers and magazines around the country, many of which cast him as the misguided boy who thought he was bigger than the Olympic Games and was being horribly abused by those around him, as if he were some kind of fool to be picked up and moved around and not a man capable of making his own choices and living with them. The local paper in San Jose was a particular thorn in his side. So, if Tommie Smith was a powder keg in Los Angeles, the fact is understandable. And if there was an element of truth to what people were saying—if Harry was running wild and taking the Olympic Project places Tommie never intended or expected it to go—that only made the matter more aggravating, giving a second pull on his poor self, now truly betwixt and between influences. He and Lee, now John and some of the other fellows, were all caught up and ready to swing at even the wind if the wind caused a riffle.

Sometimes it is better for a man to just be quiet rather than attempt even a few conciliatory words. The few seconds after the 200 meters were such a time for Stan Wright, but he didn't realize it. Something in his nature made him reach out, maybe to relieve the tension, or to encourage a release of grievance. After Tommie won the 200 from Hines, Wright felt compelled to tell Tommie that the 200 was the best race he had seen him run, that his curve was the most successful. Promptly, Tommie lit into him. John lit into him. Harry Edwards lit into him. The professor's entourage lit into him. Even Tommie Smith wife's lit into the befuddled Stan Wright. Mrs. Smith, in specific, told him that he should start being a black man first and an American second. These insults were excessive, without question, because Stan Wright was a decent fellow who meant no harm and whose principal offense was to be out of step with the more militant, West Coast athletes, so different in sensibility from southern blacks, many of whom refrained even from wearing the OPHR button, much less supporting the boycott or allied demonstrations. Wright himself had been successful in his good life by being patient and by working hard. If patience was now a vice and another way of selling out, the coach had a lifetime behind him that created blame, and therefore he had no choice but to take what was handed out. Personally, Lee Evans did not see Stan Wright as a bad man, and he had no desire to see him threatened. Lee even called the coach once to warn him to be more cautious. Stan Wright was in a box, Lee knew; he was in the same box that every American man and woman of African descent was in. It was stupid, really, that black people had to choose between being black and being American when they had a right to be both. Be that as it may, Lee was "with the protest," in the vernacular of the day. And he had no trouble at all seeing the anger of Tommie and the anger of John as legitimate. The deal with John Carlos in the 100 meters was particularly outrageous. Thirty-odd years later, Lee still thinks John Carlos would have been Olympic 100-meter champion in Mexico City had he been permitted to qualify for the event. And under all this is a second belief, and that is that Carlos was denied his opportunity precisely because he was too close to Harry Edwards, Lee Evans, and Tommie Smith.

:

The 400-meter final in Los Angeles was a gathering. Larry James had been at the NCAA but Vince Matthews had not. Vince had been at the AAU but Larry had not. Both men were in Los Angeles. In the ordinary course, Lee Evans qualified along with the two challengers for the final. In contrast to his friends in the 200, he got a good lane. Running from lane six, he had Vince inside him and Larry outside. With the race underway, he could see Larry go out quickly, and he could watch him closely. Completing the backstretch, he knew that Vince was moving up, and that Larry was still running well. He knew that he was fine, too, that he was where he needed to be and doing what he needed to be doing. Lee actually took a lead at the head of the homestretch, as if the victory might be as easy as slipping into a lake or a stream, a gradual wading with no need for a hard swim. But this was not to be the case. The challenge in the final 100 meters did not come from

Larry, as he was falling back, nor from Vince, who was straightening again and even leaning backward, but from Ohio University's versatile Emmett Taylor, who seemed to think that he might win. This was the time, of course, to light the sky, to put in Emmett's mind the possibility of a great storm, the effect of lightning, as a way to acknowledge the possibility that Emmett had hesitated on the verge of derailing Lee's express, and that he had ducked for cover as any reasonable man would. On the other hand, he might have run just as hard and fast as he could, and could do no more, and therefore lost to Lee Evans in the last few yards, which is what happened and which is what always seemed to happen, to someone or the other, in 1968.

"I was very happy with lane six," Lee explained later, "especially with Taylor in the next lane. He took me out real nice, so I didn't have to worry about Matthews and James. Sure enough. They were in back of us as we hit the stretch and they never could catch up." Graciously, Lee added that he was surprised that Emmett was as tough as he was. Lee ran 45.1. Emmett had the same time. Vince was third in 45.4, while Larry finished fourth in 45.7. In his diary, Lee recorded his relief that the big races were over, at least for a while. Within the next weeks, he and John Carlos would head for Europe, run a few races, make a little money, maybe look for a chance to take the world record down a peg, and they would recharge. Upon return, a new season—the second season in the long run-up to the Olympics—would begin with laying a new base and adjusting speed and strength, looking to the actual Olympic Trials in South Lake Tahoe and then to the important day in Mexico City. Along the way, Lee would study the effect of altitude. He had heard the stories. He would not be able to breathe. He would not recover. He would not be able to surge at altitude the way he could at sea level. Altitude was going to shake up the deck, throw the cards entirely into the air. That was the suggestion. Of course, maybe none of this was going to happen. Reasoned opinion was that for events of less than sixty seconds, the effect of thin air would only make the times faster. But no one seemed certain, and that was worrisome even to a man accustomed to overcoming adversity.

:

One important decision was made in Los Angeles. There would be no boycott. America's black athletes would be in Mexico City if they made the Olympic team. Lee Evans made the announcement on July 31, 1968. He said that a unanimous decision had been made to compete, although "the vote was also almost 100 percent that we make some kind of protest." The form of protest was unstated. Most people accepted Lee's statement as sufficient to dispose of the matter, but Harry Edwards would not relent. Edwards said that Olympic officials could rely on Lee's statement if they wanted, but "if I was in Payton Jordan's or Hilmer Lodge's place, I wouldn't put too much stock in what anybody says." Payton Jordan was the head coach of the United States Olympic team, Hilmer Lodge was the president of the USOC, and "anybody," in this instance, was Lee Evans. Edwards's response to Lee Evans was a sign that Harry would not accept even what the athletes decided. He was the actor. He was the decision maker. He and only he would say when the threat of boycott was over. Edwards also claimed that Lee had misstated the case when he said the boycott vote was nearly unanimous. Edwards told the National Conference on Black Power that of the twenty-six black athletes favored to make the team, twelve had supported the boycott, thirteen had opposed it, and one had abstained. Because the boycott lacked consensus, the Olympic Project had "released" its athletes to compete. The notion that the loose-limbed OPHR claimed the authority to either maintain or release athletes is remarkable. The claim reveals that included within the OPHR's idea of human rights was control, a stripping away from the athletes their right to make decisions for themselves. This was not a hidden hand, or an unseen agenda. Rather, the black press in particular saw what was going on. Here is one expression of opinion from a newspaper directed to a black audience:

*Harry Edwards and his disciples tried to sell the idea to Negro athletes. Most of them turned thumbs down on the plan, but Edwards browbeat them and vilified them and insulted all writers, Negro and Caucasian alike, who criticized the plan. The plan had no merit at all. But these are tedious racial times and it's rather easy to make the unthinking people feel that they are "traitors to the race" if they don't fall in behind every publicized scheme proposed by people who make a profession of hollering at "Whitey." Fortunately, though, some of the athletes wouldn't cave in.*

Lee Evans never "caved in" to Harry Edwards. Neither did Tommie Smith. They spoke for themselves. The two said from the inception that if the other athletes wanted to boycott, they would join it. They said that no personal sacrifice was too painful if it meant greater freedom for their people. It is now apparent, as it was then, that someone else was shouting over the words they spoke and over their shoulders. The question remains whether the two athletes intended the effect or countenanced it. But the boycott was a dead idea in either case. It was time to make other plans and time to move on. Doing so, the friends from San Jose would leave Harry Edwards behind. But they would never, not through the many years and not through the recording of memory, be free of him. He was simply too loud.

# .33

*A rolling stone gathers moss.*

By the end of June, with consecutive victories in the NCAA, the AAU, and the putative Olympic Trials in Los Angeles, Lee's summer could already be considered long and successful. But this year the summer was only prelude to a series of last days. The Olympic Trials were scheduled for the middle of September. The Olympic Games would follow in October. Ordinarily, in those two months, Lee would be recovering from the previous year and setting a base for the next one rather than pausing in a long course, but this was not any other year, and Lee had a lot of work left to do. A day after the nontrial Trials in Los Angeles, he and John Carlos went to New York to be fitted with national uniforms, and then they flew to Paris. In Europe, Lee competed in a series of meets; at one or more he thought he might try to set the world record, but rain and then a certain miscasting of circumstances made that impossible. As it happened, he ran the 400 meters four times and won four times, but slow, by his standards: 46.1, 46.7, 47.3, and 47.5. He also contributed to several victories in the 400-meter relay, on teams cobbled together for a night or a day, and ran some 200-meter races for sharpness and because he wanted to. Competing in different European meets, Vince Matthews was running faster times than Lee was: 46.0, 46.3, 46.0, and 46.1, a fact Lee was keenly aware of. Vince was apparently coming into his own late in the season, as he had done in 1967 when he had beaten Lee in successive races. Ron Freeman, who had trained in San Jose with Lee between the meets in Berkeley and Los Angeles, was improving, too, and Larry James,

Jim Burnett, and Jim Kemp were doubtless making similar efforts to get better fast. All of these runners, these aspirants for Lee's crown as the best runner in the world for a lap, would get together late in the summer in South Lake Tahoe, California, to train at altitude and ultimately to compete for selection.

Theron Lewis's season had not fulfilled its early promise, and he would not be a factor in the Trials, but memory of his 1964 Olympic Trials experience would cast a pall over the days and the weeks in Lake Tahoe. In 1964, Lewis had been fourth in the Olympic Trials 400, but he was left off the 4 x 4 at Tokyo in favor of 200-meter champion Henry Carr. The men this year were wondering whether the Olympic coaches might make a similar decision with regard to Tommie Smith. If so, the margin of comfort would be reduced from first four to first three across the line on September 14, the day of the final. In all events, the summer was ending like this, with the talk of the future in a season that ordinarily would have been in the past. During the work and the planning for the Trials, Lee was visiting one evening with Bud Winter, a person for whom he had developed real affection as well as respect. The early scraps that had almost driven them apart were mostly forgotten. On this evening, the two had been at Bud's home where the coach, unusually, was relaxed. Drinking a glass of wine, he allowed himself to grow reflective, even sentimental, proof, if any were still needed, of trust and sympathy. In this mood, Winter was talking about the Olympic Games. More specifically, he was talking to Lee about what had happened at the Olympic Games in 1960 with Ray Norton. Ray had been a treasure to him in his career, but on the occasion so much had gone wrong. Before this night, Lee had never seen tears in his coach's eyes. He had never seen disappointment so close to the surface, and so enduring. Seeing his coach in distress, eight years after Rome, Lee vowed to himself that he and Tommie would win in Mexico City. They would not be the cause of their coach's future remorse. Anyway, as Lee saw it, the coach deserved a bit of extra credit. As pressure had built on him and on Tommie, another coach might have been tempted to edge away from them, or at least to find a way to protect his own, different positions. Bud Winter had not done that.

He had been steady. He had not needed to agree with everything his two athletes said, he only needed to honor their right to say what they believed. The coach had done that.

# .34

*blue skies mountain views*
*calm before*

This was the time of the unclenched fist, the time during the season within a season for reestablishing the base, or tinkering with the workouts to correct a flaw or a weakness revealed by the championship season; it was the time to take a deep breath, to grow relaxed, and then return to work. In Lee's case, he had nothing new to do, of course, because everything had worked, but he had the difficult job of hanging onto what he already had. As always, he had the footsteps behind him. In 1968, the fastest sixteen times in the world had been recorded by American quarter-milers, and Lee's three major victories over three separate adversaries came with a total margin of 0.4, all of which came in the NCAA, a fact that left him with no room for error. If he had been perfect, as arguably he had been, he had to keep being perfect or he would lose everything, his old victories washed away. If that happened, Lee would become irrelevant, in late years, an old man claiming accomplishment that no one recalled and no one wanted to hear about, a Eulace Peacock in a world of Jesse Owens. Lee was in a precarious state, indeed. Many stories tell of the hero who has trouble after trouble set upon him until the end when he springs like a mouse from his trap and escapes, triumphantly. But in this case the people suffering the troubles were Larry James and Vince Matthews, among others, who kept getting beat by Lee, and if they sprang from the trap, they would do so at his expense.

Wisely, Lee started by taking it easy. He went up to Tracy Walter's running camp in Washington state to be one of the instructors. There, he ran longish, he gave lectures, and he fished. He returned refreshed to San Jose just in time for Linda to break a tooth. After seeing the dentist on August 5, he and Linda immediately drove to South Lake Tahoe, population 14,000. South Lake Tahoe, California, was on the border with Nevada, where the boundary darts southeast from the southern route. The actual demarcation between California and Nevada was—and presumably is—directly in the middle of Lake Tahoe, the pristine attraction that brought tourists to the area in profusion and assured that the community would be dotted with small hotels, mobile homes, and shops. On the Nevada side was South Shore, where people could gamble, eat, drink, and be entertained twenty-four hours a day, enticements that were, however, of little interest to Lee and Linda pulling into town shortly after eight o'clock in the evening. They were looking for the apartment rented by Jim Kemp and Mel Pender, where they were going to spend the night before looking for a place of their own. That done, Lee was going to get serious.

Lee and Linda, and Mel and Jim were in South Lake Tahoe, California, because the USOC had chosen to bring together potential members of the Olympic track and field team for high-altitude training before the Trials. In fact, the track itself was 1,000 meters higher up the mountain, at a place called Echo Summit, in order to match the level of Mexico City. In an unusually sensitive decision, the contractor for the six-lane tartan track and aprons was asked to leave as many trees as possible. Even on the infield, so many remained that every runner racing more than 200 meters disappeared eventually behind a screen of them. The interlude of the disappearing runner was highly valued by spectators, and a suitable image for a trial designed to eliminate from sight the many in favor of the few.

:

Lee and Linda arrived at South Lake Tahoe before the facility officially opened, and they had to fend for themselves until it did. The couple got an apartment for $100 a month; Lee took a part-time job as an auto mechanic's assistant, where with close

*In the critical days, Ron Freeman of Arizona State accelerates.*

supervision he learned to take out Y and replace it with X; the couple toured and fished and sometimes, alone or in company with others, gambled lightly, limited generally to pools of money collected from the two-dollar per diem stipend the USOC allowed. During the day, Linda and Lee, or Lee alone, would wander among the athletes, just looking around and getting a sense of what was going on. Lee noticed particularly Bill Toomey and Russ Hodges, who seemed to train all day and often lifted weights, something Lee had not done. In other respects, Lee turned to his own preparation. When trailers on site became available, he moved into one with Ron Freeman, and the two increasingly trained together. This unusual stretch of time, in which all the athletes were together, is an opportunity to emphasize how fortunate Lee was to have been well coached throughout his career. In these critical days, he took a little of this and a little of that from each of his former and current coaches. A reader of the diary from Tahoe can see the hand of Stanley Dowell in the longer intervals, detect Charlie Baker's legacy in the speed work, and see Bud Winter everywhere, his technical advice a reminder of what separated Lee from the talented but unschooled athletes who were also in the camp. In every respect, Lee was methodically preparing himself. The first two segments shown here are preliminary stages of his training, and the third is the sharpening work.

:

*Tuesday, August 13: Ran 6 x 220. Ran first 3 with 220 walk; then last 3 with 330 walk. Times were 26.7, 27.0, 25.5, 24.0, 23.5. Jogged a warm-down. I got very tired between intervals.*

*Wednesday, August 14: I have increased my sit-ups and push-ups to 25 from 20. Today I did my toughest workout up here. I ran 5 x 330. The first 3 with 220 walk; then the last two with 440 walk. Series 37.5, 37.5, 38.1, 37.5, 40.6. I was very tired. I was getting a cramp in my right calf.*

*Thursday, August 15: Today I ran 4 x 550. The 440 times were 57,*

58, 56, 57. *The 550s were around 71-72. I walked a 660 for rest in between.*

:

*Tuesday, August 20: Today I ran 5 x 330 with Ron Freeman. Nick Lee ran 4 with us. The times were 38.5, 38.5, 37.6, 41.0, 39.0. Very cold and windy* [it snowed]. *I was very tired on the last two. Ron ran his last one in 38.5.*

*Wednesday, August 21: Today, I did a step-down. 550-330-220-110.* [On] *the 550, the 440 was 55. The final time 69. The 330* [was] *36.5. The 220, I caught a cramp in my calf and stopped at the 110. Ran 23.2. I ran 2 x 110 to make up for the 220. Every day I do wind sprints on the last lap of my mile warm-up, and the sit-ups, and push-ups and high knees.*

*Thursday, August 22: On way to Oregon. Got 35 minutes left to go* [diary written in flight]. *Linda and I won $8 in slot machines at the Reno Airport.*

:

*Friday, August 30* [Tahoe]: *Just jogged today because of meet tomorrow.*

*Saturday, August 31: Puma has its new shoe out today. I ran in it. I broke the world record in the 600 meters today by 2.3 seconds. I ran 1:14.3. Winzenried* [Wisconsin freshman half-miler, Mark Winzenried] *was 2nd, James 3rd, Freeman 4th. They all bettered the old record. I was real upset because Matthews broke the world record in the 400 meters today, 44.4.*

*Sunday, September 1: Did not practice today.*

*Monday, September 2:* [Lee ran 45.2 for 400 meters in Toronto, Canada, to beat Ron Freeman, who was second in 45.7 and Vince

*Lee Evans and Larry James practice handoffs at South Lake Tahoe.*

Matthews who was third in 45.9. Lee does not mention this race in his diary, so fixed was his attention on the Trials.]

*Tuesday, September 3: Today I ran 10 x 150 with Kirk* [Clayton] *and Tom* [Smith].

*Wednesday, September 4: Ran 6 x 110, no time.*

236

*Lee finishes his world-record 600 meters ahead of Larry James and the University of Wisconsin half-miler Mark Winzenried.*

*Thursday, September 5: Ran 10 x 110 and some wind sprints.*

*Friday, September 6: Ran 2 x 352 fast and practice finishing.*

*Saturday, September 7: Ran 10 x 110 and practice tape breaking.*

*Sunday, September 8: Ran 6 x 150 buildups.*

*Monday, September 9: Ran 3 x 220 finishes; 1 x 330 in 34.0.*

*Tuesday, September 10: Jog.*

*Wednesday, September 11: Rest for Trials tomorrow.*

:

Between Lee's arrival at altitude and the Trials, he ran five races. He lost two of them. He lost in Walnut, California, to Ron Freeman on August 10 and lost again to Ron on August 23. He didn't care much about either loss. Ron was a friend and also, perhaps not

*At South Lake Tahoe, Vince Matthews enjoys his moment of triumph at Lee's expense.*

coincidentally, someone he was confident of beating at the Trials and later at the Games. Two races Lee won were at altitude. On Saturday, August 17, Lee beat Vince Matthews, Henry Smothers, Hal Francis, and Jim Kemp in a race his diary describes as follows: "I went out fast, was very relaxed on the backstretch. I pushed the 330, came off the curve with 2 yd. lead. Felt good and kicked away to a ten yard lead. My time was best this year, 44.9. Was pleased. My chest was in great pain. Doctor said my lungs had too much carbon dioxide. I was in oxygen tent for about 5 minutes." The other race at altitude, of course, was the 600 meters on August 31. Although pleased with the result, Lee was, as he indicates in the diary, angry. Later, he confided to a writer that he had never been so mad in his life, so far as track and field was concerned. While he was fiddling around with the little-run distance and toting up a world record no one bothered about, Vince Matthews was claiming the major prize. Lee could not stand the thought of Vince holding a world record that ought to be his. The victory over Vince two days later in Toronto apparently did nothing to assuage the pain, judging from Lee's failure to record it even in his own notes. The Trials were yet ahead, however, and the day of reckoning for Vince and Lee, as well as Ron and Larry and the others, of course, who were thinking of upsets. Unlike in Los Angeles, this time the Olympic Committee was serious, as it finally had to be. The Olympic team at 400 meters would be the first three runners across the line, with the fourth to sit and wait for a decision on Tommie Smith, who might or might not join the 1,600-meter relay team at Mexico City.

# .35

*the life and death of water (cf. the wasteland.)*

On reflection, the recital of Lee's experience has been the river overflowed, with the bank of dirt and grass covered and no sense of direction from the swirling water except the general motion downward to the sea. Those in the water bob past, as in a storm or the immediate aftermath of one, Theron Lewis, Thurman Boggess, Robert Johnson, Dale Bernauer, Hardee McAlhaney, Dave Morton, and Martin McGrady along with the many more long forgotten, unlike these, but with ambitions that sustained them for a while until they went under. But now it is time to return the river to its channel, to pinch the waterway, and let it become direct, time to make the water flow a single course, onward to release. Lee and the other survivors were in the heats of the Olympic Trials for 400 meters, arguably the deepest and richest event on the schedule. If they were still afloat, they might hope to remain in that condition, some more than others. But the common experience is that the most unlikely people clamber up out of danger, the weak and the strong side by side, the bold and the shy sharing a ride, and no reason except the event itself. So, there will be no more talk of mice and traps, and of man against man, but of all the men in ordinary straits. If the imagery of water and rivers, and submerging, seems mean, recall that we are talking of people's dreams and therefore of life itself. We are talking about Lee Evans. In September of 1968, Lee was looking around. He was nurturing his dreams. He felt sure that he was fine. But he was in the river with the rest, and that could not be denied.

The living look upon a corpse with delight; once upon a time Walt Whitman said something along that line, to capture the relief of survival, or, at least, of continued being. The 400-meter trials started on September 12. The athletes were to run four rounds, culminating with a final on Saturday, the 14th. As in Mexico City, the four races in three days would test the athlete's nerves, judgment, strength, and speed. Even the apparently insignificant first round, which permitted every athlete to advance who ran faster than 48.0, had meaning. Emmett Taylor, for example, ran extravagantly in the first round and was eliminated in the second. Wayne Collett followed Emmett closely in his first race, then ran 44.9 in the second, before failing in the third. More routinely, people ran as well as they were able, race after race, until the progressively faster times ran them off the track and the Olympic team. Only the runners who were both steady enough and fast enough moved into the final. Listed from lane one to lane six, the finalists were Jim Kemp, Ron Freeman, Larry James, Hal Francis, Vince Matthews, and Lee Evans.

:

Lee used to say that if Jim Kemp was in the field, you could be sure the race would be fast, the way he would start his engine and rip along. But now, in the critical race, Jim was in the first lane, and carrying the weight of two tight turns, a curb rather than a lane to cut along, and a psychological battle. He had to tell himself that everything was fine, that he could do it, that he should pay attention, not panic, run hard, watch the runners in front, save something for the stretch, and hope for stragglers. Doubtless, meanwhile, the other runners were looking at Jim in that tight lane of his, and they were thinking, "Better him than me." No way was he going to make this. Nonetheless, Jim did run for it! By 200 meters, he had passed Freeman and had the other runners fanned out in front of him, ready for the taking if only he could accelerate or if they would slow, or better yet if both would happen, if he could go faster and they would lean toward him. Come back to me, Jim seemed to be saying with each strong stride. Come along. Come back here.

Sometimes Baldy Castillo at Arizona State would give the runners a piece of paper on which the workout was written, and leave it at that, but Ron Freeman needed more, and lately he had been getting more. He and Lee were tight now, and he and Lee had been working out together. So, if Lee had the advantage of three good coaches going for him, now at least Ron had those three coaches once removed. Today, he could see the race as it developed. He was watching Larry James one lane out, and Larry was gliding along, and Jim Kemp was coming up to him on the inside. Now Jim was going past at the half lap. Ron was unperturbed. The smallish crowd might go, "ooh" as one and lightly, "aah," but he was waiting for the homestretch where he could find his friend Lee Evans, who was moving along in the outside lane. Ron knew well what Lee intended to do. He would join him when the time came.

Larry James was fast in the early running. He came out of the blocks and into the first turn like a sailing ship leaving harbor, the sensation of weight giving way to speed as the canvas caught the wind. Larry was not pushing or pulling but being carried along, as if in the circumstance the effort to stop would be more difficult than the effort of running. He was moving, as ever, with the gracefulness of dancing, water, flight, sound. He was running to take the breath away from the unseasoned observer. Once set in motion, he would run swiftly to completion. Larry James was going to make this Olympic team; his talent left no doubt about the matter. That he had been soundly beaten in Los Angeles was forgotten.

Hal Francis already had his great victory for the year. At the NAIA, he had beaten Arkansas AM&N teammate Henry Smothers, as well as Prairie View's Fred Newhouse and Thurman Boggess. Here, he was fortunate to be in the final. Of course, he didn't see it that way. If he gave himself a chance, he might slip through as well as any of the finalists. All it would take was one or two to fall and he would be there. He had a personal best in these Trials, two to be precise, so why not one more? Hal was in the slipstream of the race, there in the middle of it, and he wasn't letting anyone go easy.

Before long, Vince Matthews knew that his legs had gone out from under him. He had come out quickly from the start, but not so fast that anyone was amazed or shocked, nor so fast that he had forfeited his chance. He should have carried the speed. He should have been alright, but he could feel the draining, and he was surprised, really. Even his arms could not drive him forward. The 44.4 he had run recently, a cause for celebration a short month ago, mocked him now. It was as if an inspiriting force had come and replaced an old self with a new self, and the new self was drawing to an end, the finish line a haze, not something to be leaped into but to draw wearily closer, as a man in a tug-of-war would handle a rope, struggling against another man pulling hard the other way.

Lee saw him from the corner of his left eye, the first eye granted the unexpected sight. Lee could not have imagined a gift from such a man! How generous! the gesture! from the fastest man in the history of the event, the man who had beaten him three times late the previous season, and who might be expected to finish this season with a similar flourish. Vince Matthews in the finals of the Olympic Trials 400 meters was running from lane five as if he were oblivious of the man off (off!) his outside shoulder, the man who was measuring him, tailing him through the first 200 meters in 20.7. Vince was running as if he did not know, or knowing, did not care, that Lee Evans was comfortably in his wake, that Lee was waiting patiently until the homestretch opened in front of him when he would reach out and take the race.

:

These six runners were crafting the memories of a lifetime. On such a day a runner might later say, here I was one thing and there the other, referring to the start of the race and its finish and the fact that at one point he was hopeful and later, not, or alternatively an Olympian. The backstretch was behind the six runners. They had emerged from the trees, had run the second turn, and straightened for the stretch. Now, each was thrown into the last 100 meters. James was leading, Vince was fading, Ron Freeman was surging, Hal Francis was striving, Lee Evans was beginning, and Jim Kemp—how like him!—was churning and hoping and bottom fishing. Oxygen debt is building, to play its part, knocking, knocking, knocking. Larry James would win, surely. He would avoid the snares of past races and glide across the line. This is what Larry would have done, that is, but for the unfortunate necessity of the last few meters and the terrible urgency of Lee Evans. Lee fought the entire homestretch to withstand the withering pace that Larry James set down. "Pigeon toed," they said. "Agonizing," they said. "Wild," they said. "Uncontrolled," they said. But Lee Evans was a pupil and a learner. Seconds before this race, the most important race of his career, Lee had settled in his lane and looked into the near distance and in that near distance stood Bud Winter. Bud was shimmying, shaking down his body from head to toe. "Relax," he was saying to Lee. Relax. In the last meters, Lee opened his mouth, opened his eyes, opened his heart, lifted his knees, twisted his body, and drove his arms in a more forceful arc. He rushed past the line as if it were not there. By contrast, Larry tightened up in the last ten yards and dipped his head ever so slightly as the line approached. Otherwise James ran as he always did. He ran beautifully. Lee finished first in 44.0, 0.4 faster than Vince had run earlier at Tahoe in the race that had so upset Lee. Larry ran 44.1 for second. Ron Freeman closed mightily in the last 100 meters to claim the important third slot with 44.6, while Vince fell to fourth in 44.8. Jim Kemp was fifth, and Hal Francis was sixth, both in 45.2. Jim had equaled his lifetime best from lane one and Hal his. In neither case was the result sufficient to earn anything but admiration.

:

Eventually, both Vince's 44.4 and Lee's 44.0 would be rejected as world records because they ran in the sixty-eight-spike Puma shoe, popularly known as a brush shoe. The IAAF decided that the shoe could not be accepted for record consideration, either because the brush created a competitive advantage or, in the more cynical view, because adidas did not have a comparable product and would lose sales. In theory, Larry James had a claim to the world record with his 44.1, but before the matter could be pursued, the time would likely be obsolete. At South Lake Tahoe, Lee Evans was already talking about running 43 at the Olympics.

# .36

*There is some kind of bump
under this red carpet!*

The talk of an Olympic boycott never revived after the first Trials
in Los Angeles. Even the talk of protest abated among the black
athletes, in part because no consensus had been reached, in part
because the nature of the future demonstration was vague, in part
because the financial implications became understood—with shoe
contracts with major manufacturers being made under the table—
and in part because the business of making the team intruded.
Conceivably, too, the athletes were just tired of all the talk. In the
circumstance, the reasonable course for Avery Brundage was
silence. Instead, he relit the fire. Speaking before the camera, in
words that would be transcribed and repeated in the print media,
Brundage said that a boycott would only "be to the disadvantage of
the boys themselves," that he didn't think "these boys" would be
"foolish enough to demonstrate at the Olympic Games," and that
if they were so foolish, they would be "promptly sent home."
Having made his remarks, Avery Brundage ducked from the
podium as if he were expecting to be hit by a brick. Body language
notwithstanding, Brundage was speaking from power and of power,
his tone not different from a plantation owner who worries about
what the field hands are doing and who threatens to fling them,
once and for all, from the shacks he has generously provided.
Predictably, this made the athletes angry. The meetings began
again; the talk of protest reemerged. Among so many different
personalities, with so many interests and concerns, from the
variety of areas in the country, with so much at stake, emotions

were high. The words were rising and falling, ideas were being tossed up and falling down. Progress was made and given up, but nothing in the confusion or the difficulty detracted from the reality. Something was going to happen in Mexico City. After what Brundage said, that was certain. An added element, too, was the fact that these men had now spent weeks and months together training and competing in South Lake Tahoe. They knew each other; they had worked past the representations of each other they had read in the newspaper or heard second hand. Tommie Smith, as it happened, did not breathe fire; Lee Evans was not a hater. Neither Tommie nor Lee wanted more than their due. They wanted to be treated with respect. This is an idea upon which true unity can be based, leaving only the method to be decided, and also an idea that permitted no person to stand aside. Everybody was involved whether they wanted to be or not.

The newly selected Olympic track and field team was being carried directly from high-altitude Tahoe to high-altitude Mexico City to control the negative effects of being up, going down, and then going back up. As a result, the only interlude between the Trials and the Games was a stopover in Denver for uniforms and administrative detail. Not entirely blessed by the USOC, one bit of organizational detail came down to the black athletes, who determined to have a last conversation to decide how the protest or protests should be conducted. In the meeting, someone said, "Black armbands," and a sprinter said, "I can't wear armbands, they cut off the circulation." And someone said, "Black socks," and someone else said, "Black socks make my feet sweat." And someone said, "Paint the shoes entirely black," and everyone laughed. If the shoes all looked alike, Puma and adidas would not pay. Finally, someone said something like this: "Event by event, decide what you want to do when the time comes." And everybody said, "That is fine. We will do that." This was fine with Tommie, who was on the team at 200 meters, and with Lee. As the two people publicly associated with the protest, they had the most invested in the outcome. But, even at this last moment, they did not impose themselves. They did not force the issues. They were but two men among equals, set apart, however, by the obvious fact that many of the threats came to them. With the Olympic Games imminent, these two had to face the prospect that they might find themselves in somebody's scope. Moments later, the back of their heads might be blown off. If it had happened to Dr. King, nothing made them special. If the possibility that an Olympic athlete might suffer mortal wounds at the Games seems outrageous, the reaction is a trick of memory and a failure of imagination.

:

Meanwhile, the larger, civil world was deteriorating, or so it appeared. Martin was dead, of course, on his way to being irrelevant in the rush of events; Bobby, too, was gone, leaving shades and shadows of himself in place; the American cities had been burned, and could go up again at any minute; the students in Paris were in the streets; Prague Spring was ended by Russian tanks; Nixon was scurrying about the country preaching his coded message of law and order; and Hubert Humphrey was being undermined by Lyndon Johnson's Vietnam and humiliated by the events at the Democratic Convention in Chicago, later identified as a police riot. With particular relevance to the Olympic Games of 1968, Mexico City was also in turmoil. What was happening in Mexico City had been seen before. An Olympic city was supposed to present itself in a clean and ordered way, the troublesome spots ironed over, covered up, or removed entirely; otherwise, the enterprise would have no purpose but sport.

Historically, Berlin set the standard for a clever and sanitized Olympics. In the period immediately before Hitler's Games, the Germans had cleaned up the city. They had painted the houses, swept the streets, and offered special loans to property holders. Workmen—dirty creatures that they were—were asked to stay off the main streets. The streets themselves were even stripped of the ordinary signage encouraging good Germans to fight against Jews. Possible Jews, the authorities advised, should be treated as an Aryan would be. A man on a bus was to give his seat to a foreigner "even if she looked like a Jewess." No one was to discuss anti-Semitism during the period of the Games. The race-baiting *Der*

*Sturmer* was removed from kiosks and reading cases. In every respect, Berlin was to look, for a limited time, like a city without a bias or a hateful disposition. It was to look like a city in which even a Jew could walk unhindered. After the Games, the citizens were told, everything would return to normal. Jews could be ostracized again, debarred from professions, stripped of possessions, kicked in the street, and limited in educational opportunities. Eventually, they could be forced to wear the yellow star, and later still completely disposed of, but not while the Olympic Games were in the city.

In Mexico City, the problem was not Jews, but students. They would protest! All summer long they were in the streets and on the campuses. Sometimes in the thousands, and more rarely in the hundreds of thousands, stirring and shifting, sometimes negotiating with the government, sometimes being rousted, occasionally being killed, more times being detained and removed, but always they were out there, apparently inexhaustible, with their talk of democracy and freedom. September came and the activity continued and the Games were closing in and something needed to be done to restore order. Otherwise the streets would be clogged with protest when the tourists came, and the television cameras would show the slogans being scribbled on the walls, and the microphones would record the voices of the discontented people. The happy message of Mexico City, the first host city in Central America, would be overwhelmed, and the hundreds of millions of dollars and the hours in preparation would be wasted. People would see the real Mexico City. No one wanted that. On October 2, 1968, at a location fifteen miles from the Olympic Village, 1,000 government troops opened fire and used fixed bayonets on 3,000 demonstrators. The massacre left many dead and wounded. At the time, the government admitted fewer than fifty dead, while more reliable witnesses referred to hundreds of victims. The exact number was difficult to say because the army took the bodies away; some people said they went in piles to incinerators, and others pointed to the ocean, but in any case, away, and impossible to count. The remaining troublemakers were taken to the mountains for the duration. Thank goodness, IOC President

Avery Brundage was reassuring. Indeed, he seemed untroubled, his ponderous image that of the big, bluff man who had seen worse. He was after all in the construction business in Chicago! Of course, the Games would go on. "I was at the ballet last night, and we heard nothing of the riots," he commented. More directly to the point of his Olympic Games, Mr. Brundage said that he had consulted with the Mexican authorities, "who [had] assured us that there will be no interference upon the entry of the Olympic flame into the stadium on October 12, nor in any of the events until the closing of the Games." After that, one presumes, so far as Avery Brundage was concerned, the violence and the deaths in Mexico City would be of no account. It is impossible not to wonder, though, in the passing of time: Did Avery Brundage ever suspect that but for his Games, the police in Mexico City would have let the students run through winter, undead? Did he see them moving through the city?

# .37

*He just thrust his arm straight up into the air!*
*This is terrible.*

When the bodies in the plaza are forgotten, the vibrant colors of Mexico City remain and the people are wildly ecstatic to have the Olympic Games as cause to celebrate and to exult, and to have the rest of the world turned, for once, their way, and away from Europe and away from America, away even from Asia and the Antipodes and Africa and anywhere else that might interrupt. The pageant is magic, impossible to resist the gathering of hope and the turning away from despair. Under azure sky, across the cobbled streets, beneath the umbrellas, in conversation and excitement, the Games open and everything else falls away. No doubt, there will still be mothers and fathers walking the streets looking for loved ones, now gone. There will be beds unslept in and tears shed, and there will be reports to complete and complaints to make and inquiries to direct, but those are such empty ways to spend a day when the festivities are begun.

If you would have the event as it happened, the marathon was run on the second Sunday of the Games. But in the imagination, which is applied, the marathoners leave the mark early, to lead the tremendous crowds from afar and into the stadium, to give herald to everything that follows. On the sunny day in smog and heat, the seventy-two men run their light and feathering way, the way of Bikila and Wolde, the way of Kenny Moore and Kimihara, and of Akcay and Adcocks, out from the Plaza de la Constitution, winding south along beautiful streets; they skim past the teeming crowds and the soldiers set to the task of maintaining the course.

253

The runners move along the green line through Chapultepec Park, reenter the city, and begin in earnest to make the stadium less distant. In dream, as if in recollection, they draw closer the 80,000 people waiting for them, the many with so little news, just the snippets of information relayed along the way, and with interest growing. If later a strong man appears among the leaders, a man who does not run as a wisp and whose stride is not light, a Mike Ryan from New Zealand for example, or a Derek Clayton from Australia, nothing is altered. The first image of this race endures. In a cluster, the runners are rotating around a turn, before the winnowing that makes one a champion. In this, the corrected schedule, the marathoners enter the stadium as the 100-meter runners come to the start for their final.

Jim Hines, once of Texas Southern and more recently of the Houston Striders, is settled in his blocks. Charlie Greene of the University of Nebraska is nearby but bandaged, and USC's Jamaican star Lennox Miller is prepared to overtake him. In the instant, they burst from the blocks and pour down the straight-away of the new artificial surface. Deep of chest, bandy-legged, Jim Hines wins. Two words—it is as fast as that—Hines wins. For all the work the men do on the start and on the mechanics of speed, the race ends as soon as it begins, and a man in a distant row who has leaned back to check the safety of his child misses the race entirely, turning too late into the back of the rising crowd. He only hears that Hines has tied the world record of 9.9. The man is made up, of course, no more true than the change in the marathon schedule, but it could have happened. A distracted man could have missed Jim Hines fulfill the ambition of a young lifetime. Because his event was scheduled early in the meeting, Hines is the first American of African heritage to win an event.

No one expected any trouble, not now, on the victory stand, and not ever. Hines had refused to associate with the threatened boycott, and had hung back from discussions about any protest. The whisper was that Jim had a contract with the Miami Dolphins to play football, and a demonstration would have jeopardized that opportunity. In the circumstance, the organizers must have seen an opportunity to take the legs from under the boycott. They

*Jim Hines shoots across the line in the 100 meters.*

suggested that IOC President Avery Brundage present Hines his gold medal, knowing that the photo of the ceremony would flash across the newswires: a smiling and triumphant Avery Brundage amicably shaking hands with the fastest man in the world at the Olympic Games. At this, Jim Hines finally blanched. After all the time of holding back, of not clasping hands with Lee and Tommie and with the putative radicals from California, Jim Hines's limit was reached. He would not permit Avery Brundage to give him his medal nor would he shake the IOC president's hand. Jim Hines might not have favored the boycott, he might not have been inclined to protest or demonstration, but he was nobody's fool, least of all that of Avery Brundage. If Avery Brundage wanted a black man to wave an American flag for the television cameras or pose for a picture, let him look to the boxers, whose occupational hazards— the many blows to the head—made any decision possible.

Tommie Smith and Lee Evans followed the controversy over the 100-meters medal presentation closely and with increasing distaste. They began to consider the possibility that Avery Brundage would try a few more times to hand out awards. He might wish, for example, to put the gold medals around the necks of the two men who had tormented him. In the carefully contrived medal ceremony he could confront the "boys" who had threatened to bring politics into his Games. He could make them bow their heads to him, and he would stick out his unsavory hand for them to shake. No, this could not be permitted. More strongly even than Jim Hines, Tommie and Lee knew that they could not shake hands with a man who had forfeit the right to courtesy or kindness, or even to reconciliation. In conversation with their wives, the two men decided to buy black gloves. They would tuck the gloves into their waistbands. If Brundage tried to shake hands, they would pull the gloves on and have him shake leather. So, this is the sequence of protest in Mexico City; this is the way events were shaped. Jim Hines, a man who was not identified with the protest, indeed who seemed to turn from it, followed his conscience when the time came. Hines boycott Avery Brundage.

:

Tommie Smith was peering into his future, but the image was hazy—or surely it ought to have been—because he was no longer an incomparable sprinter. If he had once been a genius, now he was only a miracle. He was just like the other sprinters capable of flight, who sought his sliver of light and the fair breeze upon which he had wafted with such ease. Jim Hines had beaten him at 200 meters early in the year. More recently, John Carlos had done it at the Olympic trials. Because Hines and Carlos had beaten him, so could someone else. Smith would certainly lose if his concentration failed, or if he flinched under pressure, if he tightened when he should loosen, the way Ray Norton had done at Rome. He might also lose if he injured himself, as he had done before.

In the conjecture, John Carlos was the watching man. The New York native was hovering, ambitious, talented, a friend, and therefore an especial adversary. At the Trials, he ran 19.7, faster than the world record. This was something a man could take back to Harlem and brag on. But the record had been wrenched from him. They said it was because he wore the wrong kind of shoes. But the people who said this also denied him—for no good reason—the

*The United States 200-meter entry at Mexico City:*
*Larry Questad, Tommie Smith, and John Carlos.*

right to contest the 100 meters at the trials. Carlos was angry, and the heat of his anger was banked by mistrust and suspicion and by history itself. In any case, Carlos had reason to feel items of value had been stolen from him. All he had left was the chance to snatch Tommie Smith's gold medal from him. If he could do that, Tommie would drift from consciousness, his prodigious stride, his grace, his relaxation, all of it swept aside in the wake of John Carlos, the Olympic champion. Politically, too, Carlos was sprinting up to Tommie Smith's shoulder.

Before the Games, Carlos was likely to skip a meeting directed to protest, sometimes asking how much he would be paid to attend a session. But in Mexico City, he was the nearest approximation to Harry Edwards, who was sitting the Games out, a long way distant. In public appearances, Carlos was unrelenting. Quote me right or not at all, he would demand at a press conference after the final of the 200, for example. And what he wanted to say was described finally, almost in exhaustion, as "a familiar soliloquy" against White America. With athletes too, Carlos was a heated figure. When the all-white Harvard crew announced its support for the Olympic Project for Human Rights, Carlos said, who needs them?

He alienated other athletes, as well, by incidental discourtesies like cutting in line at the lunchroom, small matters that would be unnoticed unless the perpetrator spent his time hawking justice.

There was disquiet. Tommie Smith was one thing, and John Carlos the other. If Tommie was threatened with death, he responded with anger of course, but a calm resolve to do the right thing as he had the light to see it. If Carlos was threatened, well, that was unthinkable wasn't it? The several previous American summers had been full of images more than faintly redolent of John Carlos's discontent.

:

The 200 meters at Mexico City was run in four rounds: a heat, a quarterfinal, a semifinal and a final. The heat and quarter were run on the morning and afternoon, respectively, of Tuesday October 15, while the semi and the final were on Wednesday the 16th. The semifinal was scheduled only two and a half hours before the final at 5:50 p.m. Smith, Carlos, and surprising Peter Norman, of Australia, emerged on the first day as favorites. Norman broke the Olympic record by running 20.2 in his heat, and Tommie matched that time in the quarterfinal. Carlos also moved forward, bothered only by a near slip coming off the rain-slicked turn of his quarterfinal. In the semifinal, too, Carlos advanced easily. From lane one, he won the first semifinal with a new Olympic record of 20.1. Tommie was equally successful, as he too won his semi in 20.1, but Tommie finished limping, a fact that cast Carlos as favorite in the final, at least until some explanation for the limp was forthcoming.

Lee saw the end of Tommie's semifinal from a distance. He was in the stadium attending to his first heat in the 400, which he won easily. When Tommie's leg clutched, he was sitting between his wife, Linda, and Tommie's wife, Denise. He immediately went down to the practice track to find Tommie. The tall sprinter was already on the trainer's table, his affected leg wrapped in ice from his hip to the bottom edge of his shorts. John Carlos was lounging nearby. Bud Winter was there, pacing and moving about the practice area. Bud had seen this before. He had a reason to be upset, the way a man shot twice might feel.

In Lee's memory the moment is captured in a quick exchange he had with Tommie. Lee said to Tommie, "I don't care if you are hurt, you are going to get out there and run, and you are going to win." The great sprinter just lay there as Lee spoke. When Lee finished, he winked at him. Oh! Lee said, to himself, that Tommie is a sly fox!

And he went back upstairs to the two wives, Linda and Denise, and he said, "I don't know if Tommie is hurt or not. He winked at me! We'll know when they come out for the final. Tommie always takes a practice start. If he takes one, he's fine; if he doesn't take one, well, then he might be hurt after all." But Tommie didn't take a practice start. Returning to the track with the other finalists, noticeable for the bandaged leg and the thin black socks pulled up over his calves, he settled in lane three.

Carlos was in four, Peter Norman in six, and Edwin Roberts in eight. The others, too, were in their lanes, Larry Questad, Roger Bambuck, Mike Fray, and Joachim Eigenherr. Even to the last, Tommie could have tested the leg. He did not. He would take what came to him. The pause at the top, the watchfulness, the prime instant, all in the balance and the silence, all the men were as one.

No, on second thought, the eight finalists were not as one. They were fanned out along the track like shells on a beach, each on his own, and nothing that happened thereafter was designed to encourage closeness—not the anxiety of waiting, not the reaction to the gun or the flash, not the first strong strides, and certainly not the barely contained power of the curve. If there was any doubt that separation was the goal, and not unity, the catapult into the last meters, which might have brought the men together at last, showed that something else was at work. In the race being run, the men were pulling apart. More specifically, John Carlos was pulling them apart.

Carlos was the leader through 120 meters in 12.2, and then again, as the finish line came into sight, he stayed the leader until it happened that the figure on his inside drew near, and the two leading runners threatened to reverse.

Later, John Carlos said that with his lead secure he had looked back over his left shoulder toward Tommie. He had exhorted him to get up, to take the victory he had worked so hard to achieve. If he said those things, Tommie did not hear them. He was too busy running for the line. He was closing on John Carlos and stretching his high stride. This was the stride that God and Bud Winter had given him. No other sprinter had this capacity—this was the genius in him—to do more, to rise up and accelerate, to do this exactly when others began to do less. Friends sometimes went out to cinder tracks to measure his stride length after Tommie did something that beggared belief. Upon measuring, they claimed that the strides grew longer in the last fifty meters, stretched to ten feet at the climax, when foes dropped behind, as stunned as if banged upside the head.

In the early days in Mexico City, people in the Olympic Village said that Tommie Smith had lost his confidence, but they also said that Bud Winter had appeared, dressed in a fisherman's vest and a funny hat, and did what he did best. They said that the coach walked Tommie over to the track and the two had practiced the drills, the high knees, the relaxation, the reaching out with the foreleg. They had rehearsed the consciousness of motion. They had worked for explosive acceleration and controlled deceleration, and Tommie had become himself again, jaunty and ready to run. He winked at Lee. He did not take a preliminary start. He waited for his time.

And here, in front of the hundreds of thousands, and the hundreds of millions at second hand, with Avery Brundage and his cronies hopeful for a different result, with his wife in the stands, with Lee up there somewhere too, his heart stopped by affection and pride, doubting everything, including even whether his friend would finish or fall to the ground, Tommie was lifting. Against logic, he was getting faster.

Did he know then that the race was only a prelude, that soon he would throw himself on his own sword, or into the fire—that he would die, surely, as one person and emerge as another? Did he know that one life would become lost in the next steps and the other takes its place, or did his dash to the line carry away all other thoughts and leave him free, if only for an instant, content? No.

*Tommie Smith at Mexico City.*

Somewhere Tommie Smith must have sensed the shadow to his celebration even as he celebrated early, five meters from the finish with the world record flying beneath his feet and the gold medal drawing ever nearer. Later, people would say, you should not have done this. You should have finished as you started. You should have run through the line. The words however were from freightless people who did not carry his burden and did not know the pleasure he took from release. Weightless as a child, he threw his thin arms into the air before he got to the finish line, in anticipation of it. He raised his fine face to the heavens and he permitted himself a final undimmed smile. He was the Olympic champion. He had not closed on John Carlos, after all, as there was nothing inexorable or gradual in what he had done, unless of course one thinks of a funnel coming across flat ground. Tommie Smith had exploded past his friend and teammate. Coincidentally, Smith set a new world record for 200 meters. Wearing conventional spikes, he finished in 19.8, a tenth slower than John's run in South Lake Tahoe but incontestably legal.

John Carlos never doubted the validity of the 19.7 he ran in the trials. But Carlos had his chance in Mexico City, as Tommie did. In fact, John Carlos did look to the left in the home straight at Mexico

City, as he says he did. In subsequent remarks, Carlos said that he let Tommie win, that Tommie wanted the victory more that he did, and that he was prepared to defer. Some people believed Carlos when he said these things. Others did not. Either way, Carlos's statements are about what he intended. They are beyond absolute proof. On the other hand, observation and experience provide some basis upon which to tell the truth. When Tommie Smith passed John Carlos at Mexico City, Carlos did not look like a man sacrificing his medal to another man. Rather, he looked like a man who had missed a bus and did not know whether to chase it down or wait for the next one and who hesitated a few seconds in making the decision before grinding to a resigned, forlorn halt. Anyway, Carlos literally staggered the last fifty meters in Mexico City after Tommie passed him. Meanwhile, Peter Norman cruised past him for the silver. John Carlos had the bronze medal. Both runners recorded 20.0, 0.3 ahead of fourth-place finisher Edwin Roberts of Trinidad-Tobago.

Lee watched all this with satisfaction. It was not that he had antipathy for John Carlos, or any like it. To the contrary, he considered John Carlos a friend. He wished him well. But, he wanted Carlos second to Tommie Smith. Tommie gave Bud Winter an Olympic championship in a way that John could not have done because he lacked the closeness of association. Further, as to the claim that John Carlos paused midrace to encourage Tommie and to the later claim that John gave way to Tommie, Lee has his own perspective. He remembers the times when he, too, late in a 200 meters thought he finally had Tommie down, only to have Tommie hit the accelerator and jump meters ahead, one second being here, off his shoulder, and the next there, flashing into the horizon. Lee had been stunned by those moves. He could imagine what it looked like from the stands. Now, he knew, from watching Tommie sprint past John. In any event, the race had been run. The winner had been named. Tommie had won. John had stumbled. Peter Norman had excelled. The afternoon was drained, and the light would soon fade.

This was a rare evening, however, with no time for sighs and none sitting back. Something extraordinary could still happen, to temper what had come before, or to remove it entirely from memory.

Throughout the course of American history, no American of African origin had been allowed to stand equal with his fellow citizens. Words had been spoken and some written, promises had been made, laws enacted, but there was a terrible gulf, and into that gulf poured righteous anger. Now, that anger and righteousness would be given form in front of the entire watching world. In the most widely televised Olympics ever, the United States of America was about to be called to account.

This is not a step lightly taken, nor without consequence. As the eight finalists left the track, many lives were about to change in a way that no gold medal can explain. The two San Jose men were together with Peter Norman under the stands. The Americans were talking about what to do now. Here, too, recollection varies. One version is that Tommie handed John one of the black gloves designed to serve as prophylactic against Avery Brundage's handshake, and asked him to do what he did, to which Carlos assented. Carlos by contrast says the ideas were his. Leave it, either way, and record what happened.

The first thing that happened is that Peter Norman of Australia risked subsequent censure, which thereafter came, by asking whether he might join the two by wearing a button in support of the Olympic Project. They gave him a button and he put it on. The three men then walked to the Olympic podium. Both Smith and Carlos had rolled their pants legs up to emphasize the long black socks. Neither man wore shoes. At the playing of the national anthem of the United States, Tommie Smith bowed his head as if in prayer and held his right hand with its black glove straight-armed into the air. In somewhat more casual manner, with the slightest crook in his left arm and perhaps an immeasurably less-distinct nod of his head, John Carlos did the same. And then the jeers and the whistles came down. They rained on the two standing men. A cut had been opened in the sky, and through that cut the vituperation flowed. Some in the stadium, distracted, did not know what was happening, and took no part in the making of the noise, but the television cameras saw everything.

*The occupation of time.*

264

:

What Tommie Smith and John Carlos did was a salute, no more offensive in itself than any other gesture. But this gesture was explosive because it borrowed other events and other emotions, and traded on them to an audience that had been prepared. The fires had burned American cities so often that white people smelled smoke and feared flame even when nothing was happening. They feared the flame because it was promised to them by a new generation of black leaders who were breaking away. In the photographs that crowded the national magazines and appeared on the nightly news, the leaders dressed in black clothes shot black fists into the air and cried for black power. Black Power! Integration and assimilation were failed remedies, they said. Force would meet force and violence would resist violence. From now on, the world was new.

Of course, no fire was burning in Mexico City. No threats were issued. Tommie and John spoke no harsh words. They issued no indictments from the stand. But their dark fists evoked all that and more. So if observers looked down on Tommie and John only to see Harry Edwards, or Rap Brown or Bobby Seale, for that matter, or maybe just some black man with a bad attitude and a match, part of the responsibility rests with Tommie and John. In important ways, they dressed the part. In any case, these two along with the other black athletes had been told not to do this kind of thing, and they had done it anyway. A roiling would begin. For the most part Brundage would keep himself hidden, but the rumors would emerge. Hard times were coming.

In this, Lee Evans was in trouble as Tommie and John were not. They had run their Olympic races, and had none left. Lee had yet to run. He had the opportunity for two finals and two gold medals. In fact, Lee was uniquely in danger, although some would deny the characterization. They would point out Ralph Boston remained, and Bob Beamon, and Larry James, Vince Matthews and Ron Freeman, Mel Pender and Ronnie Ray Smith, among a great many others. But the list of other black athletes is distorting. In the national media, the protest by black athletes began with Tommie Smith and Lee Evans, not with any of the others. Even with the late advent of John Carlos, Lee and Tommie remained the face of the Olympic protest, and that is where the events settled. Tommie and John had done what they had done. They would face consequences. So, too, in a different way, would Lee.

In the forty-eight hours that followed, Lee's experience would pass as a dream, as a drowning, a drifting through water, a sequence seen through the glass darkly, in the slow motion of an accident, but sharply and clearly, as if not a dream, not a drowning, not a drifting through water, not seen through the glass darkly, but fast, with separate incidents driving into each other until only one remained, cohered. In the end, Lee would be required to stand apart. He would have to separate himself from the seamlessness of the experience and to make a supreme effort in the final of the 400 meters. This could not possibly be done.

# .38

*Most roads eventually narrow.*

This happened and then this other thing happened, and then some people did this other thing and made this other decision, and Lee was at first quiet and rested and running well, and he was concentrating and controlled, and then when these other things started to happen he was worried and upset and puzzled and turned around, and suddenly he was crying, and he was angry, and he wasn't going to run at all, but he was going to go home and be bitter for the rest of his life, and he was going to know that he had done the right thing and feel like a fool at one and the same time, and then friends came to him and said go ahead and run, and he straightened himself out as best he could. He straightened himself out for the Olympic final, where eight men stood on the line. Lee was nervous, tugging at the loose ends, quavering, and already drained, words and thoughts crashing, not that he had too few, but that he had too many and too much emotion as well. If he were not careful, he could panic and get everything wrong. He could soar and then fall. He had to concentrate, now, as never before. I have been working all my life for this opportunity, he says. And I can hardly feel my feet under me. I have been working all my life, he says, for this opportunity. And I can feel everything. Gun.

:

*Question: What did the Olympic authorities do to Tommie and John after they made their protest?*

The USOC rebuked the two of them. A representative of the USOC made a tearful apology to the IOC.

*Question: Why did the USOC initially respond so cautiously?*
For the same reason one refrains from putting a stick into a hornets' nest.

*Question: Did the IOC accept the apology?*
No. The most frequently cited version of events is that the IOC called upon the USOC to take stronger action against Tommie and John and vaguely threatened the disqualification of the remaining members of the United States Olympic team for track and field if that stronger action were not taken. Some reports said that the threat of disqualification extended to U.S. athletes in all sports.

*Question: Was Avery Brundage in the Olympic stadium when Tommie and John stood?*
This is not known. It might be possible to find out. Somebody knows the answer.

*Question: Was the event televised?*
Yes. The Olympics in Mexico City were the first Olympic Games to feature the enveloping coverage now considered normal.

*Question: Do you believe that Avery Brundage either saw the demonstration personally or saw the coverage that included Tommie and John?*
Yes. He saw it. He definitely saw it. He saw Harry Edwards walk right on up there and get his medal, and then he saw Harry Edwards jack that fist of his up into the air.

*Question: How fast did Harry Edwards run the 200 meters at the Olympic Games in Mexico City?*
His time was not recorded, but it was extremely fast.

:

Close the door, the IOC was saying to the USOC, send some out, keep others in, but put conditions in place to prevent a recurrence. Do something to punish Tommie and John, and do something to warn the others. With the pressure building in this way, Lee Evans was the man most likely to get caught, but his first concerns were competitive. Having easily won his first heat on the day of Tommie's 200-meter victory, he had to run a quarterfinal and a semifinal the next day, and the final on the day after that. Unless he was required to think about other matters, he would concentrate only on the three races. Lee was determined to do first things first, and the first thing was to win the Olympic gold medal. After that, he could protest.

The two preliminary races went well. Still excited by what Tommie and John had done but with no sense of imminent harm— the jaws being opened on his two friends but not yet closing—Lee qualified easily by finishing a relaxed second in his quarterfinal and then by slashing the Olympic record to 44.8 in his semifinal, which he obviously won. In the semifinal, Lee finished a tenth ahead of Larry James. Third American, Ron Freeman, qualified in the other semi, making the 400 meters a good bet for a sweep. And this, of course, is when events started to slip away as athletics become further entangled with race and the politics of power. Not that Lee could complain about the matter of race. He and Tommie had raised the question. But power was another matter. And here the question was whether the two young men were old enough to understand the nature of it. They recognized words as instruments of power, of course, and exhortations; they heard the ministers from the pulpit and read the books and articles. They learned the polemics and the threats and the promises about race and equality. The two men understood the force and power of people in the streets, and of broken glass and burned homes, and they knew too the changeable laws of the land, the shift of them to follow and lead to or away from social justice. As well, they appreciated the role of funding, sometimes given and sometimes taken away, but all of this is less power than a reaction to it.

Power is where power goes, and the most dangerous kind of power is stealthy—the tailored suits, the pressed shirts, the slightest rustle of fabric against fabric accompanied by the sound of good shoes against hard wood and marble floors, and the act of walking down the corridors to have a private word. This is the power that moves events. Privileged men are in motion. Avery Brundage was not a man to care for the moral principles that drove Tommie and John, and Lee, nor for the power that allegedly came from the exercise of moral authority. Moral principles were messy and situational. Judged by his record, Brundage preferred to make one decision only, and bluntly: the Olympics, for example, were good, politics were bad. Ambiguity eluded him, as apparently did his own vast hypocrisy, given that politics made Brundage, and politics sustained him. Brundage preferred institutional power, which was orderly and most often held by people who looked, acted, and felt as he did. On the occasion provoked by Tommie and John, IOC President Brundage would speak—or have someone speak in his behalf—to Douglas Roby of the USOC. In turn, Mr. Roby would talk to some of the others in his organization, and then something would be done. Meanwhile, to hold the line, a minion could be sent out to talk sense to the black athletes.

:

Once upon a time, a long, long time ago in a world away, Jesse Owens had been a hero. At Berlin in 1936, he won four gold medals as a sprinter and a jumper. But that was not why Jesse Owens was a hero. Many people have run fast and many have jumped far. These accomplishments are merely remarkable, as many athletes have discovered, and they are not enough to cast a lasting light. Singularly, Owens was a hero because he put the lie to Aryan superiority, because he brought the Germans off the high horse. That is what people said. Perhaps closer to the truth, Owens was a hero because he failed to recoil from the hypocrisy. Too often he failed to state the obvious: that he was subject to systematic discrimination in much if not all of the United States, that he would not have been permitted to vote in many jurisdictions, that many restaurants around the country would have turned him away, and that he could not travel freely, buy any home he could afford, marry anyone who would have him, and socialize without criticism. He had been born wrong: the wrong color, the wrong race. For these reasons, there was a falseness built into the popularity of Jesse Owens, as if the popularity required Owens and his admirers, each, to embrace the pretense of unmitigated good and unmitigated bad, and to ascribe the good to the United States and the bad to Germany, and therefore Owens was an American icon even though he was denied the privilege of being an American at all.

Transplanted from Alabama to Ohio as a boy, he was so passive that he gave up his own name after a schoolteacher mistook J.C. for Jesse. In the years that followed, coaching and talent made him special, but nothing made him wise. He remained a man who did what he was told. After Berlin, there had been so many demands, so many compromises, so much to swallow, so much humiliation disguised as opportunity. Somewhere deep he must have known it had been mistake to let them race him against a horse. He must have known that the spectacle was more demeaning in its way than a minstrel show, but he raced the horse anyway. He ought not to have done it. He had thought, probably, that the incident was minor, but now it hung like a weight around him, like something that identified him as weak and malleable, someone who came from another time and place where such things could be casually made to happen, that a black man could be demeaned for the amusement of other people, who winked at each other to see what the great Owens was doing. In one way the detractors were correct. He was a man of his times. That was the pity. Sometimes, a person could get another sense of Jesse Owens, a glimpse of the private person, a sadness in the eyes, especially as he got older, like a man who wanted to be left alone, but who would not know what to do with himself if he were.

He was out of favor now. He knew that. The young boys and men were burning, they were setting fires, and he was wearing his suit and shaking the wrong hands and saying the wrong things. He was sitting in the wrong counsels, and taking directions. It was his way of getting ahead. As the militancy spreading across the United States found expression in the possible Olympic boycott, for example, Jesse Owens contributed a thirty-minute video to tell the American public what was wrong with the idea. In various forums, he argued that bad as race relations were, they had been worse. He contended that he had softened the effects of race and ethnicity in Nazi Germany by his participation in the 1936 Olympic Games, a doubtful proposition when millions of people had died in and under cover of the war precisely because they were Jews or gypsies or homosexuals, or of the wrong political stripe. Over and over, unaware of the paradox, Owens contended that the Olympic Games should not be mixed with politics. He never said whether the Games could safely be mixed with morality or social justice, those concepts being different from politics, and he did not reveal how it was possible for him to manipulate the Olympic image for one purpose while denying the right to others, for other purposes.

In any case, Jesse Owens was wearing his Olympic laurels in Mexico City. He was in the city as a guest of the Mexican government and was also engaged to assist the USOC in "athlete relations." More specifically, he was there to hold the line if black athletes acted up. After Tommie and John took the stand, he was deployed. Go talk with the brothers, or words to that effect, and off he went on the afternoon after the demonstration to see if he could cool the fire, talk the rabble down. He met with approximately twenty-five athletes; most were black, but some were not. As individuals, they were diverse enough to promise a complex reaction to the events that brought them together.

Owens's message was that the Olympics should not be politicized. But he had no answer when people noticed that the Olympics were already deeply affected by politics, and he had no answer when they said that the question was not whether the Olympics should be politicized, but by whom, for what purpose, and how. Was it politics, Hal Connolly asked at this meeting, that prevented the United States from dipping its flag in the opening ceremony? Owens should have been able to answer this question, as it was unexceptional, but either he could not or would not. He attacked the speaker instead. Noting that Connolly was white, he asked him to leave the room so that he could talk to the "brothers" alone. This was the instant when the meeting defined itself. The champion of 1936 was calling the bluff of the black men with their black gloves, their black berets, and their unforgiving, often separatist rhetoric. Owens was saying, essentially, that he was the black man now, blacker than they. He was the militant who called for the ouster of the whites, and they were the ones for whom a white man was holding the floor and asking questions. If he had compromised, so also had they. Connolly's presence was the proof of it.

True, these were black men he was addressing, for the most part, and they were angry. But they were not lost. They, and not Jesse Owens or anyone to whom he reported, were driving this agenda. They were setting the issues, controlling the arguments, and deciding how best to proceed. In that context, if they decided to listen to a white man speak and to judge the temper of the man, it was not for Jesse Owens to say boo. The color of a man's skin made him neither friend nor foe. Hal Connolly could stay, said Vince Matthews. Furthermore, he added, you are not listening to what the man is saying. What is the answer to his question? John Carlos spoke, too, in favor of Connolly, who he thought should stay. With this, the meeting reached another, deeper, break point, in which the question was whether Owens would let the matter rest and get on with the meeting or hold his issue and destroy the very purpose of coming together. He would do the latter. Perhaps from his own hurt feelings or from instinct, or maybe because he was a street fighter after all and was ready to forego any charge the USOC may have given him in order to have revenge against these men, now so clearly his tormentors, people who loathed his pattern of behavior, who rejected his past, and disrespected his present, Owens turned on Carlos. The great demonstrating sprinter, he pointed out, was letting a white man speak for him! Now we see! Disorder came, as it must have done, for Owens had settled on a central issue of the civil rights battle: whether the exclusion of even well-meaning whites was a necessary step in the journey. Many of the men in the room had gone both ways on the issue, sometimes wishing to be entirely alone and other times suspecting that this was not the right choice and not one that would work. Anyway, here the issue was again, with Owens raising it, others deriding him, Connolly in the middle, and no one very happy.

Lee was at the meeting. He heard nothing that surprised him from Jesse Owens. The ploy with Connolly notwithstanding, Jesse Owens would hold no sway with this group. In truth, Lee felt sorry for Jesse Owens, the hero of Berlin now like a bear being baited. Still, the meeting was disappointing. Lee had wanted Owens to listen to the athletes, to understand what was at risk, and what was not at risk, and to deliver a message to the USOC to calm down. The demonstrations, Lee felt, were not against the Olympics, they were in favor of civil and human rights, two related matters entirely consistent with the Olympic oath. The USOC's reaction was outgrowing, in other words, the slight provocation. From Lee's view, the meeting with Owens, the controversy about Hal Connolly, the various insults that had been traded, the brinkmanship, all were normal. Owens had botched it. He had not listened. He wanted to lecture instead. He wanted to claim a prize that was out of his reach. More comically, in the middle of all the deep talk and the feisty taunts, the old Olympian had even warned the sprinters against the loss of circulation that could be caused by high, tight, black socks. Still, the governing bodies had no need to overreact. Lee had been in a year's worth of meetings. This was just one more, heightened maybe by what Tommie and John had done, and by Owens's antic, but not sufficient to change anything. This exchange was more like a stirring or a sifting of what was already in place. Feeling this way, Lee left the wasted meeting with no sense of foreboding. He would get a good night's sleep, and tomorrow he would run for the gold medal.

:

When Lee went down to breakfast the next morning, the reporters surrounded him. In a decision made after midnight of the previous evening, the USOC had given John Carlos and Tommie Smith twenty-four hours to get out of the Village. Lee was shocked. In the first minutes after hearing what the USOC had done, he repulsed an official who said hello, he pushed another nearly to the floor, and he cried and screamed aloud, not so much for the loss of his friends who, after all, had no more events to run, but against the sheer injustice of it. The marvel is that Lee was devastated. The marvel is that he was damaged at all, because he should have seen this coming and protected himself, using anticipation as a shell, a hard surface to deflect the blows that came his way and the way of his friends. He had the life for it, that's for sure. He was born poor and worked for small sums of money. He was born black in a society that valued white people. He had read of South Africa, and he knew discrimination in his own country. He had been denied apartments. He had been stared at on the streets. He had been passed by, heckled, insulted, and derided. His life was threatened so often that it was commonplace. For all these reasons and a thousand more, Lee Evans should have expected Tommie and John to get the boot. He should have expected that they would be treated harshly. But he had not expected it. He had expected the two men to be treated fairly, for there is no other way to explain the terrible pain he felt when they were not.

Among other things, the decision to oust Tommie Smith and John Carlos was a warning for those who remained, and, most particularly, for the man whose name appeared with Tommie's in every report of dissension and protest. The people who made this decision knew that Lee Evans's final was the afternoon of the announcement; they knew that the decision to throw Tommie and John out of the Village as unwanted and undesired would strike him like a bludgeon or a whip. They knew he would be angry and that he would react. Before he could run, therefore, they must have wanted to do him harm, to draw from him the reserves of his energy and to leave him spent on the track, to see him beaten. In a second pondering, after reacting to the loss of his friends, Lee understood all this. How they would have smiled to see him straggle, to see him removed from the chance for protest by running an abysmal, depleted race. There he would be on the track after the disaster: drawn, exhausted, humiliated, cried out, and alone, reduced finally to the single man he really was, and friendless.

If this result was not what the USOC intended, it was at least the predictable consequence. They had strung out Lee Evans. Lee simmered. He went over the situation time and time and time again. He was thinking about not running. He would go home with his teammates. He would turn away from a life's work and forego the near certainty of a gold medal, for this is the way he saw it. He would forfeit the chance to demolish the world record in this altitude-affected city. Like Achilles, he would leave the field and sulk in his tent. And he might have done exactly that, too, but for the intercession of three men, the first of whom was Bud Winter, who whisked Lee away, coming from the back, from nowhere, in the instant after his second altercation with an official.

:

Lee Evans believes that Bud Winter hypnotized Navy pilots in World War II, that he took men who had completed one mission and prepared them to go out for another and another, and that the techniques of relaxation that Bud used with his track men was a product of that experience. Based in part on this knowledge, Lee thinks that Bud Winter hypnotized him the critical morning in Mexico City as they started to work though the problem. Lee was not going to run. He said so. Bud said that he knew, he knew that Lee would decide what was best. Lee said that he would not run. Bud said, yes. And then the next thing Lee knew, he was relaxed, and then he was asleep. He awoke refreshed. Of course, he still wasn't going to run. The idea of staying behind while Tommie and John were thrown out of the Olympic Village chilled his blood. And then Tommie Smith and John Carlos appeared. Asked by Coach Winter to talk with Lee, Carlos took the initiative. He and Tommie had run already; now it was time for Lee to run. He must stay. Run and win. Tommie agreed.

Lee Evans would not have stayed without Tommie and John. That is what he thinks now. He would have packed his bag and left. But as it was, he decided to stay. And he decided to use his anger to build his normal fire even hotter. For days, he had been concentrating on his race. When Tommie and John left, he returned to the task with intensity. He was going to take these people who had struck such a blow at him, and he was going to strike one of his own. If they wanted to degrade him, he would be strong. If they wanted to reveal him as sullen and withdrawn, he would be true to his own nature. If they wanted to humiliate him, he would not assist them. Unavoidably, every decision changes the person who makes it. By degree, some decisions make the person stronger, some weaker, some wiser, some kinder, some more cruel, and some less capable of caring. Some decisions detach the person entirely from the prior self. This day, Lee Evans was going to become stronger and wiser and better than he had been the day before. He was going to oppose the USOC. He was going to throw force back at them. He was going to do it on the track for all the world to see. For once, the magnificent finisher, the quarter-miler with the supposed kick, was going to drive from the front. Even if he controlled nothing else on this difficult day, he would control the race. There remained, though, the matter of lane assignments, but even that concern was released when Larry James visited the room that Lee shared with Ron.

As soon as Larry entered, Lee knew what was going on. Lee said, "Oh, I can tell from the look on your face that you've got the lane assignments and yours is good and ours aren't!" With this exchange, the three men in the room were back to the pleasure of sports. Lee was still mad, but Larry had released some of the pressure by the mere act of showing up and letting the tug of a smile appear; he had made the day seem good, if only for an instant, because he had made it seem normal, the usual prerace routine of quarter-milers haggling over lanes. In the spirit of the question, Larry answered Lee, "Yes. I have two, Ron has one, and you have six." There it was. This was one of the small strokes of fate that had the potential to change everything. Ron would be handicapped by the tight turns and Lee would have Larry at his back. Larry was right to be pleased, and maybe on another day Lee would have been unhappy, but he was thinking of running hard anyway. From lane six, he could have a clean run. When Larry left, Lee looked at Ron and said, "I'm going to win that race this afternoon," to which Ron replied, "Me, too." When Ron spoke, Lee knew that something funny had been said, because two people cannot win an Olympic final, but he also knew that Ron meant it. The young man from New Jersey by way of Arizona State intended to win from lane one. As fast as Ron had been improving, the challenge was not insubstantial, and Lee marked the significance. "Now, I have to watch this guy!" he said to himself. The truth is that Lee was happy about Ron's attitude and proud of him. Then and later, Lee Evans acknowledged the debt he owed to Ron Freeman. As the two men had trained together in the late summer and fall, Lee had written the workouts, but Ron had been the one who made sure they ran them completely. For Ron, 3 x 500 meant 3 x 500, even if Lee said he was too tired. Now the conditioning was going to pay off for both of them. At least, they hoped so!

After Larry left, the rest of the day passed slowly in the usual way. Lee ate a light lunch. He relaxed as much as he could. And he rehearsed the plan. He was going to explode the first seventy meters; he was going to work the second 100 meters hard while staying relaxed. He was going to run an angry and vigorous third 100-meter stretch, and then he was going to hang on for dear life, for gold, and for the record. Then, at last, the time had arrived to leave for the stadium and make the final preparations. One thing Lee needed to do was to meet with Coach Winter. He wanted to share his plan with Bud Winter, to get whatever tempering advice the coach might give, but more centrally to etch it in stone, to make a thing from which he dared not depart for fear of later criticism. When he saw him on this occasion, Lee even gave his coach the projected splits. The coach suggested that he be more cautious, especially in the first 200. Despite his low boil, Lee agreed. He would slow the merest degree. Or maybe he wouldn't, but he would think of slowing, and maybe that would be enough to prevent a spectacular blowout on the homestretch. The last thing he wanted was to end up dangling on a line for Larry James to reel in, a terrible result for a fisherman to contemplate.

Lee and other others warmed up at the appointed time and place, and then made their way to the stadium. As the official representative of the U.S. coaching staff, Stan Wright was the shepherd. His presence could have been a source of tension,

*Coach Wright, Lee Evans, Ron Freeman, and Larry James en route.*

because some athletes criticized the coach as "old school" or a person who accommodated too often. Lee however was past that. He realized that Stan Wright had his own view of the politics— knew, for example, that the coach had never supported the boycott, and that he had expressed reservations about what Tommie and John had done. "They will regret that decision for the rest of their lives," the coach had said. But this was just sorrow, the voice of an older, more experienced man who worried about the people he valued. So, Lee was not unhappy to have Stan on hand. He was less happy with the man who showed up next. USOC President Douglas Roby came to the area just off the track to lecture the three 400-meter runners about manners. This really was outrageous. The three men were minutes from the start of the Olympic final. They were all nervous, the surest indicator being Ron's oddly twisted shorts that he was too preoccupied, at first, even to adjust. Lee was upset too; surprised by his reaction, he reminded himself that the other runners were nervous too. And the third man on the U.S. team, Larry James, might reasonably be more nervous than the other two. He was the easterner from the storied track school, posh, cool, settled in the suburbs. People had the impression that Larry James was less militant than Lee was, and by extension Ron, but Larry was just young and had not fully expressed his views. That is, he had not done so until Mr. Roby appeared. It was mild Larry James, the quiet man, who emphatically warned Stan Wright to get that man away, which Stan thereafter did. No doubt content to have done his silly and pointless task, Roby acceded.

With Roby gone, the representatives of the United States in the 400-meter final were free to do what they had come to Mexico City to do. After all the turmoil, the doubts and suspicions and anxiety, they could now run. Entering the track, the three of them were joined by finalists from other countries. The names flowed. Along came Amadou Gakou of Senegal—a poem in itself, the man and his country—and Martin Jellinghaus of Germany, Tegegne Bezabeh of Ethiopia, Andrzej Badenski of Poland, then Amos Omolo of Uganda. So many vowels for so few people! Uniformly, they were lovely names for such a brutal event, brutal especially the way Lee Evans had sworn the race would be run. The runners were on the edge of the track when Bob Beamon jumped. When it happened, Lee was bending down to adjust his practice spikes, which he was wearing after seeing Carlos slip while wearing the new Puma model. So, maybe Lee was being careful with the shoes, or maybe he was only fidgeting, but either way he was too preoccupied to give Beamon's prodigious jump more than a darting look. Lee saw the jump the way a young boy looks up to see south-flying birds go past, high, high above, but nothing that had not been seen before.

Later, the newspapers and magazines would dissect Beamon's long jump as a scientific advance, like a trip to the moon, photographs from Mars, an experiment in lightness, and a result of the correlations of drag and weight and gravity. But there was none of this from Lee at the instant. He was thinking of the Winnipeg Tip. He was thinking of his lane. He was thinking of the critical first seventy meters. He was thinking about lengthening his stride on the backstretch. He was thinking of a torrid final 100. With twenty meters to go, he was going to relax, to roll his hips, to push off in the last strides. He was going to overlook nothing, for if he overlooked anything, he would lose, because Larry James was on his shoulder and Ron was there, too, with his lean and hungry look despite the disadvantage of his tight lane. Lee was going to remember the fundamentals: looser, faster. In sum, Lee was thinking entirely and absolutely about what he was about to do in his Olympic final, for sure the only one he would ever have. The day was for accomplishment or loss. Bob Beamon had nothing to do with anything.

Of course, in Lee's response to the situation in Mexico City, there is much that marks Lee Evans as a man. More than others, he depended on concentration. He prided himself on the long period of preparation and visualization that preceded lesser races than this one. Lee's dungeon, the place to which he withdrew to prepare, is inadequate to capture the danger of what he was doing. His process was like diving more deeply than others did, and staying there longer. He would not come to the surface until he had won. In the effort, he might know pain, he might do harm, he might black out, or he might die. And he didn't care. He was going to win. If the water was dark and cold, failure was darker and colder. And yet, on this day, the most important day, the day of days, he was unsettled, lonely even as he approached the starting line. He was questioning himself and his place among others. If he put all the people he could trust inside a circle, for him to see them and take comfort from their presence, who would be there? Whom could he trust? Had he trusted wrongly in the past? Was it all and ever about race? Could he trust anyone who was not of African descent—a group that included, for instance, Dowell, Baker, Winter? Could he trust all those who were? All black people? He could trust them all? What was it? What was it that brought these things to mind now, of all times? He had friends, of course; he had people he trusted. Not everything was about race. It could not be so, surely.

He wrenched his attention back. They were setting their blocks, all of them doing the mechanical task to make sure that the job was done right, of course, that no slip would take the place of talent and providence, but also they were doing the job to gather to themselves the comfort of familiar routine. Each of them had done this thing countless times, placing, hammering, kicking, checking, striding out from, adjusting. They had done this on cinder tracks in Fresno, tartan tracks in Tahoe, in sandy soil, and on surfaces so hard they were as concrete. Now, they were here, and they were doing it again, together, tying themselves together forever. From the inside, Freeman, James, Jellinghaus, Bezabeh, Gakou, Evans, Badenski, Omolo, all of them were engaged until all of them became aware that Bob Beamon was on the track celebrating his big jump. The television showed him one minute kneeling with his hands on his face, in disbelief, and then sailing around the stadium in delight. As a result, the start of the 400 meters was delayed. Standing behind his blocks, Lee was talking to himself in irritation, Get him off the track. Get him off the track. Bob! Bob! Bob! And then he was saying, Do not worry yourself about such matters. Be relaxed. Stay calm. Be prepared. Forget about Bob, and do what you are doing.

They were called to their marks. Lee was heavy. He was angry. He was not, in the critical moment, himself. On his mark, his interior voice asked: Why do you do this to yourself? In the stands, Linda was watching. Linda knew how upset he was. She knew he was in turmoil. If he won, Linda had freed him to do what he wished: You can burn down the victory stand if you like. Do not hold back for me. Lee was the one with the reputation for harshness as a competitor, but Linda was fierce! Of course, she had put him on the spot by letting him loose. He had so many choices to make, with such imponderable consequences. Lee! Lee! Why do you do these things to yourself? Get set, the runners were told. On this last command, the favored man returned to his body. The disconsolate, questioning impostor was gone. Lee Evans smiled, as everything extraneous fell finally away. He took two deep breaths, settled in his blocks, and went with the gun. In a series of strong strides, just a few really, he took half of Badenski's stagger and surged into the race. He had never run like this—unleashed, excited, powerful, controlled. He hit the turn hard, swung left, and

*Lee swings into the homestretch, at left, while Larry and Ron surge ahead in lanes two and one, respectively.*

fought to hold himself in the lane from which he might, if he lost his attention, be drawn inside and risk disqualification. Now the runners in the two lanes outside him were falling into his wake, and he was not concerned with them and not concerned, in any conscious way, with the runners behind him either, not with Ron in lane one who said that he, too, would win, nor with Larry, whose challenge had figured to be severe. Lee was concentrating on his own work, his own relaxation, his own checklist: the chin, the neck, the shoulders, the arms, the hands, the trunk, the torso, the drive, the knee lift, the turnover, the stride length, the count. He was on the backstretch.

They would calculate the splits later, to show where Lee Evans had been in his furious charge around the track. They would time him through the 100-meter mark in 10.4 and the 200 meters in 21.1, and they would not know that he had expected to go out faster and would have but for Bud Winter's caution. They would time the 300 meters at 32.2, and then they would marvel at his homestretch. Which is to say, they would marvel if he could complete it. In that event, they could safely say that this man was the true heir to Herb McKenley; he was the blend of speed and strength that they had been looking for, the perfect man for a race of one lap! Of course, it went without saying that McKenley had buckled, but that was a small matter, really, measured against the magnificence of what the Jamaican had attempted. Lee was sprinting up this homestretch, no doubt as Herb had done, both of them, in their time, hunters turned to prey. This was a painful way to run a quarter. Having known in advance that it would be so helped only a little. To make matters worse, the effect of what he had done was by no means certain; Lee might still lose this race because Larry James was back there, a stride or two removed, no more than one mistake on Lee's part, or one stumbled stride, from the gold medal he could add to the one Charlie Jenkins of Villanova won in 1956. The smooth, elegant easterner had let Lee do the work. Now, presumably, frighteningly, he was prepared to rip the homestretch.

Cream on a dance floor, Bud Winter had said. James had dispatched Roby. He had steadied his nerves. He had been unflustered by the presence of 80,000 excited people in the stands, and untroubled by the thought of the hundreds of millions watching in homes around the world, or in the pubs and cafes and taverns where beers would be spilled in the tumble of arms and legs as patrons shouted first for one and then the other runner coming down the stretch. Larry James was as ever. The Mighty Burner indeed! Between fire and ice, James was ice, uncommonly cool under pressure with no sign of tension or straining anywhere in his motion. The young man had no business exhibiting such calm! He had not even been ranked in the United States the previous year at this distance, much less in the world, but now in the most important meters, he was streaming home. Let us give the game away, here at the very end. If the race had been ten meters longer, would James have won? Twenty? Three? How many meters more would the 400-meter race have had to have been to permit Larry James's surge to carry him past Lee Evans? No one can say. In the last five meters of the race, Lee recalled Bud's training. He pushed hard off his ankles and then he leaned, a beguilingly simple exercise.

Lee Evans slipped across the finish line in first place. In legal shoes, he had crushed the world record. His winning time of 43.86 would remain in the books nearly as long as Beamon's jump. For all the chinks in his amateur status, the minor under-the-table payments to run meets in Europe, the rumors of payouts for wearing this shoe or that, Lee was essentially a scrambler making his way. At that, he was one of the last of the kind, and his record is the more remarkable for that fact. By the time Lee's record fell, quarter-milers would replace V-ups and push-ups with specialized weight training, performance-enhancing drugs would proliferate, and money would be openly paid. Larry James was second in Mexico City with 43.97, and Ron Freeman completed the sweep from the unfair inside lane in 44.41.

Now what does one do when the award ceremony is ahead and good friends have departed? The 200-meter sprinters had left the question of demonstrations and protest delicately posed between the eliciting of sympathy, on the one hand, and damage to the Olympic Games, on the other. So far, international reaction appeared to fall the way of the protesters, especially after the ham-handed punishment meted out to the Americans, but a wrong move would tilt the affair the other way and leave the IOC the aggrieved party. All the good that had been done could be undone; against all odds, the light would be unlit and the bell unrung. This was the time that had approached. This was the time that had been on the horizon. It was time to decide. How much was a person willing to risk to preserve what Tommie and John had achieved? How much to sacrifice? Or was the game up? Would it devolve finally to the personal interests of three men who wished, at all costs, to be received as heroes by an estranged and bitter community, or the fragment of one, that had sent them forth, and Lee in particular, to burn, baby, burn? Would they, burn, baby, burn?

:

Lee and Ron and Larry garbed themselves in black berets and gloves and went to the award ceremony together. When the anthem played, they took the berets off and stood silently. When the music stopped, they raised their black fists in greeting to all those predisposed to understand the meaning of the gesture. Also, they smiled. They did not glower. They brightened the stadium

*Lee raises his closed, black fist. He is Olympic champion.*

with evident, heartfelt humanity. The three men had sought the middle way, after all. They had done no harm. Later, Lee added a slight jibe of his own, his personality peeking out. Asked about the black berets, often the symbol for the Black Panthers, he said that they were protection from the rain. Yes, that is often why a person wears a beret, not a cowboy hat or a fedora with a brim, not a sombrero or a ball cap, but tiny acornlike headgear plopped rakishly on heads made for the cafe life. Protection from the rain, indeed! And yet the reporters dutifully took his answer down.

:

Looking back after more than thirty years, the image of two black men standing in Mexico City like dual shadows of the Statue of Liberty has an elegiac quality. The men have bowed their heads, as if to mark a passing. By 1968, the old civil rights movement was coming to an end. Much of what Americans of African descent could accomplish together had been done. The opposition would retrench. Efforts would be made to divide, or destroy, voices and organizations. The people might rise occasionally together on isolated issues, but they would not experience the moral clarity that enfolded them and protected them in earlier days. Soon, even moderate academics like Daniel Patrick Moynihan would join Nixon's new administration to encourage a period of benign neglect in race relations. Funding for social programs might increase in Nixon's truncated two terms, but the attitude was sour. People were being left behind, and the civil rights struggle was moving through dusk. Largely unseen and unremarked, new foundations were being built, new economic strengths discovered, and an emerging middle class was being encouraged, but the excitement was missing, and the sense of destiny too. People were now going to talk of gray areas and gray issues and of balance and of pendulums swinging. They were going to talk and talk. White people were even going to say that black people were disenfranchising them. And they were going to mean it.

If what Tommie and John did in Mexico City was the last protest of the waning era; if it was the last universal protest emanating from a morally unambiguous, mass civil rights movement, and the last one that was a knock on an opening door and not a futile attempt to put a foot in a closing one, the two men produced a striking farewell image. The image stands among photographs showing strange fruit hanging from southern trees, alongside scenes of the burned-out church in Birmingham, Alabama; it is next to the photograph of students rolling on buses into the Freedom Summer, and there with the photograph of the young man being bitten by a German shepherd. Too, the photograph fits nicely into a montage showing Martin Luther King addressing the multitudes on the Mall in Washington, D.C. For the sake of inclusion, the picture of Tommie and John is also paired with that of Senator Robert Kennedy stunned and stricken in the basement of a Los Angeles hotel. Among these images from the civil rights movement, the photograph from Mexico City remains a singular memorial. Tommie and John rightly own that memorial. They were in the right place at the right time, and they seized the opportunity as no one who came later could do. Lee, Ron, and Larry, who did come later, also have a monument, although it is often denied them. Their monument is in the race they ran and thereafter in the wisdom to leave well enough alone. Conceivably, they could have done more. They could have become violent on the victory stand, or simply made a spectacle of their anger. But that kind of protest was not right for the day. So they did what they did. They touched, borrowed, and associated with the image of Tommie and John, but they did not intrude. They did not make a second image to compete with the first. They hoped to be understood. This is the way of young people.

Avery Brundage would later edit Tommie and John out of the official film of the 1968 Mexico City Olympic Games. There would be no picture of them on the stand, no picture of them with fists uplifted, and no picture of their dignity and their defiance. He was altering history, as best he could, as he had done at least once before when he manipulated the stories and images from Berlin in 1936. History, however, was catching up with Avery Brundage. If he had railed against Tommie Smith and John Carlos and Lee Evans and Harry Edwards in 1968, the Olympics in Munich would teach him what politics really was. But that was murder. And Tommie Smith and John Carlos murdered no one. Nor did they countenance it in the name of the Olympic ideal. Avery Brundage had done so. In 2003, the stories and revelations were rising out of Mexico City. The bodies of the many people killed in the police riot in 1968, as the city was cleaned up in time for the Games, were finally being located and the count estimated. In this way, the victims were returning from the oceans into which they had been dumped, from the common unmarked graves that held them, and from the pyres and fires that had burned them. Though Brundage and the officials in Mexico City had swept them out of time and out of history, the young people were coming home.

# .39

*All the days in all the ways
I am watching you.*

If the papers and magazines had reported that Lee and his 400-meter teammates had been cheeky or taunting or teasing in their protest, Lee would have been fine. He could have gone home to San Jose a hero. If the reports had said that Lee and the two others had provided a denouement for what Tommie and John had done, Lee would have returned to a boisterous welcome. If the reports had emphasized that the protests of Lee and Ron and Larry were hinged or connected to Tommie and John, in that event, too, Lee would have been chaired home, high again in the esteem of his friends. But a relieved press accorded to Lee other words and characterizations. Lee, said the newspapers, was exemplary, humble, and sportsmanlike. He had not acted to force his removal from the Village, nor to bring disgrace to his country. These words split Lee from his people, who had been prepared to receive a seething militant and got this instead. Tommie Smith might spend unhappy days washing cars and being trotted out to greet the customers, before setting himself right, and John Carlos might see his marriage end and his education stopped, he might scuffle in the streets and remake himself in the shape of what people said he had been, but nothing the two men experienced would match, for sadness, the empty space in which Lee Evans would find himself. But all that would happen after the games. First, Lee had a relay to run.

The early talk was that Tommie Smith would run the 1,600-meter relay instead of Vince Matthews. Indeed, Smith might anchor. That talk ended when Stan Wright concluded that Vince had earned his slot. Lingering controversy dissolved when Tommie left the Village. So, the four men who finished first at Tahoe were the team. Beginning in Tahoe and continuing in the Olympic Village, the men didn't talk of winning. Barring accident or injury, they knew that they would win. Aside from deciding to take blind passes, they did not talk much about tactics either. Instead, they talked of the final time. No jive, they sang, we will run 2:55! This was at a time when the world record was 2:59.6.

World records inch down, they eke and claw along. What these audacious fellows had in mind was a planned assault on the world record nearly as sensational as the one Bob Beamon had achieved in the long jump by serendipity. Giving each of the last three runners 0.5 advantage for a running start and taking into account the personal records for each of them, mid-2:55 seemed reasonable. What could not be predicted was how tired the runners would be. The heats and final of the relay were on the two successive days after the 400-meter final. This meant that Lee, Larry, and Ron would run six races in five days. The effect of politics and the controversy was also hard to figure. A great deal of nervous energy had been exhausted by anger and indecision, the riffling through of possibilities to find the correct ones, to say nothing of the distraction itself. In other words, however fast the four friends ran on Sunday, they would have run faster if rested and left alone.

The Americans looked tired in the heat on Saturday afternoon. They looked like they were running hard. And all they got out of it was an Olympic record of 3:00.7. It was a reminder that these were not supermen. They were just as tired as any reasonable person would have expected. Nonetheless, the performance opened up the conversation. Maybe another team could slip in, after all. The Kenyans, who finished only a tenth behind the American team in 3:00.8, looked particularly good. The question was whether they were at the limit, however much they might benefit from being born at altitude.

On Sunday evening at 4:50 p.m., the qualifying teams lined up to answer the questions: Was the United States unbeatable? Could the Kenyans surprise? Was David Hemery of Great Britain, after his stunning victory over Ron Whitney, among others, in the 400 intermediate hurdles, fast enough to bring Great Britain into contention? Was the consistency of the German team enough to win them a medal? If the United States ran well, how far down could they take the record? Running in lanes one through eight respectively, France, West Germany, Trinidad-Tobago, Italy, Poland, Great Britain, Kenya, and the United States were ready to go. In the lane for the United States was Vince Matthews.

Matthews was upset before the race even started. He had missed his medal in the individual race by failing at Tahoe, the world record he once thought he owned was long gone, first as a result of the Trials final and then the explosion by Lee Evans in the Olympic final, he was separated from his teammates by the fact that he had not run the individual event, and, as a last straw, he had the outside lane leading off, with everyone able to see how he would do against the other runners. More intimately, he had the pressure of the little song they had sung together, the one that promised 2:55. If this team were going to run that, he had to get them started. And, at last, there was more one thing: Vince was haunted by a recollection of the 1964 team. There, three members of the team had run 44s or 45s except Ollan Cassell, who had a 46. Vince was mortified by the possibility that he would run a similar, incongruent time. Set!

Matthews jumped. It would all be done again. The runners who had departed would return. They would coast, walk, or canter back to where they had been, stretch and idle a bit, then settle and await new commands, a ritual that looked the same as the one that had occurred seconds previously, but was in fact altered. Seven teams now had an advantage and one a disadvantage. The one with the disadvantage, the team that might go out with one more false twitch, was the favored team. Vince knew that his teammates were watching him closely now. They were watching him the way the owner of a house does when he finds a burglar half in and half out of an upstairs window. If Matthews jumped again, they were all gone! The relay and the 2:55 and the world record and the laughing and the jiving would be washed away as surely as paper wrappers in a rainstorm. With seconds like minutes, and then again, mere flashes, the race was set once more.

In the tension, no one was waiting for the gun. For the 80,000 in the stands and the hundreds of millions tuned in, the blank interval between the getting set and the going now was all about the leadoff

American. Would he do it again? Would he jump? Would he write his name alongside that of Budd and Norton? Would Vince Matthews prove to be a person capable, indeed guilty, of throwing away a perfectly good gold medal because of a nervous tick? Was he going to leave early? And take his mates with him?

Vince Matthews was capable of extraordinary running. He had proved that in previous races, and he would later confirm his ability, indeed he would later be an Olympic gold medalist in his own right, but this was a difficult day. He did get off on the second attempt, but he did not have his usual vigor. Far too early, his legs went rubbery and he had to push rather than flow along. He was driving the nail blow by blow, and covering the distance stride by stride. He was fast, for sure; he would never be anything but fast, even on his worst day, but on this day, one that was important to him, one that he had hoped would spare him any comparison with other relay runners who had seemed not to belong with faster teammates when splits were calculated, he was not fast enough. In the last strides of the opening leg, Daniel Rudisha-Matesi of Kenya went past Vince Matthews. The opening legs were 44.6 to 45.0.

This was only a slip. Perhaps, for Vince, the question of pride was involved. But even that wound was assuaged when Ron Freeman blasted the second leg in 43.2, faster than anybody had ever run the distance. Kenya was twenty meters behind when Ron passed to Larry. After Larry responded with a quicksilver 43.8 of his own, the victory was secure, and so also was the world record. The remaining question was by how much the record would be broken, a matter to be determined by Lee Evans who, however, was mighty tired. He was too tired to bring his team to 2:55. The new world record holder for the open distance managed a solitary 44.1, normally scintillating running, but modest compared to what he might have run. Still, the relay was complete; the world record was established. The final time was 2:56.1, which was slower than the song but still fast enough to destroy the old standard. Kenya finished second in 2:59.6, and West Germany closed for third in 3:00.5.

Afterward, the four Americans celebrated quietly. Asked whether he wanted to take a victory lap, Lee demurred. Too bushed, he said. As to the award ceremony and the standard question of action and

*A weary Lee finishes the world record that would carry him
and his three teammates into history.*

reaction, the men had a bit of fun but did not stir controversy.
They merely tucked their gloved hands under their sweats and
pulled them out for surprise. But, by now, a fist was just a fist, and
not a call to arms, and the men were left laughing, even as the boos

and hisses came down yet again from the more excited fans. Texans, one of the relayists opined. All joking aside, the animosity directed toward the athletes was serious. In the mailbox at the Olympic Village, the death threats still came in. By the conclusion of the week of competition, Lee could count fifteen or twenty of them directed to him. Sometimes, the correspondents named a time and a place, and sometimes they did not, leaving the cloud to over-hang every moment. Lee did not feel safe even on the victory stand. He smiled on the dais, he said in answer to one questioner, because it is always more difficult to shoot a smiling man.

# .40

*Keep your eyes down, and walk on by.*


In this circus, he was not a star, but a foil for the star. The star was Martin McGrady. It was the winter of 1970, more than a year having passed since the Olympics, and Lee Evans was yet again chasing Martin in Martin's favorite distances on indoor tracks around the country. Three times he raced him and three times he lost. The press was calling McGrady the chairman of the boards, in part because he dominated the great Lee Evans, whose last chance to beat McGrady would come at the National AAU indoor meet in New York City at the end of February. Lee needed this victory. He needed a springboard for a successful 1970. More to the point, he needed the win so he could put 1969 firmly behind him.

The disappointment started immediately upon his return from Mexico City in October 1968. As a double gold medalist and the holder of two new world records, one in his own name and one from the relay, he was supposed to be welcomed home with a celebration. This was not an unreasonable expectation. Larry James got a parade, for example, and Ron Freeman a good job. By contrast, he had no parade. He got a cold shoulder, and the job they offered him was an insult. He initially thought that the San Jose police department wanted him to work with young people to lower the dropout rate. On closer evaluation, he realized that the police really wanted him to stop the riots. Next thing you know he would be the well-dressed black man encouraging other black folk to "cool it." He backed away fast, but not fast enough to stop the publicity that made him look like a man being used. Worse, the publicity made him look like a man willing to be used.

Tommie was out there somewhere. In some ways, Lee could envy his fellow Olympian. On matters of race, Tommie Smith was on one side of the line, and everybody knew what side that was. This perception was in some ways a response to the decision by the USOC to throw Tommie from the Village. If the USOC had taken similarly stern action against Lee, Ron, or Larry for what they did, or against Ralph Boston for receiving his medal barefoot, or Bob Beamon for rolling his pants up to show black socks, they too would have been honored. As it was, all of these people lacked the credential Tommie Smith and John Carlos had. They were not victims. As a result of his prominence, moreover, Lee was a special case.

Lee, some people said, had straddled the race line. He had not been sufficiently militant in Mexico City. He had not burned the stand down. He had not gotten himself disqualified from future Games. As annoying, Lee had acknowledged a debt of gratitude to his white coach, Bud Winter, in Mexico City, and had dedicated his victories at the Olympics not only to all the black people in the United States, as he had said after the 400, but also to his many "white friends," an aside he added when candor overcame discretion. And finally, in the list of offenses, Lee had smiled, not once but several times. He had enjoyed himself. He had conveyed joy. All in all, this was no way to conduct a protest! What kind of Black Panther laughs on camera?

:

Lee had a stark view of all this. He smiled in Mexico because he was happy. He felt grateful to Coach Winter, so he said so; and he did have white friends. So why was any of this a problem? The business of friendship was particularly troubling. Did his critics not have such friends? No such associations? They lived in a cordoned off and controlled world free of white people? They had no white people who had been kind to them, and none to whom they had been kind, they worked for none, and none who worked for them? They loved and appreciated no few white people in the turmoil of life? None loved them? Did the talk of a separate black community mean that black people had to pretend that such a world existed and that they lived in it?

Malcolm X had once said that whites and black could not live together without violence, and that therefore they must separate, but he changed his mind and then black men killed him. So, no, Lee was not a separatist. Lee was in the world as it existed, although his version was idealized to the extent he wanted everyone treated with respect and care. That was how far his radicalism went. As to the personal quality of his critics, they merely made him angry. These were the people who did nothing for themselves, but pushed others forward. They took no risks; they published and spoke no recorded words. They stood in front of no crowds. Rather, they watched and judged others in the cover of anonymity.

Lee was furious. He was also frustrated, because there was no remedy. If a person wanted to defend himself from damage to his reputation, to whom should he speak? To the streetlight? To the mailman? On the corner? A few mumbles let loose in the course of a long walk? For a year, Lee had stood shoulder to shoulder with Tommie. He was the one who had done that, not any of these. He had said what was on his mind. He had called for freedom and fairness for his people. He had accepted the indignities. He had borne lightly the insults and offenses written and said about him. He had received the regular threats on his life. He had smiled, indeed laughed, in the face of the danger. He had gone about his business without compromising his beliefs or his associations. He had run, finally, at the Olympics and won twice. This is what he was intended to do.

Lee had come from the fields and from schools that ignored him on account of race. He had made himself a better student by his own effort. He had read, thought, and considered. Cogito, ergo sum? Lee Evans was at least one answer. He was a man. As he saw it, this record was sound. Now that people turned away from him, he was hurt and he was surprised. But he could not see that he had made mistakes, nor that he had moved a foot to the wrong side of any line. None of this helped. He still had no way to make things better. All he could do was wait, and hope for a long life. He needed the long life so that attitudes could shift and he might be understood.

Meanwhile, Lee had his senior year to complete at San Jose State. While strangers might doubt him, his teammates did not. He was selected to serve as captain for the San Jose State team for the 1969 track season. The job figured to be important because Coach Winters was thinking of a national championship. Carlos was eligible and fit. Sam Davis, Olympic gold-medalist Ronnie Ray Smith, and Kirk Clayton rounded out the sprinter corp. Future Olympian John Powell had the discus. Martin McGrady might run for the Spartans, and George Carty was an excellent hurdler. If several of these men could win events, San Jose had a chance.

Lee took his responsibility seriously, and this was a distraction. But he was also a little careless with his own preparation. His weight, for example, edged up from 162 to 167, and from time to time, he did not concentrate with intensity. He was making himself vulnerable, a fact that was not initially obvious. Prior to the NCAA outdoor championships, Lee won important races in Long Beach, at the California Relays, and at the Kennedy Games. At Kennedy, he beat Southern Cal's Edesel Garrison who, along with UCLA's Wayne Collett, figured to be national contenders. Beyond those two, Lee was not much concerned. He barely noticed when LSU freshman Al Coffee ran a 45.6 in his first effort; nor did he look with more than desultory interest at Texas A&M's Curtis Mills, who ran 46.1 on the University of Kentucky's new, soft all-weather track.

Of course, Larry James was active. Larry had his usual Penn Relays to open up; he ran four quarters in various relays: 45.3, 45.1, 45.8, and a 47.2 leadoff leg in a heat. He also won competitive races at the Martin Luther King Freedom Games in Philadelphia—a meet supercharged by the fast sprinting and showmanship of John Carlos—and the IC4A. James was not entirely himself, however. At the IC4A, he ran a fast first 110, and then struggled in with a 46.6. Twenty minutes after the race, observers said that he was still struggling for breath. "I wanted to try this [the quick opening 110] because I've never done it before. I want to learn to run a faster first half of the race." This tactic would be interesting to Lee Evans, but not a matter of concern. He would follow any pace and then he would win.

:

The University of Tennessee hosted the NCAA outdoor track and field championships on the weekend of June 19-21, 1969. With temperatures steady in the mid-eighties and sultry, Lee spent a good deal of time and energy worrying about his teammates. The points kept draining away. George Carty was a nonscoring seventh in the hurdles, Kirk Clayton was disqualified for running out of his lane in the 100, Ronnie Ray Smith misjudged the finish line in a 220 semifinal and failed to advance, shot-putter Richard Marks had foul trouble, and steepler Darold Dent, like Carty, finished seventh. And then, of course, there was Carlos. Carlos was supposed to win the 100 and 220 and anchor a winning relay, but no matter what he was supposed to do, he was always John Carlos, and that opened a world of possibilities.

So, Lee was chasing John and the others around a bit. At the same time, he was keeping an eye out for Coach Winter, to make sure that he was working well with the coach, and he was keeping another (the last available) eye out for Kansas, a team that had Jim Ryun, a trio of excellent throwers, and a supporting cast. With all this on his mind, Lee never did give his race much thought. The customary hours of concentration on his race fell to catch as catch can. Nonetheless, the slightly oversized, scattered Lee Evans told reporters that he not only expected to win, but set the world record for the imperial distance to go along with his metric time from Mexico City.

:

After easily qualifying, he lined up for the final in lane three with Larry James in lane four. He had no intimation of an approaching calamity. After a delay for television and a false start, the race was underway, and James put his new tactic to work. He went through the 220 in 21.0, a sufficiently quick split to give him a commanding lead, which however he lost shortly to a hard-charging Al Coffee, who was fast enough and new enough not to realize the snare into which he had fallen. Meanwhile, Lee Evans was trawling. He was happy to be in the speedy wake, and picking up the people who came back to him, as James did and then Coffee. Lee was even with the two leaders ten yards into the homestretch, and his victory seemed assured. The Olympic champion could accelerate the last 100 yards in his usual way, and that would be that. Or, it would have been, but for Curtis Mills, the first black athlete to compete on an athletic scholarship at Texas A&M. About this race, Mills had said: "You wait and see. My name will be in the papers." My name will be in the papers?

Time was running out. If Mills wanted to erase the headline that said, "Lee wins," and to replace it with words that said, "Unknown Aggie upsets Oly champ," he needed to move immediately. Mills unwound his tall frame into a sprint.

Lee never knew what was happening until it was too late to do anything about it. One minute he had his victory secure, and the next he was walking off the track with a "who-what" look on his face. Lee had eased slightly approaching the line, something he never did, and a flash of maroon stole past him. This was a very bad result, of course, but worse news soon came. Taking advantage of Lee's lapse, Mills not only beat him, but broke Tommie Smith's world record of 44.8 by a tenth. Curtis Mills was the world record holder. At the NCAA, Lee was credited with 45.1 and second place. He might as well have been kicked in the teeth.

:

Lee was mad at himself for the loss in the NCAA, but at least San Jose, assisted mightily by John Carlos, cobbled together enough points to win the national championship. SJS beat Kansas by a point after Villanova's Liquori outkicked Ryun in the mile, and Ryun dropped out of the three mile, in which he had been entered to pick up a few extra points. The team title aside, Lee's attention was fixed on Curtis Mills. All he wanted was for the Aggie to show up the next week for the AAU meet, where the few extra pounds he was carrying, the relative lack of intensity he had exhibited, and the burden of being an underdog to the new world-record holder would mean nothing. He wanted revenge, and he wanted it right now.

"If I run all summer," the NCAA champion said, "I won't be ready when the Aggies start competing in indoor meets." And Texas A&M coach Charlie Thomas added, "He still has two collegiate seasons remaining and those guys wanting to run against him will get their chances later." In other words, Mills was going to pick up his marbles and go home. He would not run the AAU.

:

At the AAU meet, James, who had fallen to fifth in the homestretch at the NCAA, again went out fast. Lee Evans again chased him down. While Larry faltered, Lee held on to win his fifth straight national, open championship in his event, a fact that could not dislodge the shard caught in his throat. No Curtis Mills!

During the remainder of the 1969 outdoor season, Lee continued to run, he continued to manufacture intensity, and he continued to win. Notably, he won for the United States against the USSR and the Commonwealth, and he won again for his country against a team from Europe. In the latter race, Lee ran 44.9 for meters, a time that becomes more (or less) impressive with knowledge that Lee eased in the last strides, unable to persuade himself to run the entire distance. Lee was entering a stage of life neither here nor there. He was not the unconquerable man he had been earlier, but neither was he substantially changed. Rather, he was changed just that tiny bit that makes all the difference at the highest levels. Be that as it may, he had a right be the world's number one ranked 400 meter/440 yard performer for 1969, as he had been in '66, '67, and '68. But the rankers thought otherwise. They put Curtis Mills first.

By the time the rankings were announced, the indoor season was already underway, and Lee was thinking of 1970, which he hoped would be better. The first job was to deal with Martin McGrady. After a season in which both broke indoor world records, Martin for 500 meters and Lee for 500 yards, they were ready for the AAU meet in New York City where each would run the 600.

Lee could not know. But it would not have surprised him. He was in for a wild ride in New York. It would be typical for the city. You get in the cab. The driver seems fine. You check his credential. And all of a sudden, he roars away from the curb and you are hanging onto your hat, maybe looking for a handle, anything for additional purchase on the turns. Then the car stops and you walk unsteadily away, exclaiming to yourself: What in the world!?

:

McGrady was determined to lead at the AAU. Later, he said that he had decided, for once, to "be the rabbit," but this shows a basic misunderstanding about how a rabbit is supposed to act. McGrady started like a rabbit, all right, grabbing the early lead and settling into a serene dash, but from that point on, he was a poor imitation of the general article. He forgot to tail off. A real rabbit would have stepped aside or slowed dramatically or given the race a kind of doff. McGrady did none of those things, but just kept sprinting into the turns and out of the turns and down the stretches, and so on, with the momentum building with each of the several passing laps. All the while, he knew that a man was on his shoulder. He knew, as well, that the man was Lee Evans, and he must have known that the presence of so strong a figure was designed to cause panic, like having a barbarian at the gates, but McGrady was undisturbed. He was doing what he was doing, Lee was doing what he was doing, but Lee was doing what he was doing a stride or two arear and so long as that was the case, all was to the good. If the two men had run all night, Lee might eventually have gotten past Martin, but that was not the deal. All Martin had to do was stay where he was for the allotted 600 yards, which he did. Martin McGrady won the national championship in 1:07.6, a time much faster than his old world record of 1:09. For a person who dominated an event the way McGrady did, this was like a man turning in an old watch for a new one, even though the old one was still good.

As for Lee, he had worked hard throughout. He had given himself the chance to win. He had run so close, so strongly that many of the excited fans doubtless believed that he would seize the lead for himself at any instant, or at least try to. If he could do it, there would be the rejoinder from McGrady. If he failed, Evans would hang up on a curve and sputter, or he would fade on one of the short stretches. Either way the race would be exciting, except that nothing like that happened, and, indeed, it was unlikely to happen after the race assumed its first order. Lee had been pinned for good in the initial strides when Martin went ahead and he slipped in behind. All the other steps in the race were futile, and that was true even though Lee's second place time of 1:08 was a full second under the old record. Far from an occasion for satisfaction, Lee's fast time served only to bring stronger praise to the winner. It didn't matter.

Lee had done what he could do in New York. He lost. Anyway, it was over. The circus was closing down, the big top folded and stored. The indoor season was complete. Martin McGrady could now fade away until next winter, when Lee could take another shot at him and his odd, overlong distance. In the meantime, Lee could reestablish himself as the finest quarter-miler in the world, outdoors, where races counted—in the ordinary estimation—for more than a weekend's amusement.

# .41

*Try signing this name in the register.*

John Smith is no name. It is the absence of a name. It is a pretend name. It is a name a person signs or says when he doesn't want another person to know his real name.

:

All this is true unless the John Smith one has in mind is an athlete, in which case knowledgeable people recognize John Smith as a fine quarter-miler. Most fans think instantly of the 1972 Olympics in Munich when an injury prevented him from finishing the final of the 400 meters, a fact that started in motion events that ended with Vince Matthews and Wayne Collett idling on the victory dais, getting themselves sent home and costing the United States the certain gold medal that would have followed in the 1,600-meter relay, on which Lee Evans was prepared to run. Oh, *that* John Smith! But no one knew that in June 1970 at the AAU meet. Before the final of the 440, for which Lee Evans was favorite, Mr. John Smith was occupying the cultural spot reserved for people with his name. He was unknown. Nonetheless, he beat the previously undefeated Lee Evans to win the national AAU title. And it wasn't so much that he had won, as the way he had done it that made an impression. While Lee was handling Larry James, Curtis Mills, and Wayne Collett, among others, John Smith ran him down in the homestretch. This never happened. Just like that, with a few strides from a man named Smith, 1970 became the second year in a row in which Lee lost a national title to an upstart.

For the rest of the season, Lee won every race he entered, a series of performances sufficient for him to regain his ranking as the number one quarter man in world, the slot he had grudgingly ceded to Curtis Mills in 1969. In perception, however, the many victories and the yearly acknowledgement barely registered. Because memory seeks the exceptional, the season remained the one in which the legend from Mexico City, the world-record holder, this most competitive man, Lee Evans, lost the national championship. The reckoning is changed only a little by an awareness that Lee Evans knew John Smith before the AAU, that he considered him a close friend, that he later said that if he had to lose to anyone, only John Smith would do, and that he considered John the future of the event.

Initially, Lee said that the "future" would begin at the end of the year because he planned to stop competing, but he changed his mind and decided to run in 1971, a year that turned out to be the one in which his marriage came apart. He ran well early, missed the AAU because of injury, came back to run moderately well later in the summer, and finally earned a top-ten spot in the world rankings for the year. But what is any of that to a man with Lee Evans's credentials, except a tailing off, an early reminder that the days were passing, and he, like everyone else, had a measured number of them. Lee tried, nonetheless, to will himself through an Olympic year in 1972. If he could get to the line, he would be defending champion at Munich. Unfortunately, he could not do that. He was no longer a man lighted with ambition, no longer the young man who knew that he would never lose a big race, no longer, even, the man who would die a figurative death before submitting. Rather, he looked like a man who didn't know whether he wanted to keep running. Stan Dowell, who returned to coach Lee for the season, captured Lee's fragility as the season began:

*Started Lee today on the first track workouts . . . The day was cold and windy, and I arrived 30 minutes late. Lee looked so alone standing on the track at San Jose State; nobody else was around.*

In the days that followed, the diary showed an athlete struggling. He had a cold. He needed vitamin C. He was tired. He was

disinclined. He was distant. He was unenthusiastic. He didn't want
to run the workout in its entirety. He wanted to do other workouts
than the ones scheduled. And then, for days on end, he fired up and
ran with intensity only to have the flame flicker again. Even when
Lee won races, something was different. At the Cow Palace in San
Francisco in February, for example, Lee finally beat Martin
McGrady at 600 yards. "Hot damn, he did it," Stan wrote:

*We walked around the Cow Palace and talked strategy. "Run your
own race and kick off his shoulder," and it worked! Lee hung on
and at the gun lap McGrady had a 2 yard lead. Lee swung wide on
the last turn and had a tremendous kick to the tape. Lee won by
inches in 1:10.3 (meet record). The quiet look of satisfaction on
Lee's face was something I haven't seen for some time.*

He hadn't seen it because his athlete had been drifting away. The
long-sought victory over Martin was misleading, like a man
grabbing a root or a branch on his way down a slope. In the midst
of this difficult period, and inextricable from it, a personal tragedy
occurred when his beloved brother Dayton died. Lee mourned
deeply. He could honor him in the season. He could dedicate races
to him. He could search for spiritual meaning and resonance. But
the loss of Dayton was a heavy burden added to the disheartening
list that included, and arguably began with, the way he had been
treated upon returning from Mexico City.

:

For Lee's sake, then, let us make a break with all of this. Cut the
chronological narrative of 1972 to the essence. Indoors, Lee beat
McGrady again at the Millrose Games. He then added the indoor
AAU title, which Martin did not contest. Thereafter, he ran an
early-season 44.6 for yards and beat Wayne Collett by inches. He
also won Mt. SAC, the West Coast Relays, and Cal, but he lost at
the King Games, at Compton, and at Vons. On June 17, he won his
fifth outdoor AAU title. Then, of course—because in hindsight this
seems inevitable—he got injured. He got injured at the worst time
to have an injury in an Olympic season. He got hurt just before

the U.S. Olympic Trials, which began on June 29 in Eugene, Oregon. First, Lee was sore, then he had a cramp in his leg, and then he had pain behind the knee. Because this injury is a farewell, of sorts, the diary should tell the story without gloss. The words are those of Stan Dowell:

*7/6: First day of trials. 7:00 p.m.—46.8 (24.0). Strided out first 220 in 24.0 (leg hurt, so he turned off sprint) and kicked like hell last 220 (22.8) to place 3rd in heat! Right ham hurts behind the knee!*

*7/7: Ran 45.4 at 1:20 to qualify for 7:30 heat. This is the tough day! Came back and ran 45.0. John Smith was 5-6 yards ahead off the turn. Lee lifted and passed JS to win by three yards.*

*Note: When I arrived at Eugene, I found Lee with a lack of self-confidence! Why? His leg was numb and he had no control for his first 220. The trainer worked on the leg for a ham pull. Gave Lee muscle-relaxers every 3 or 4 hours. No help—what is wrong?*

*We ate together about 6 hours before the final. First time I ever heard Lee say, "I wish the race was over now." Lee warmed up and looked loose—but I could feel he was not really ready to push a 44.0 race.*

*The dumb trainer said, five minutes before he walked to the blocks, "If it starts to go..." and he put a ray of doubt in Lee's mind.*

*Final: Lee was in lane six and had Collett [in lane eight] to key on. Lee went out very conservative and was 10 yards behind the early leaders at 300. My heart sunk!! Then he started to rally about 100 yards from the tape. He ran on guts and a half-numb leg. He passed everybody and almost nailed Vince for the third spot. First time he ever placed 4th in the quarter in his life.*

*1  44.1 Wayne Collett*
*2  44.3 John Smith*
*3  45 [44.9] Vince Matthews*
*4  45.1 Lee*

*Collett ran the greatest race of his life. 20.6 first 200? Well, Lee made the 1600 meter team. He didn't even care about this.*

In not caring about the relay, Lee was wise. He would never run in Munich. Through the combination of injury and International Olympic Committee discipline, he would have no teammates to run with. In the Olympic final, John Smith ran with a bad leg and had to stop midrace; Vince and Wayne then ran to gold and silver, but subsequently drew the ire of Avery Brundage for their performance on the victory stand. Here is the way *Track and Field News* described the aftermath of Vince Matthews's greatest triumph:

*So exactly what happened up there? (1) Their apparel drew criticism. Both had their sweat tops open, Matthews with an old gray t-shirt beneath. Collett wore neither sweat pants nor shoes, carrying his footgear with him. (2) After the medals were presented, Collett jumped onto the top rung with Matthews. (3) The pair did not exactly maintain the status quo while the anthem was playing. Matthews put his hands on his hips, smiled, talked to Collett, scratched his nose, looked around twice, scratched his chin twice, generally fidgeted, and folded his arms. Collett also talked to Matthews, while neither looked at the flag but stood sideways to it. (4) Upon leaving the stand, Matthews twirled his gold medal around his finger by the chain. (5) Collett later emerged and gave a 'black power salute.'*

Brundage said that what happened was disgusting. Out the two men went. With Matthews and Collett gone and with Smith injured, only Lee remained from the intended United States 1,600-meter team. Under the rules then governing substitution, there was no way to put a representative team on the track. Lee Evans's third gold medal was gone by the hair on Vince Matthews's chinny chin chin; gone by the twirl; by the T-shirt, the shorts, and the absence of shoes.

Lee's gold medal was gone with the hopping about, with the casual conversations, and with the salute at the end, this last item the dollop of political expression that dovetailed it into what was happening at these Games. The plain fact is that Munich, no less than Mexico City, was churned by the politics of race, but on a grander scale. Two weeks before the Games, the African Sports Council, which represented most of the African nations for Olympic purposes, threatened to withdraw all the African nations unless Rhodesia was expelled. Although Rhodesia's participation had been negotiated and approved, the IOC could not risk a mass withdrawal, so Rhodesia was removed from the list of participating nations.

Of course, Lee was a keen observer of the African situation. He was also prepared to lead a U.S. response if Rhodesia competed. But that was not necessary with the IOC capitulation. Otherwise the Munich Games mark an insistent, acknowledged end of innocence for the world's most famous athletic and social festival. It was one thing to have blood in the water-polo pool in 1956 as the Hungarians and the Soviets traded blows, and another to have Tommie, Lee, and John use politics as an expressive device in Mexico City, but when the Palestinians used the occasion of the Olympic Games to murder eleven Israeli athletes and coaches as well as a German policeman, a point had been reached from which there was no return. Not even a man as willfully ignorant as Avery Brundage could misunderstand the meaning of what had happened, although he could and did insist, as ever, that the Games must go on. But his Games were shrouded now in black and were gloomy for the present and the future.

As for Lee, his career as an amateur athlete was drawing to an end. Before the next outdoor season opened, he would sign with a professional track circuit. While it lasted, he would run well. But the circuit did not last long, and therefore neither did Lee's career. After a couple of years, in which he won many races but not much money, his professional experience was finished. Lee retired from the track with two Olympic gold medals. He held the world record in the 400 meters, owned or shared a total of eleven world records, and had a reputation as one of the supreme competitors in the history of the sport. For the long period between 1966 and 1972, it was impossible to consider the 400 meters without thinking first of Lee Evans. He ran in a tangle of arms and legs. He had to concentrate to run a straight line. His arrival was imperiled. The result was often in doubt. But in the years of his prime, he almost always finished first.

Because he won so many races, his career has a fixed quality. Even in critical races that he won by the thickness of a singlet, a different result is difficult to imagine. But Lee Evans competed at a time when the United States produced dozens of world-class quarter men, any one of whom, on the days he won championships, could have beaten him. That they did not is the history Lee wrote. Over the years, friends and fans sought a psychological explanation for Lee's desire. They found it in his esteem, which they said was low. They found it in the way he had been treated when he was young, and they said that had been hurtful. They found it in the experience of his people, which was unjust. They found it in his father's stories and his brothers' examples and in his mother's irreplaceable love. Perhaps it is easier, and more certain, to say that Lee was looking for home. He was forever searching for the single place where he could relax and feel at peace. For him, as it happened, home was a circle, a single circuit of the track to be defended at all costs.

Time was passing, however, through every race in every season. Lee could not stay forever young, always fast, and always strong. He needed to find something else. In this critical analysis, he was a man of two worlds, the America where he was born and the Africa from which his people had been taken. As far back as Mexico City, he was enticed by the prospect that the African nations could produce sprinters as well as distance runners, and hoped he might coach there. On the advice of fellow Olympic gold medalist Mal Whitfield, who was already established in Africa, Lee decided to delay until his education was complete and his running days were done. By 1975, the time had come. After a stint at Essex College in New Jersey, Lee left. Rather, Lee returned. With few interruptions, he spent the next decades coaching in Nigeria, Cameroon, Qatar, and Saudi Arabia. In addition to national coaching responsibilities, he gave seminars, lectures, and clinics widely. This is the way Lee exhausted his remaining youth and the first years of his middle age. This is the way he honored his heritage and reached, as nearly as possible, back through the generations to find himself and to contribute.

Lee could never be African, of course. That experience had been severed from him hundreds of years before he was born. But he

311

could be of Africa. He could receive from it and give to it. That would have to be enough for one man's life.

# two epilogues and a dream

*The first exaggerates the importance of a single day.*
*The second makes short shrift of Lee's many years in Africa.*
*The dream is not perfect, but it is not a nightmare.*

The year is 2003. Lee Evans has taken a job as the head track coach at the University of South Alabama. On a day in the spring, he is doing what track coaches do. He is standing in the center of a green field. He has a clipboard on which he is making notes. The throwers are throwing, the vaulters are vaulting, and the jumpers are jumping. The jumpers are especially hard to overlook. They are posing, dashing, measuring, rising, and landing. They kick up sand and ostentatiously brush themselves off. On the track, the sprinters and middle-distance runners are running repeated intervals. Broken into groups they are taking off at different times from different places on the track, and finishing at different places on the track. Every now and again, they pass each other, resting or sprinting. Sometimes they acknowledge each other and sometimes they don't.

Stan Dowell, who has joined Lee as an assistant, is monitoring the men. Dowell is smaller than the imagination makes him, but he is still fit, and imposing. When he calls the splits, the words have an authority, like they really mean something else, something like "get moving," for example. Women are on the track as well. One of the women is from Ireland or Wales or Scotland or one of those tiny countries with an attitude. The woman from etc. is leading other women in long intervals, and the line of them stretches a fair way along the track. Nearby, the women sprinters have finished their workout and are off to the side, near the building where the equipment is stored, speaking conspiratorially, in whispers.

Occasionally, one of the women reaches out and softly touches another, like a tap on the shoulder, and then all of them react. One thinks: They are talking about their boyfriends. One thinks this because the women are laughing. On the infield, perhaps 200 feet away, other women are clustered. Several are throwing a weighted ball, while others stretch idly. In another area, a woman from Africa, who lived with her family in Paris before coming to run with Lee, is near tears and surrounded by teammates. Her mother's watch is missing, a fact she discovered when she was packing to leave, switching spikes for flats and retrieving sweats and T-shirts.

It is not twilight, not in the South, not in the spring when the afternoons are long and night delayed, but the workout is coming to an end. The movement of the athletes calls to mind a migration across a wide plain. Singly and together, the students join Lee as he walks slowly in the direction of the modern field house where he has his office.

A quiet young man comes up, ducking his head as students for generations have done. He hems and haws before he tells the coach that he has fallen behind in a course and is thinking of dropping it. Lee now looks into the young man's face. In a firm but respectful way he talks about eligibility and scholarship. He tells the fellow that he needs to work harder, and he wonders if a tutor would help. Chastened, the man retreats. Maybe he will drop the course later, but not without additional thought.

A woman runner, who is notable for thinness and lightness of foot, sees an opportunity and approaches. She is flirtatious, there is no way around it, the slight tilt to the head, the wide eyes and smile, the shamble of crossed feet and rocking. Perhaps she is incapable of acting any other way in the peculiarity of her circumstance. She is young, healthy, and pretty. Long accustomed to this, Lee ignores the woman's manner. He talks to her about her training. He talks to her about her family. He redirects her. She has approached a boundary and been turned away. When a teammate comes along, the two walk away together, talking about food. Lee is alone for only a minute before the woman who has lost her mother's watch arrives, as inevitably she would. Her eyes still brimming with tears, she tells the coach about the watch and about

314

her mother. She is talking about lost time. What would a girl from Paris talk of but that?

By now she is convinced that the watch has been stolen. Lee talks to the young woman the way a man would who has lost a lot of watches. Lee says that it is possible that the watch has been taken, but maybe not. The watch may reappear. The watch-losing woman is not happy, of course. She will be happy only when she gets her watch back. But as she leaves she is pleased to have the scrap of hope that the older man has offered.

The phone rings the instant Lee enters his office. Before answering, he has just time to lay down his clipboard and find a place on the floor for the starting blocks he has been carrying. The call is from the mother of an athlete Lee has dismissed from the team. Lee has given the athlete many chances, but the mother is still angry about it. Lee is hearing words that are meant for the mother's child. He tells the mother what she does not want to know.

:

Lee is proud of the time he spent in Africa. On the first day that he was there, in the country of his new residence, there was a coup. That is Africa for you. A person knows that when he (or she, as may sometimes be the case) goes to Africa, things happen! Even when they do not happen, the imagination rages with possibility, for beauty and splendor, and tumult, and violence and serenity and natural wonder, and for the effect and force of oppression and resistance, for the pull of a continent, split into nations by borders that may or may not have meaning to the people who live inside them. Anyway, on Lee's first day there, his country was in turmoil, and then it settled down. Lee stayed and prospered. By the time of the 1976 Olympics, he was a coach of the Nigerian team. The team traveled by plane to Canada, but when they got there, they found that the African nations were going to boycott rather than run with people who entertained the apartheid South African regime. The undying issue was bubbling again, and this time the Africans acted. Everyone seemed surprised that so many wonderful athletes would refuse to run and jump and throw, but they had. That was what it was like. The expression is old, the one that says that there is always something new from Africa. This time it happened to be a certain balky recondite feeling that African people should not be denied a fair opportunity to live freely in Africa. That is a very very odd thing for people to think, or at least it has been for centuries. After all the years, Lee returned to the states from Africa because he needed to put his economic situation in order. He also wanted to see what the wide opportunities were. Still, he misses Africa. One day he may go back. Anyway, that is enough of this. One man cannot explain Africa to another man, much as Lee has tried.

:

Lee is the head coach of a university in Alabama, funded by the State of Alabama. He is surrounded by young men and women for whom he is at least partially responsible. Some of the young people are of African descent; many are of European descent. Every day, these students talk to each other, they run together, and they share goals. In fact, they share lives. They do not think, often, about a time when what they are doing would have been unthinkable. Of course, they know it. But they do not *know* it, and that is good. Once upon a time, the coach of this Alabama team lived in a different world. This man's father, who was from Louisiana but lived in California, did not want, ever, to go back south. Jim Crow down there, he said. The son saw that much and more in his youth, and he grew angry. He was by nature a quiet boy, and he was on his way to becoming a quiet man. But his anger required expression, and for that he needed a voice, and for that he needed to change, and change he did. He spoke often and loud, and suffered the reporting of his words. He enjoyed the vitriol of people who hated him and the respect of people who loved him. He was in danger, that much was evident. In the strangeness of the time, the fact that he was in harm's way was his greatest strength and also the source of his well-being. And then the turn came. There is little to be said about that. People do get lost in the folds of time, and no one is ever promised a just life. But Lee Evans has earned the right to solitude, if ever he chooses it. When he was young, he was in the movement. Two generations before his current students were born, he did his part to change their lives. He was one part among the tens of thousands of parts. This seems a modest boast only if a person forgets what it was like when Lee Evans was coming of age.

There was a time when a black man driving from one end of a southern state to the other, Alabama for example or Louisiana, would pack a lunch and carry his drink in a thermos.

# endnotes

Lee Evans is the primary source for those sections of the book dealing with his experiences. Lee's descriptions and characterizations join those gathered from third-party sources. From the material reviewed, the author decided what to include and what to exclude, and what weight to assign. The opinions expressed herein are those of the author, unless otherwise indicated.

Chapter 1

The vignettes are drawn from general reading as well as from a review of the literature and periodicals for the subject years.

Chapter 2

The emergence of Larry James is documented in two *Sports Illustrated* articles that appeared in the spring of 1968: Pete Axthelm, "Big Blaze in the Mighty Burner," *Sports Illustrated,* March 25, 1968, at page 30; and Johnathan Rodgers, "The Mighty Burner Blazes On," *Sports Illustrated,* May 6, 1968 at page 63; as well as by ongoing coverage by *Track and Field News* and particularly the cover story from May 1, 1968, "James Rockets 43.9r." The description of Lee Evans as a man who ran like he was struggling out of a corset comes from the article by Joe Jares in *Sports Illustrated,* "Lee Cools the Mighty Burner," May 20, 1968, at page 71, an article also consulted in the reconstruction of the race. I reviewed the articles appearing in II May 1968 of *Track and Field News*, "Evans' 44.9r Tags James (News Roundup)" and "West Coast: Evans' 44.9r Handles Villanova, James."

Chapter 3

The youthful reminiscences are those of Lee Evans. The comments and characterizations are those of the author.

Chapter 4

For description of Arthur Wint and Herb McKenley as well as a general background in the history of the event, see Roberto Quercetani, *Athletics: A History of Modern Track and Field Athletics (1860-2000)*, (Milan, Italy, SEP Editrice, 2000). Also, Roberto Quercetani, *A World History of the One-Lap Race, 1885-2004* (Milan, Italy, SEP Editrice, 2005).

Chapter 5

The introduction of Tommie Smith is influenced by two video presentations: *Fists of Freedom: The Story of the 1968 Summer Games*, HBO Sports, Sports of the 20th Century; and TNN's *Fame for 15; Episode #010;* by Gay Rosenthal Productions. *Fist of Freedom* included a version of Tommie Smith's story about purchasing ice cream.

Chapter 6

The careers of Hal Davis and Ray Norton are developed with the assistance of Mr. Quercentani's editions, above. With regard to Ray Norton's experience in Rome, I reviewed the *Track and Field News* Olympic edition for 1960. As noted in the narrative, I quoted Bud Winter on Bud Winter from his two books, *So You Want to Be a Sprinter* (San Francisco, Fearon Publishers, 1956), and *Relax and Win: Championship Performances in Whatever You Do* (San Diego and London, A.S. Barnes, 1981).

Chapter 7

That Tommie did not know Bud Winter when he entered San Jose State and that he was recruited as a basketball player is from the May 22, 1967, edition of *Sports Illustrated* in an article titled "He is Built for Chasing Beyondness," at pages 33 to 43, by Frank Deford, as is the statement that the young sprinter ran "on top." Mr. Deford also captured the unique physical properties of Tommie Smith, with particular reference to the long lean thighs, after which, it was said, "there seems to be hardly any room left for the rest of the leg...." The long quote from Bud Winter regarding his opinion that Tommie Smith was possibly the world's fastest sprinter "right now" came from an article in the April 1965 edition of *Track and Field News*. *Track and Field News* also included a feature on Tommie Smith in the May 1966 edition, one prominent feature of which was a discussion of stride length, acceleration, and the lack of deceleration from the athlete. The description is part of the background to this chapter. The coverage of the 1965 NCAA Outdoor Track and Field Championship by *Track and Field News* included Smith's remark about being wrapped like a mummy. *Time Magazine*, March 10, 1967, and *Newsweek* for the week of June 12, 1967, had articles highlighting the sensational young runner. Although the two articles were written at least two years after the sprinter's arrival on the scene, they were part of the analysis that appeared in this chapter. Also, Gwilym S. Brown, "Sad Music from a Stradivarius," *Sports Illustrated*, June 27, 1966, was generally helpful.

The dispute between the NCAA and the Amateur Athletic Union (AAU) was described with particular interest by *Track and Field News*: "Track Power Struggle—NCAA-AAU War Revives," December 1964; "An Editorial, T&FN Views the War," "NCAA-AAU War— Temporary Moratorium," and "More on Sanctions," all of which appeared in the January 1965 edition; "Track's Civil War— The Boycott, with Hope," February 1965; "Track's Civil War, Late War Developments," March 1965; "Track Civil War—War Begins to Hurt," April 1965; "Track Civil War—Concern over War Grows," May 1965; "Track Civil War—Athletes to Defy NCAA," "Track Civil War—Now What Happens?," and "A Disgusting Chapter (editorial)," July 1965; "Track Civil War—Senate Investigates," August 1965; "Track Civil War—Solution up to Senate," September 1965; "Track Civil War—Finally There's Hope," October 1965; "Track Civil War—Unrestricted Competition," November 1965; and "Track Civil War—NCAA, AAU Agree!" December 1965.

Chapter 8

The material is primarily developed from interviews with Lee Evans and conversations with Stanley Dowell. Mr. Dowell was featured in a February 2001 edition of *The Consolidated Press* in an article titled "The Coach: Another in a Series of People Who Made a Difference," by Guy C. Klitgaard.

Chapter 9

The athlete's performances are recorded in *Track and Field News* for the relevant periods.

Chapter 10

Charles Baker was kind enough to describe his year coaching Lee Evans at San Jose City College. Mr. Evans added his impressions. Together, the two retellings form the basis for the first part of the chapter. The reference to Tommie Smith as more than "just fast" comes from Dick Drake's feature in *Track and Field News*, May 1966. Otherwise, the people, the races, and the times come from *Track and Field News*, with the characterizations being that of the author.

Chapter 11

I referred to the original program for the 1966 AAU meet; to Gwilym S. Brown, "A Doleful Day for Ryun," *Sports Illustrated*, July 4, 1966, at page 22; and to *Track and Field News*, in developing Lee's first national championship, and to *Track and Field News* for the race results for the remainder of the year. The quote by Stan

Wright is from the *Track and Field News* reporting for the LA Times International Games, August 1966.

Chapter 12

In the March 1967 edition, *Track and Field News* has an extraordinary description of the mile relay in the 1967 AAU Indoor National meet. Bud Winter's descriptions of Tommie Smith's performance as "beyondness," "wayoutness," "Superman," and "Green Hornet," appear in that article. The remark attributed to Ken Shackelford is from Deford, "He is Built for Chasing Beyondness."

Chapter 13

The times and distances are from *Track and Field News*.

Chapter 14

Adolph Plummer's world-record run in May 1963 was reported in the June 1963 edition of *Track and Field News*. The good-natured statement attributed to Tommie Smith that Plummer's record was "humbug" appeared in Deford's, "He is Built for Chasing Beyondness." The statement by Lee Evans that Plummer's time did not seem "worthy" of a world record was taken from the May 29, 1967, edition of *Sports Illustrated*, in the article titled "Tommie in a Breeze," by Gary Ronberg, at page 22. *Track and Field News* covered the dual between Tommie Smith and Lee Evans in May 1967.

Chapter 15

Times and distances are from *Track and Field News*. The quote attributed to Jim Hines about beating Tommie Smith "ten times if they raced ten times," is from *Sports Illustrated* coverage of the 1967 Coliseum-Compton Invitational, June 12, 1967, in the article titled "Two Guys Named Jim Had the Same Idea," by Tom C. Brody, at page 34.

## Chapter 16

Lee Evans now describes Vince Matthews as one of the most competitive and talented athletes he raced. His admiring recollection is a subtext to the chapter. Vince Matthew's reaction to being left off the world-record 1,600-meter relay team is described by Vincent Matthews with Neil Amdur, *My Race Be Won* (New York, Charterhouse, 1974), at pages 105-106; the fact that Vince sought advice about the best way to beat Lee is something Lee heard at the time, but also is recorded in *My Race Be Won* at pages 142-147, as is the importance of leaning into the finish, at page 142.

## Chapter 17

Tommie Smith's statements in Tokyo were reported in the November 1967 edition of *Track and Field News* along with extensive interviews with Tommie Smith and Lee Evans regarding the possibility of an Olympic boycott. Generally, refer to Amy Bass, *Not the Triumph but the Struggle: The 1968 Olympics and the Making of the Black Athlete* (Minneapolis, The University of Minnesota Press, 2002).

## Chapter 18

The weekly and monthly national magazines of the era—*Life, Time, Newsweek, U.S. News* and *World Report*, among others— closely tracked race relations in major articles in 1965 to 1968. For a description of the disturbances in Newark, see the cover story, "Races: Sparks and Tinder," in *Time*, July 21, 1967, at page 15; and *Newsweek*, "Newark Boils Over," July 24, 1967, at page 21. For a recounting of what happened in Detroit, see "An American Tragedy, 1967, Detroit," *Newsweek*, August 7, 1967, at page 18. More generally, see "The Black Mood: A Survey," *Newsweek*, August 21, 1967. The description of the rural South and the statements appearing in the section are from *Newsweek*, July 24, 1967, at page 23.

Chapter 19

The following were consulted: *The Modern Olympic Games*, by John Lucas (South Brunswick and New York, London, A.S. Barnes and Co., 1982); *Hitler's Games: The 1936 Olympics*, by Duff Hart-Davis (New York, Harper and Row Publishers, 1986); *Jesse Owens, An American Life*, by William J. Baker (New York, The Free Press, 1986); *The Olympics: A History of the Modern Games*, by Allen Guttman (Urbana and Chicago, University of Illinois Press, 1992). Also, *The Games Must Go On: Avery Brundage and the Olympic Movement* (New York, Columbia University Press, 1984).

Chapter 20

On leadership styles, refer to *The Kennedy Imprisonment: A Meditation on Power*, by Garry Wills (Boston/Toronto, Little, Brown and Company, 1981), at page 164, 165.

Arnold Hano, "The Black Rebel Who 'Whitelists' the Olympics," *New York Times Magazine*, May 12, 1968, included the statement that Edwards and his followers would have burned the San Jose stadium to the ground had the game been played against UTEP. For a description of the Thanksgiving meeting, I relied on Johnathan Rodgers, "A Step to an Olympic Boycott," *Sports Illustrated*, December 4, 1967, at page 30; also, Bass, *Not the Triumph but the Struggle*, at pages 89-91. The long quote from Harry Edwards is from "A Step to an Olympic Boycott." The list of grievances came from contemporaneous reporting but was included in Bass, *Not the Triumph but the Struggle* at pages 135 and 136. Also, Harry Edwards, *The Revolt of the Black Athlete* (New York, The Free Press, 1969), appendix A, at page 128.

Chapter 21

The opening paragraph is a suggestion of the abuse that Tommie and Lee endured. In its December 1967 edition, *Track and Field News* reprinted some mail from the outpouring prompted by the proposed boycott. Here are samples of the species defined as "hate mail."

* "Incredibly good news. When are you leaving?"

* "You are a fine nigger specimen—just another agitating militant. Hope you and your followers get your bloody heads bashed in."

* "Why in the hell don't you and all the jigaboo so called athletes boycott all things American and try the Congo. Now, there is a leading country—cook pots and dung piles everywhere, but that is black culture. If you can't stand that, try Biafra, Nigeria. I think you colored folks would be better off in your own tribes with your own unprounounceable names."

The times and distances for 1967 appeared in the January 1967 "Annual Edition" of *Track and Field News*, as was the reluctant ranking of Lee over Tommie as the number one performer for 400 meters/440 yards. The emergence of Speed City is highlighted in I March, 1968, *Track and Field News*, and the reference to John Carlos as a "big farmer" and a "comedian" is from the October 1967 edition of the same magazine. I also referred to John Carlos's biography, written with C.D. Jackson Jr., *Why? The Biography of John Carlos* (Los Angeles, Milligan Books, 2002)

Chapter 22

The notes are from the contemporaneous diary Lee Evans maintained. The description of the San Francisco Examiner Games is from Pete Axthelm, "Smashing Start to the Season," *Sports Illustrated*, January 5, 1968, at page 46. The quoted statement from Charlie Greene is from that article.

Chapter 23

The Los Angeles Invitational Track Meet was described in the article by Pete Axthelm in the January 29, 1968, edition of *Sports*

*Illustrated,* "Boos and a Beating for Tommie," at page 56. Here is how Smith described his reaction to the boos: "I think I expected it to happen, and in some ways maybe I'm kinda glad. I think I would have been disappointed if I had gotten no reaction from people *like these.*" (Italics added) The adjustments South Africa agreed to make in order to secure Olympic participation were reported in the February 16, 1968, *New York Times* with a dateline Grenoble, France, February 15, 1968, as were the remarks by Col. Westeroff. The excerpt from the editorial by Robert Lipsyte was in the February 17, 1968, *New York Times* the same day the newspaper reported the withdrawal of Ethiopia and Algeria, in the first wave of reaction. The phone calls made to Mike Goodrich, John Thomas, Jim Hines, and John Hartfield, and the fact that James Dennis was "roughed up", were reported in a *New York Times* article by Frank Litsky on February 17, 1968, "9 Negroes Appear in Garden Action." That same article referred to the bomb threat. The *New York Times* article, "Militants Lose 7th Ave. Scuffle," was by Homer Bigart and appeared on February 17, 1968. Mr. Bigart's article also described the experience of the Holy Cross and Providence athletes, the exhortation that the group break into "twos and threes and go in and tear that goddamn building down," as well as the statements by Harry Edwards that the crowd had his endorsement if they wished to rush the arena, and his preference that they "let the damned thing (the Garden) rot."

In his subsequently published book *The Revolt of the Black Athlete* at page 68, Dr. Edwards with regard to the alleged threats made against athletes in New York wrote: "However, upon checking with athletes who were supposedly threatened, such as John Thomas and others, the accusations were not confirmed." The language is artful, but does not amount to evidence that the threats were not made. I credited contemporaneous reporting. I found no magazine or newspaper that issued a correction, denial, retraction or clarification to the reported threats. Further, remarks attributed to Harry Edwards are probative:

*"[John] Thomas would be very foolish to cross that picket line. There are some brothers in Boston who would be very upset with*

*him. They might not show it that night, but within a week John would regret his decision. Hines says he wants to play pro football some day. If he runs in that meet, he'll never be able to play football for anybody. Some cats in Texas have personally said they'd fix it so he'd be on sticks if he's crazy enough to run New York."*

Robert Terrell and Paul Zimmerman, "Picket Plans Present High Hurdle To NYAC," *New York Post,* February 15, 1968; and see *Time,* February 23, 1968, at page 61.

The statement that "any black athlete who does cross the picket line could find himself in trouble" is from Gerald Fraser, "Black Athletes are Cautioned Not to Cross Lines," *New York Times,* February 16, 1968.

Reports of intimidation continued at least up to and including the Olympic 'Semi-Trials' in Los Angeles, from which event the following scene emerged: "At the athletes' training quarters at Cal Poly in Pomona and in hotel lobbies in Los Angeles there were whispers of black lives being threatened by black hands....One prominent Olympian stayed in his room rather than go to dinner with two white men and two other athletes. Asked about the reason for his change in plans, the athlete made the sign of a gun with his thumb and index finger. He said he had been threatened." John Underwood, "The Non-Trial Trials," *Sports Illustrated,* July 8, 1968, at page 10, 13.

The radical language, and the resulting radical image, of Harry Edwards: America must change "or we will destroy it," "I will use whatever tool, political or otherwise," and the claim that the young Edwards pulled his own teeth and stayed in school in order to have access to a shower are from Hano, "The Black Rebel Who 'Whitelists' the Olympics." The statements attributed to Richmond Flowers and to Roscoe Divine both come from Paul Zimmerman, "Under the Gun," *New York Post,* February 17, 1968. The commentator to whom reference is made is Amy Bass, *Not the Triumph but the Struggle,* at page 156.

## Chapter 24

The discussion of coercion as an instrument of social action has as a point of reference two books by Hannah Arendt: *The Origins of Totalitarianism* (New York, Harcourt Brace Jovanovich, 1948), and *On Violence* (New York, Harcourt Brace and Co., 1969). The idea that victimized groups can claim innocence beyond individual virtue is from Arendt, *Essays in Understanding: Hannah Arendt* (New York, San Diego, and London, Harcourt, Brace and Co., 1994). The essay in which the idea appears is "The Image of Hell," at page 199.

The reference to "crackers," "pigs in blue," "Lynchin' Baines Johnson," the presence of "traitors" among the ranks of black athletes come from Hano, "The Black Rebel who 'Whitelists' the Olympics." In that article Harry Edwards describes himself as a "black rightist," a description that is revealing. The young professor may have been referring to "rights," as in rights and interests, but he unconsciously called to mind the tactics typically associated with the "right" wing of the ideological perspective and with which tactics someone like Avery Brundage would have been familiar. The quoted statement from Harry Edwards, to the effect that he did not think any black athlete would go to the Olympics, is from the same source. Lee's reaction to the Cal-Berkeley runner is from Lee Evans's diary. That Lee opined that another athlete was a "Tom" is cited by Bass, *Not the Triumph But the Struggle*, at page 150, with further attribution to Milton Gross, "TV's Eye in Storm Center," *New York Post*, February 16, 1968.

The reference to an illimitable remedy—"by any means necessary"—is a common thread, indeed the arguable anthem, of the militant black power movement of the 1960s. To have a sense of the ubiquitous employment of the phrase, see, for example, Harry Edwards, *The Revolt of the Black Athlete*, at page 101, in which Professor Edwards issued a statement on behalf of the OCHR to a group of students at Mexico City University who had requested support. In part the statement reads, "The anti-human governments of the world must be made to understand BY ANY MEANS NECESSARY (capital letters in the original), (sic) that the rising tide of youth will use *any means necessary* (italics added) to stop the generation to generation flow of inhumanity." Also, see the forward by Samuel J. Skinner Jr. to *The Revolt of the Black Athlete,* in which Mr. Skinner summarizes Edwards's purpose, beginning with the planned protest of the San Jose State–University of Texas at El Paso football game: "From this moment on, Edwards' theme was written. The desire, the motivation, all centered on one word—"justice"—justice for the black man; justice for the black athlete—BY ANY MEANS NECESSARY." The capital letters appeared in the original text. Also, variations on the theme carry the same message, as the following statement by Harry Edwards illustrates: "The crackers are losing all over. In Vietnam, Thailand, Laos, Bolivia, all over. The blue-eyed devil is in trouble. The third world power—black, red, yellow, brown—is taking the white man apart in chunks. We must get the cracker off our backs, by Olympic boycott, by out-and-out revolution, by whatever means." Hano, "The Black Rebel who 'Whitelists' the Olympics," at page 41.

For the limits Tommie Smith and Lee Evans placed on their right to influence other people or the nature of protest, see, for example, Kenny Moore, "The Black Athlete Revisited," *Sports Illustrated,* August 5, 1991, in which Tommie Smith describes his actions: "It [the Olympic protest] had to be silent—to solve the language problem—strong, prayerful, imposing. It kind of makes me want to cry when I think about it now. I cherish life so much that what I did couldn't be militant, not violent. I'll argue with you, but I won't pick up a gun," at page 72.

Chapter 25

The responsibility of leadership—the scope and reach of a leader's liability—is a rich area for discussion. That a leader should account for the predicted effect of what he or she says or does would not seem controversial. The fact that a particular word or a deed may have uncontrolled consequence is itself predictable and encourages the exercise of caution in all but the most private utterances and acts by a public person. *Track and Field News,* I March 1968, includes a description of the race between Lee Evans, Martin McGrady, Jim Kemp, and Ron Whitney. Also see Pete Axthelm, "Three on the Line in the 600," *Sports Illustrated*, March 4, 1968, at pages 20, 21.

Chapter 26

The meeting in Chicago, the statement by Avery Brundage, and the clarification by Don Hull are from the *Track and Field News* editorial, "Daring Dozen to the Rescue," I February 1968. The quote attributed to Larry James is from Pete Axthelm, "Big Blaze in the Mighty Burner," *Sports Illustrated*, March 25, 1968, at page 30.

Chapter 27

Larry James' story about what happened in Knoxville, Tennessee is reported by Kenny Moore in "A Courageous Stand," *Sports Illustrated*, August 5, 1991, at page 70.

Chapter 28

Lee describes the jubilation, of course. Also see, for example, Joe Jares, "Lee Cools the Mighty Burner," *Sports Illustrated*, May 20, 1968, at page 72.

Chapter 29

Lee describes the workout routine in his diary. Contemporaneous reporting is from *Track and Field News* for the subject track and field meets; also see Mark Mulvoy, "The Boys from Speed City Burn Up the Town," *Sports Illustrated*, June 17, 1968, at page 62. Vince Matthew's reaction to the death of Dr. King is based on a review of his performances and on the statement in his book, *My Race Be Won*, at page 166: "Dr. King's death seemed to drain some of the enthusiasm from my spring season, and I could sense that I wasn't alone, because the trip to the Penn Relays wasn't the same that year."

Chapter 30

The loss of the athletes, coach, and staff from Lamar Tech was reported in *Track and Field News*, I May 1968, "On Your Marks," a column by Dick Drake.

Chapter 31

The finish line photograph of Lee Evans and Vince Matthews at the AAU appeared in *Track and Field News*, II June 1968, at page 5.

Chapter 32

See, John Underwood, "The Non-Trial Trials," *Sports Illustrated*, July 8, 1968, from which the long quote ("There was mounting evidence that the boycott movement,") is taken, at page 13. The end of the boycott, Harry Edwards's response, and the citation to a newspaper article are reported in Bass, *Not the Triumph but the Struggle*, at pages 226-229, with the article attributed as follows: A.S. "Doc" Young, "Good Morning, Sports!" *Chicago Daily Defender*, September 10, 1968, at page 24.

Chapter 33

Lee describes the meeting with Bud Winter to which reference is made.

Chapter 34

The workouts and descriptions come from Lee's diary.

Chapter 35

Lee's recollections are the heart of this chapter, along with contemporaneous race reports, especially those in *Track and Field News*, September 1968. The 200-meter split for Vince Matthews in the 400-meter final at the Trials is taken from *My Race Be Won*, at page 186.

Chapter 36

The peremptory threat made by Avery Brundage is from *Fists of Freedom*, which also provides the visual evidence of Mr. Brundage's departure from the podium. The threat is reported in Bass, *Not the Triumph but the Struggle*, at page 197, by way of U.S. track coach Stan Wright, who said: "I heard him [Brundage] make the remark that if the black athletes demonstrated in Mexico City, we'd be rushed back home. A lot of the fellows here thought the remark was derogatory, intimidating and completely out of line." The meeting in Denver was reported, among other places, in the article by Kenny Moore, "A Courageous Stand," *Sports Illustrated*, August 5, 1991, at page 72. Vince Matthews describes the meeting in his biography, *My Race be Won*, at pages 188-189. Lee Evans's recollections also form part of the description of that meeting. Bass, *Not the Triumph but the Struggle*, at pages 112-130, provides a concise and well-documented description of the student demonstrations in Mexico City and the violence directed against the demonstrators. Avery Brundage's statement that his group had conferred with Mexico City officials and been assured that the violence would not "interfere with the peaceful entrance of the Olympic flame into the stadium" is reported in *The Games Must Go On: Avery Brundage and the Olympic Movement*, at page 242. Also, see Bob Ottum, "Grim Countdown to the Games," *Sports Illustrated*, October 14, 1968, at page 36.

Chapter 37

That Jim Hines refused to accept his medal from Avery Brundage is reported in daily news reports from the Games. Readers are referred to Bass, *Not the Triumph but the Struggle*, at her text pages 236-237 and footnote 12 thereto. Jeremy Larner and David Wolf, "Amid Gold Medals Raised Black Fists," *Life*, November 1, 1968; and *Newsweek*, "The Olympics Extra Heat," October 28, 1968, at page 74, also reported the events.

John Carlos's familiar soliloquy, his dismissal of the Harvard crew team, and his unwillingness to accept cafeteria protocol are reported by John Underwood, "A High Time for Sprinters – and Kenyans," *Sports Illustrated*, October 28, 1968, at pages 19 and 22.

With regard to the loss of his world record for 200 meters: "Officials were out on the track before I'd come to a stop, telling me it wouldn't count," John Carlos said of his Olympic Trials performance at South Lake Tahoe. "They loved telling me that." Kenny Moore, "A Courageous Stand," *Sports Illustrated*, August 5, 1991. Carlos's claim that he could have but preferred not to win the Olympic gold medal is featured in *Why?* particularly at pages 195-208. Moore repeats the story in the article to which reference is made above. "I made up my mind," Carlos says about his decision, "Tommie Smith gets a gift," at page 72. In "Why?" John Carlos also says that he originated the protest and its particulars, pages 195-208. By contrast, Moore attributes the planning to Smith. For more contemporaneous reporting see "The Olympics Extra Heat," *Newsweek*, October 28, 1968. Also refer to Jeremy Larner and David Woolf, "Amid Gold Medals Raised Black Fists," and John Underwood, "A High Time for Sprinters – and Kenyans." The *Newsweek* article is of special interest because the storyline appears to be based on information John Carlos gave: "But coming out of the turn, Tommie was in high gear. Carlos, his own calf starting to hurt, looked around and yelled, 'Come on up here, Tommie.' The words hung in the air as Smith whipped past...." at 74. Tommie Smith denies hearing any such shouted encouragement. Moore at page 73. On one point, there is agreement. John Carlos looked around as Tommie Smith came at him. Underwood describes the instant as follows: "In the final, two hours later, Carlos held the lead with 50 yards to go. At that point, as he is wont to do when he is on the verge of victory, Carlos looked around. He need not have bothered. Smith, settling down, was streaking past him." Underwood at page 22. *Track and Field News* reported the conclusion of the 200 meters in similar terms: "Smith, showing no signs of his injury, was also off quickly and entered the straight in second. Tommie then shifted into his unmatchable straightaway speed, caught Carlos at 140 meters, and the race for first was as well as over." As to the glance, *Track and Field News* quoted Stan Wright: "Carlos lost his cool and looked to his left at Tommie. This probably lost him second to Norman, who was on his right." October/November 1968, at page 8.


Chapter 38

The interplay between the USOC and the IOC is described in John Underwood, "A High Time for Sprinters – and Kenyans."

In his time, Jesse Owens, including his early background, was as easily identified as a brand name. William J. Baker's book, *Jesse Owens: An American Life* (London, The Free Press, 1986) is a sympathetic portrait. At page 212, Baker gives a version of the Mexico City meeting and particularly the taunting message Owens delivered to John Carlos. Vince Matthews, *My Race Be Won*, at pages 191-195 describes the black athletes meeting with Jesse Owens: "To me, running against horses is degrading, and it's interesting that I never see white athletes being asked to run against horses," Matthews added as explanation for his reaction to Owens's "lecture," as he described it. Also see, "Amid Gold Medals Raised Black Fists," *Life*, November 1, 1968, an article that also has a vivid retelling of Lee Evans's Olympic experience in the wake of the protest. In other respects, Lee's memory is the source. I referred to Roberto L. Quercetani, *Athletics, A History of Modern Track and Field Athletics (1860–2000)* at page 206 to develop the splits for the 400 meters at Mexico City. I considered but did not use the different splits attributed to the race in Roberto L. Quercetani, *A World History of the One-Lap Race (1850–2004)* at page 79.


Chapter 39

Vince Matthews, *My Race Be Won*, at pages 202-205 was helpful in reconstructing the relay, especially the anxious moments after the false start: "All I could see were these six eyes staring straight at me." The quip regarding the boos and the fact that they probably came from Texans appears in Matthews's book at page 205 and is attributed to the young Mr. Freeman.

Chapter 40

Race results are from *Track and Field News*.

Chapter 41

The primary source is the diary maintained by Lee Evans.

:

General

In the three books that I have written about running, this book is the closest to my personal experience. This generation of athletes is the last to compete before the great changes swept through the sport of track and field. As a young teenager, I watched these performances with an interest bordering on obsession. Upon completing the first edit of the manuscript, Annette Pierce was astute enough to recognize the essential message in this book. These guys, she said, you love.

# the photographs
*:credits*

The photographs are credited as follows, by the page numbers on which they appear: AP/Wideworld Photos 19, 31, 74, 105, 106, 121, 131, 148, 163, 189, 214, 221, 236, 237, 238, 255, 257, 261, 264, 279, 286; San Jose State University Sports Information Office 42; Track and Field News, 99, 104, 113, 233. The photographs on pages 283 and 293 are privately held by Mr. Evans and are reproduced with his permission. Those photographs maintained in Mr. Evans's private collection did not include information sufficient to identify them further.

# index

# about the author

Frank Murphy is the author of *A Cold Clear Day: The Athletic Biography of Buddy Edelen* (1992) and *The Silence of Great Distance: Women Running Long* (2000). He is an attorney whose practice emphasizes the representation of people with disabilities. In his career, he has been the Public Administrator for Jackson County, Missouri, the executive director of a bioethics center, the first executive director of a managed care company serving a Medicaid-eligible population, and an instructor in sociology at the University of Missouri at Kansas City. He speaks widely and often on social issues.

# about the book

The book design and cover design are by Nick Kroeker. Annette Pierce edited the book. The text was written in Microsoft Word. The layout was designed in Adobe InDesign 2.0.2 on the Macintosh computer and output to PDF files. The body text is set in Aldus Roman. The headings and page numbers are set in Palatino Roman. The chapter titles are set in Palatino Bold, and the chapter subtitles are set in Palatino Italic.

Printed in the United States
59445LVS00003B/1-51